LIVING THROUGH LOSS

D0407645

GRIEF
The Mourning After

GRIEF
The Mourning After
DEALING WITH ADULT BEREAVEMENT

SECOND EDITION

CATHERINE M. SANDERS

JOHN WILEY & SONS, INC.

New York • Chichester • Weinheim • Brisbane • Singapore • Toronto

This book is printed on acid-free paper. ⊗

Copyright © 1999 by John Wiley & Sons, Inc. All rights reserved.

Published simultaneously in Canada.

No part of this publication may be reproduced, stored in a retrieval system or transmitted in any form or by any means, electronic, mechanical, photocopying, recording, scanning or otherwise, except as permitted under sections 107 or 108 of the 1976 United States Copyright Act, without either the prior written permission of the Publisher, or authorization through payment of the appropriate per-copy fee to the Copyright Clearance Center, 222 Rosewood Drive, Danvers, MA 01923, (978) 750-8400, fax (978) 750-4744. Requests to the Publisher for permission should be addressed to the Permissions Department, John Wiley & Sons, Inc., 605 Third Avenue, New York, NY 10158-0012, (212) 850-6011, fax (212) 850-6008, E-Mail: PERMREQ@WILEY.COM.

This publication is designed to provide accurate and authoritative information in regard to the subject matter covered. It is sold with the understanding that the publisher is not engaged in rendering professional services. If legal, medical, psychological or any other expert assistance is required, the services of a competent professional person should be sought.

Library of Congress Cataloging-in-Publication Data:

Sanders, Catherine M.
    Grief : the mourning after : dealing with adult bereavement / Catherine M. Sanders —second edition
        p.   cm.
    Includes bibliographical references and index.
    ISBN 0-471-12777-9 (hardcover : alk. paper)
        1. Bereavement—Psychological aspects.   2. Grief.   I. Title.
BF575.G7S26   1999
155.9'37—dc21   98-21034

Printed in the United States of America.
10 9 8 7 6 5 4 3 2 1

Preface

I T HAS BEEN ten years since the first edition of *Grief: The Mourning After* was published. Since that time, much has been written on the subject, more research has been carried out, and many changes have taken place in the development of various syndromes. For example, different types of complicated grief have elicited much attention in the past decade. There has been a stronger focus on those family members who survive suicide, homocide, multiple deaths, horrendous deaths of all kinds. These deaths are shattering situations, carrying with them the pain and suffering of family members and friends struggling to survive the awful ravages of grief and overwhelming devastation. This new edition looks at these types of death as well as at AIDS-related bereavement and the domino effect that this disease has on surrounding friends, partners, and families.

So many wonderful people have helped me in the writing of this book. One of the most pleasant parts of writing a book is the opportunity to thank all those friends who have given me generous support and encouragement over recent years. First and foremost, however, I wish to thank all the bereaved people, those in the Tampa study as well as my own patients, who out of the goodness of their hearts gave generously of their time and energy at a period when neither of these commodities were very accessible. Each one voiced the wish that what he or she had experienced and were willing to share would in some way benefit another bereaved person. Out of the depths of their pain and suffering and through their willingness, I have gained a broader understanding of grief and its process.

Over the years, many colleagues in the field of thanatology have shared their work with me, especially my dear friends and fellow travelers in the

Association of Death Education and Counseling (ADEC). As they discussed their work with me, I have gained a deeper understanding of the entire field of thanatology. My thanks to friends and cohorts like Shery Schachter, Edie Stark, Ken Doka, Terrie Rando, Gene Knott, Ellen Zinner, Judy Stillion, Lu Redmond, Charles Corr, and Sally Featherstone. I could list indefinitely the wonderful people who have made a difference in my work and in my life but I would finally run out of space. To those who have stood by me, shared in my work, and offered important insights, I extend my deepest gratitude.

I am especially indebted to my dear, long-time friend Mary Howerton, who stepped in at a moment's notice when I was at a low period in my life, took me by the hand, and lifted me back into sanity again. Being a wonderful researcher and writer, she ferreted out information on the lifelong effects of childhood bereavement and then wrote Chapter 11. It is included in its entirety. I am forever grateful to her for giving me that boost when I desperately needed one.

I wish to thank my good friend John Beeman, who was in class with me at the University of South Florida way back when we were both music majors. We both got out of music, thank goodness, and went different routes after graduate school, I in the field of psychology and John in library science. John's career was a great help to me because he has spent endless hours tracking down references for the book and faxing them to me. His orderly training made the difference in helping me stay organized.

I would like to thank my publishers, John Wiley & Sons, Inc., and in particular Jennifer Simon, whose patience and gentle manner have been most helpful in keeping me on track. And I would be remiss if I didn't thank Herb Reich, a special mentor who edited my first two books and encouraged me all the way through their writing. Herb has since retired, and I will always be grateful for the boost he gave me in getting started. My thanks are also extended to Kathleen Wirscham, who tirelessly typed the manuscript, which was often a cut-and-paste operation. Kathy didn't flinch whenever I handed her a new chapter including the references (always a headache).

From the bottom of my heart I wish to thank my children, Sue Labella, Sally Bowers, and Catherine Bodnar, for their encouragement and support over many years. Their love has given me strength and made it possible for me to stick to the task of writing this revision and seeing it through to completion. My sister, Mary McKinney, has always been available to me, sharing whatever grief we may have experienced. Our long-time bond has created a deep-felt love and respect.

To those special departed loved ones who have contributed to my life and most especially to my work in bereavement, I offer my dearest love and undying gratitude; my son, James Sanders; my mother, Alma Alling; my husband, Herschel Sanders; my brother, James Gallion. Their deaths were the heartbreaking reasons for my seeking the awful answers to my plaintive cry of "Why?" I still search.

Catherine M. Sanders

Contents

Introduction

B EREAVEMENT IS A fact of life. In the typical life cycle of most Americans, losses will occur for one reason or another. Yet strangely, if not surprisingly, grief is denied by most of us until we are confronted head-on with a loss of our own. If we form attachments to family members, friends, spouses, homes, jobs, we will eventually have to relinquish that person or thing to whom the attachment was made. Letting go represents the ultimate pain of grief.

This book has several purposes. First and foremost, the material presented here is for clinical use. It is not a research textbook. The focus is to provide caregivers and health professionals with pertinent information on grief and loss. Through this information, it is hoped that a better understanding of the process and reactions to bereavement will be gained. Second, this book reviews major writings of others on the subject of grief and details the five phases of my own Integrative Theory of Bereavement to provide caregivers with an appreciation of the basis for interventions appropriate to various situations. Increased knowledge of bereavement will help eliminate some of the negative stereotypes that have prevailed in the past.

The material used in this book is intended for clinical application, but it may be helpful to describe the research on which my model of the phases of bereavement is based. In order to add clarity and validity to the concepts presented, I have drawn heavily on the information supplied by participants in a study performed in the Tampa, Florida, area, hereinafter called "the Tampa study."

Although I began working in the area of loss and bereavement in 1968, the Tampa study reported in this book began 21 years ago, when 115 bereaved individuals were followed through the first 2 years after the death of a close family member. In beginning the study, I felt that it was necessary to derive the information based on measurable empirical data and not solely on anecdotal or subjective evidence. But how does one go about measuring grief? If grief is indeed multidimensional, then the instrument would have to examine the various components of grief rather than indicate a single unidimensional score.

From this concern, the Grief Experience Inventory (GEI; Sanders, Mauger, & Strong, 1977) was designed to objectively and quantitatively describe the grief phenomenon. The GEI is a 135-item true-false instrument developed to discern the multidimensional aspects of grief. By using standard scales (three validity, nine clinical, and six research) that represent the separate components of grief, it is possible to compare and contrast objectively the experiences among individual bereaved persons as well as groups. Three years went into the reliability and validity measurements before the actual bereavement study could be started.

In determining differences in types of grief, I needed to compare individuals who had suffered losses to matched controls who had not experienced a loss. But this comparison posed a problem. When I searched for individuals who had not experienced a loss, I found few people. Most persons have experienced some personal loss through death. I finally settled on individuals who had not experienced the death of a family member within the previous 5 years. The types of grief I chose to differentiate among were the death of a parent, a spouse, or a child.

A third major research question revolved around the notion that individuals react to stress in ways that are truly *personal*—yet functionally integral (i.e., each person's pattern of response is consistent within the individual, yet uniquely different from any other person). For this problem I used the Minnesota Multiphasic Personality Inventory (MMPI; Hathaway & McKinley, 1951) to look at various personality typologies. Obviously no prebereavement personality measures of the bereaved group exist, but I made the reasonable assumption that the basic MMPI profile configurations are indicative of premorbid adjustment strategies that have been exacerbated by the stress of bereavement. Thus, the person who manifested disturbed reactions as a trait syndrome displayed the same disturbed reactions in an exaggerated form as a state syndrome. Similarly, those who used denial as a protective defense mechanism displayed those same characteristics to a greater degree when coping with a loss or inordinate stress. This hypothesis was borne out in the study, and it was possible to show that rather than a single stereotypic response to grief, many coping strategies are used by individuals and that these coping strategies are both fairly predictable and based on lifestyle adjustments.

Although many differences were noted, common threads were also seen among the bereaved. They each suffered a significant unique personal loss, yet they all felt pain and the deprivation of living without that particular person who had meant so much to them. The bereaved in the Tampa study had lost a spouse, parent, or child, and it is from this perspective that this book gains its meaning.

The grief process comprises a series of phases. The actual content of the phases of grief set forth in this book was developed both from observing the longitudinal aspects of the Tampa project and from studying the work of many theorists who have contributed to this field. Each phase of grief can be characterized by a wide variety of possible human responses. Although all the symptoms described for any one phase are rarely experienced by any one person, the list does provide a cluster of possible responses that one could expect to encounter during that particular period of grief. The phases, then, can provide a benchmark by which to position the bereaved individual in the grieving process without forcing the person into a mold.

Yet the phases are not static discrete entities. Rather, they imply a continuous progression, a blending of each phase into the next or, as Parkes (1972) describes, "a succession of clinical pictures which blend into and replace one another" (p. 7). Symptoms overlap as the bereaved person moves through the grief process. Further, regressions are inevitable. Even when the grieving person has clearly moved to the next phase, he or she may return to earlier patterns during times of stress or extreme fatigue. This experience is often frightening in that the person may fear a permanent regression. Instead, the regression generally passes as soon as the stressful situation ends or the bereaved person has rested sufficiently. Grief clearly does not follow a linear progression.

Thus, the process of grief outlined herein implies movement with definite bridges connecting one phase to another. The motivation to move to the next phase, to cross the bridge and go forward, is an important element of the Integrative Theory of Bereavement, which is introduced in Part Two. Indeed, the concept of motivation sets this theory apart from previous ones in that I have attempted to do more than simply name the phases; I also indicate both the psychological and the biological reasons behind the movement from one phase to another. I am not saying that a person does not sometimes get stuck along the way. For many bereaved, it takes months or even years before progress can resume; in such cases, professional help may be beneficial in order to move forward and complete the process.

That grief is a major stressor is clearly indicated. What is not often recognized is that caregivers who work with the bereaved face stresses of their own. Time is one stressful element. Whether the caregiver is involved in individual, couple, or family therapy or counseling, the progress through grief is generally slow and time-consuming. The process cannot be hurried. The caregiver's own grief may be challenged at times. Because every past grief is reawakened through all subsequent losses, caregivers working with bereaved people are reminded over and over of these painful prior losses. If the caregiver does not have adequate knowledge of the grieving process or has not developed personal coping skills, this type of counseling can be debilitating.

We experience losses throughout our lives: separation, divorce, transitions, all kinds of changes. Yet our culture has not prepared us well to deal with them. Instead, a rampant sort of denial implies a fairy-tale world, a world of bliss and easy continuity with few changes. This world is not reality. It takes a brave soul with an adventurous outlook to prepare for the inevitable losses that are to come. This book is offered as a guide to help prepare for the aftermath of those losses. But most particularly, this book offers an optimistic view not only that growth and new life are possible once the grief process has been completed, but also that they are within reach of each of us when we face change and separation with faith and courage.

CHAPTER OVERVIEWS

Part One deals with background and theoretical considerations. Chapter 1 presents a general overview of the state of bereavement as it is dealt with today. It emphasizes the fact that each individual has a need to experience her or his own grief in a distinctively characteristic way. To understand the present state of the art, Chapter 2 traces the theories of bereavement, beginning with the early psychodynamic analytic approaches and progressing through the apparent evolution of the concept to the current understanding of grief as a psychobiological process. Each theory builds on the one before it. Chapter 3 describes the Integrative Theory of Grief, taking the theory one step further by outlining phases as well as psychobiosociological symptoms useful in understanding the motivation to move through grief.

Part Two focuses on the phases of grief. Chapters 4 through 8 discuss each phase separately, moving through (1) shock, (2) awareness of loss, (3) conservation-withdrawal, (4) healing, and finally, (5) renewal. When the phases are completed, the individual may be free to reinvest in another object relation. Grief is viewed as a complex time-consuming procedure that, once begun, must be worked through to its conclusion. Within this process is a series of phases, each carrying its own symptoms and tasks that must be completed before the person is ready to move to the next phase. These delineated phases make it possible to determine the progress of the bereaved and plot the course of the journey. Each phase, with its accompanying symptoms, carries biological as well as psychological implications for the bereaved. The chapters focus on helping the caregiver understand the elongated completion of the grief process and the social implications of loss.

The multidimensionality of grief is the focus of Part Three. Moderator variables work to exacerbate problems in grief resolution. Chapter 9 shows how premorbid personality characteristics act to create varying responses to grief. Heretofore, bereavement has been examined primarily as a single process with little latitude for individual differences. Yet most persons do exhibit idiosyncratic, though personally characteristic, responses to stress. Because these broader responses to grief do exist, no single intervention strategy meets the needs of all bereaved individuals; a wide range of useful intervention approaches proves helpful.

Chapter 10 looks at social and situational factors that often interfere with grief resolution. These factors include age, gender, socioeconomic status, religiosity, sudden versus chronic illness, concurrent crises, disenfranchised grief, and lack of social support. Many times these variables can complicate bereavement.

Chapter 11 discusses early childhood and the effect that childhood experiences often have on emotions and behavior in adulthood. Chapter 12 focuses on family interaction in bereavement. Grief is typically a family affair. Important strategies for family intervention can be missed if caregivers lose sight of major effects within the family constellation. It is important for caregivers to know how to draw on the resources of mutual support within the family. This chapter uses case studies from the Tampa study and outlines intervention strategies for mobilizing the family into a more unified whole.

Part Four looks at complicated grief as it examines three types of especially traumatic griefs: suicide, homicide, and AIDS-related deaths. All three of these deaths present inordinate situations with which the grieving survivors must deal: The first two represent sudden, unanticipated, violent situations; the third represents a slow, often painful and debilitating death; all three represent bereavements that fall into the category of very complicated mourning. The first section of Chapter 13 focuses on suicide and the effects it has on the surviving family. The next section deals with homicide and the mental imagery that the survivors must contend with that could block their way to bereavement recovery. Finally, a third section focuses on AIDS and AIDS-related diseases. Bereavement overload in the gay community is discussed, as are the family conflicts. Friends of the deceased often present a different lifestyle, further causing the biologic and chosen family to enter into conflicts. The threat of potential HIV contamination further contributes to difficult bereavement.

Part Five examines three types of loss that have been known to cause inordinate grief: loss of a child, loss of a spouse, and loss of an adult's parent. Chapter 14 discusses the difficulties known to persist when a child dies. Said to be the most intense and long-lasting of all griefs, this type of loss has predominated recent bereavement research in America. Implications for all family members are included; however, bereaved parents are the primary focus.

Chapter 15 deals with the death of a spouse. Grief felt by widows and widowers differs in detail from that felt by a bereaved parent. The relationship with the spouse before death affects the quality and length of grief. Individual variations can be affected by the ages of the spouse as well as the length of time the couple was married and the attachment that was formed. Loneliness affects these survivors more than any other type of loss and may present problematic sequelae for the bereaved.

Chapter 16 reviews the literature on the death of a parent in adult life. In some ways, the death of a mature parent is less painful to an adult than the death of a spouse or child. The surviving children have usually formed families of their own to lend support. But the death of a parent changes the relationship of the surviving child to the family and to the world. This chapter contains suggestions to help cope with the loss of a parent.

Part Six discusses the rituals of loss. Rituals have been an integral part of life since the beginning of human existence. They are traditionally among the most powerful sanctioned methods available to offer symbolic guidance to the human spirit. Chapter 17 deals with a review of the properties of rituals in our world and how they fit into our culture today. The vast social changes seem to call for a return to solid rituals, both in community living and in solitary soul searching. Included here are guidelines for developing meaningful rituals. The chapter also points to the importance of marking more rites of passage in our time and discusses various options available for ceremonies that might help the bereaved offer respect to the deceased. This chapter also offers insight into the therapeutic properties of rituals and instructions for building an appropriate self-generated ritual that can offer a sense of sanctity.

Part Seven deals with practical applications for caregivers in helping both the bereaved person as well as themselves. Chapter 18 is about the need for intervention and how best to discern the needs of the bereaved. Support groups and their therapeutic enhancement are discussed. Chapter

19 addresses the problems of caregivers themselves. Working with the bereaved requires enormous empathy and patience. Also, because death in and of itself is an extremely stressful topic with which to deal, caregivers place themselves in a vulnerable position of continued exposure to stress. Finally, in Chapter 20, the positive aspects of grief are presented; what can the bereaved teach us? Suggestions include the acquisition of strength and courage, compassion, and a gentle tolerance of grief and foibles of others. In this light, grief is seen as a maturing factor rather than a destructive one.

PART ONE

BACKGROUND AND THEORETICAL CONSIDERATIONS

CHAPTER 1

Grieving

All love leads to loss. If we commit ourselves to another person, form an attachment, we will surely have to relinquish that attachment. It may be through death or some other form of separation. Either they leave or you do. That is not the issue, however. What is important is that some time in our life we must face and deal with loss and separation. For some, it may happen in later life, for others it may occur earlier and more frequently. Frequency, however, doesn't make it any easier. When separation occurs, we will grieve, we will suffer. No one is immune. It's the price we pay for commitment.

Author

G RIEF SO IMPOSSIBLY PAINFUL, so akin to panic, that ways must be invented to defend against the emotional onslaught of suffering. There is a fear that if one ever gives in fully to grief, one would be swept under—as by a huge tidal wave—never to surface to ordinary emotional states again.

ASPECTS OF GRIEF

Grief is multilayered; the pain is felt on many levels at once. For example, when a beloved person dies, the bereaved not only must feel the physical hurt of the broken heart (Lynch, 1977) and the emotional pain of separation (Bowlby, 1960a) but also must contend with the social deprivation of having to live without that special person (Parkes, 1971a).

Grief is a natural phenomenon that occurs after the loss of a loved one (Shuchter & Zisook, 1993, p. 23), but Shuchter and Zisook caution that grief

3

is an individualized process, varying moment by moment as well as person to person. Too, grief cannot be seen in a static or linear perspective in that the process must be viewed in a diverse, multidimensional timelessness.

Because of the pain, grief is obscured to the extent that there are few words in our vocabulary to describe it. Four of the most commonly used terms—bereavement, grief, loss, and mourning—are often used interchangeably; however, because of the broad usage today, the differentiation between them is less important than it used to be.

BEREAVEMENT

Bereavement represents the experiential state one endures after realizing a loss, and as such, it is an objective fact (Kastenbaum, 1977). Bereavement is a blanket term to describe the vast array of emotions, experiences, changes, and conditions that take place as a result of the loss. The length of time spent in a state of bereavement will depend on many things. For example, a large determinant could be (a) the intensity of the attachment to the deceased or (b) whether the death was anticipated with enough time to allow some leave-taking. What remains stable, however, is the fact of bereavement. If one has experienced a significant loss, one is in a state of bereavement.

GRIEF

Whereas *bereavement* represents the state of loss, *grief* represents the particular reactions one experiences while in that state. Reactions or symptoms experienced as grief might include anger, guilt, physical complaints and illnesses, despair, and sadness, to name only a few. Like bereavement, the intensity of these symptoms and reactions varies, depending on the type of loss, the situation surrounding the loss, or the attachment to the deceased. C. M. Parkes (1993) describes grief as "an emotion that draws us toward something or someone that is missing. It arises from awareness of a discrepancy between the world that is and the world that 'should be'" (p. 92).

LOSS

R. S. Weiss (1993) uses the term *loss* to refer to an event that produces persisting inaccessibility of an emotionally important figure. He adds, "the experience of loss may be produced by such different events as the death of the emotionally important figure, estrangement from that figure, even geographic distancing from that figure. Bereavement represents the experiential state one endures after realizing a loss saying 'In all these instances there is likely to be distress; where loss is viewed as permanent there is likely to be pain and disorientation' " (p. 272).

MOURNING

Mourning represents the culturally defined acts that are usually performed after a death (Rosenblatt, Walsh, & Jackson, 1976). As would be expected, different societies have different mourning customs. Americans mourn in a way quite different from those who mourn in Greece or India. For most individuals in our culture, mourning is on a small scale, private, and personal. It is usually over too soon for bereaved persons to realize the full impact of the loss. Nevertheless, general rules are usually followed. Most often, there is a visitation period before the funeral and a short graveside service before the burial. The funeral itself is usually stylized and brief. On the other hand, prominent figures require more outward signs of mourning, such as large military displays or, at least, flags flown at half-mast.

ACTUAL AND SYMBOLIC LOSSES

Losses can be actual or symbolic (Schmale, 1958). An actual loss is involved when a significant person dies, when a limb or body part is amputated or lost through trauma, when there has been a separation or divorce, or when an important job or position has ceased. These concrete losses can be seen. Symbolic losses are generally enmeshed within an actual loss. For example, when one loses a job, much of the feeling of loss is caught up in a sense of depleted ego identity. Jobs define our roles. Without a job, a sense of self that had been attached to that role is lost. When a child dies, the parent is caught up in a different identification problem. A child is an extension of the parent. When a child dies, part of the parent dies as well.

Symbolic losses are difficult to define but important to recognize. Caregivers need to be alert to symbolic losses that encircle an actual loss because much of the work of grief is enmeshed within symbolic losses.

CASE STUDY: LOSS OF IDENTITY

Mrs. Bryant had been married to a prominent physician when he died at age 48 in an automobile accident. His death shocked the entire community, and a tremendous amount of support was offered to the family. Strangers wrote letters telling her of the wonderfully kind things he had done for them. Flowers and gifts continued to arrive weeks after the funeral. Friends and acquaintances made themselves available to her constantly. Mrs. Bryant managed to get through the first year with amazing courage and strength. She even offered support to others as well as help to ease the children through their grief.

However, after slightly more than a year, support diminished. Mrs. Bryant was suddenly left with only a few close friends, and even they were reluctant to talk with her about her husband any longer. If she wanted company, she felt that she needed to talk of other, more pleasant topics, but small talk was exhausting because it was such an effort. Mrs. Bryant felt more alone and isolated than she had at any other time in her life. She told me that she felt as though she had been buried along with her husband. She felt that her sense of purpose and need had gone out of her life, and only a shell was left. The emptiness that Mrs. Bryant felt had to do with work before his death. Without him, she was devoid of personality. She suffered the actual loss of her husband as well as the symbolic loss of herself.

It was several years before she could begin to work on ego replenishment. Learning to live for herself was not nearly as easy as it had been to live for her husband. Often, caregivers are asked to help the bereaved not only to deal with the pain of actual loss but also to understand the extent of more covert symbolic losses.

PROCESS

The process of bereavement is not a linear one with concrete boundaries. It is instead a composite of overlapping fluid phases that vary from person to person and situation to situation. The phases of bereavement are meant to be general guidelines to assist the clinician as well as the bereaved in understanding the emotions and physical symptoms endemic to a loss. Freud (1917) spoke of the phases as the "work of mourning," as did Lindemann (1944) when he shortened the term to "grief work." The process demands that the bereaved deal with the pain of grief, release the lost person, readjust to a world without the deceased, and form a new identity with new relationships and roles. As such, it is time-consuming and arduous, involving much deprivation and psychosocial change.

SYMPTOMATOLOGY

Rarely does one escape (for very long) the painful experience of grief. It is the most profound expression of loss. As Freud pointed out in an early paper, *Mourning and Melancholia* (1917), grief follows every loss, whether it be the death of a beloved person or the loss of either material possessions or an ideal such as a particular philosophy, religious conviction, or patriotic dream. The symptoms vary among individuals, and the outcome may be adaptive or debilitative, but one thing is certain: The person is affected by the experience.

This facet of grief is made especially clear in Erich Lindemann's important study (1944). In what is still one of the best accounts of the syndrome of grief, Lindemann deals with the specific symptomatology of grief. Lindemann evaluated anecdotal accounts of acute grief reactions by a series of 101 subjects who were survivors of relatives lost in the Coconut Grove nightclub fire in Boston (as well as other patients who had experienced the death of a relative). Lindemann identified a specific syndrome that still stands as an accurate description of grief:

> Common to all is the following syndrome: sensations of somatic distress occurring in waves lasting from 20 minutes to an hour at a time, a feeling of tightness in the throat, choking with shortness of breath, need for sighing, and an empty feeling in the abdomen, lack of muscular power, and an intense subjective distress described as tension or mental pain. (p. 141)

In addition, Lindemann noted among the bereaved a loss of warmth in relationships to others, a tendency toward heightened irritability and anger, and a desire to socially withdraw at a time when friends and relatives were making a special effort to maintain relationships (Lindemann, 1944).

Lindemann noted five characteristics that are pathognomonic for grief: (1) somatic distress, (2) preoccupation with the image of the deceased, (3) guilt, (4) hostile reactions, and (5) a loss of the usual patterns of conduct. These characteristics are corroborated by other researchers (Maddison & Viola, 1968; Parkes, 1965). Further, many persons attempt to avoid the pain connected with grief by a flight into activity or any other method that keeps the mind off the deceased.

C. M. Parkes (1971a) describes the pangs of grief as episodes of restlessness, anger, and anxiety brought on by any reminder of the loss. He relates the pangs as closely approximating the separation anxiety that Bowlby (1960b) observed when young children were separated from their mothers. C. S. Lewis (1961) gives a personal account of this symptom when he writes in his book *A Grief Observed*, "No one ever told me that grief felt so like fear, I am not afraid, but the sensation is like being afraid. The same fluttering in the stomach, the same restlessness, the yawning. I keep on swallowing" (p. 7).

Clayton, Halikes, and Maurice (1971) found that depressed mood was seen more often in their sample of widows than was anxiety. The researchers noted that sleep disturbances and crying were reported significantly more often than were other symptoms. Marris (1968), studying bereavement in 72 London widows, delineated many physical symptoms that were aggravated by their husbands' deaths: weight loss, rheumatism, asthma, bronchitis, cramping pains in the chest, hair loss, headaches, and recurrence of duodenal or gastric ulcers. Like Clayton et al.'s findings, the most common of all symptoms is difficulty in sleeping.

VARIANTS OF COMPLICATED GRIEF

The term *complicated grief* is used when extenuating factors confound the process of normal grief, factors that stem from a variety of circumstances ranging from premorbid personality problems to situational stresses. These variables cause the bereavement to be more severe and long lasting than one would expect, or on the other hand, they cause the bereaved to avoid or not even acknowledge their grief, which hampers grief resolution.

Therese Rando (1993), in her portrayal of complicated grief, explains that the bereaved attempt to do two things: They either deny or repress the pain and even sometimes suppress the realization of the loss, and they show great difficulty in letting go of the lost one. She adds, "no matter what treatment is used, there will be a need to address these two issues" (p. 149).

Several variations of complicated grief have been identified. Rando (1993) has noted that these symptoms group into seven notable syndromes. These symptoms may occur independently or at the same time. The seven syndromes are:

1. Absent mourning.
2. Delayed mourning.
3. Inhibited mourning.
4. Distorted mourning.
5. Conflicted mourning.
6. Unanticipated mourning.
7. Chronic mourning. (p 151)

DELAYED REACTIONS

Both Deutsch (1937) and Lindemann (1944) observed that a delay in which the bereaved actually shows no grief reaction for weeks or even longer is a problem not only for the bereaved but also for the health professional because of the difficulty of noticing and addressing it. An individual can then carry an unresolved grief, which may erupt at a later date into what Lindemann termed "distorted reactions." As a matter of fact, it has been suggested that a delay in mourning is one of the strongest predictors of future complicated grief (Parkes, 1978; Parkes & Weiss, 1983). Yet, Siggins (1966) warned that a temporary absence of emotion may provide a respite from the initial strain of shock. She compared it to what James Agee (1957) called "phases of exhaustion or anesthesia in which relatively little is felt" (p. 304).

DISTORTED REACTIONS

Lindemann (1944) described several reactions as overreactions that occur after a loss:

1. Overactivity without a sense of loss.
2. Acquisition of symptoms belonging to the last illness of the deceased.
3. Symptom formation by the process of identification closely following upon the death, such as ulcerative colitis, rheumatoid arthritis, and asthma.
4. A change in relationship to friends and relatives in which there is a withdrawal of social integration.
5. Hostility toward others, with feelings of distrust and suspiciousness.
6. As a result of trying to hide anger, the development of a wooden and formal demeanor resembling a schizophrenic masklike appearance.
7. Lasting loss of patterns of social interaction—inability to initiate activities or to make decisions.
8. Activities not in the best social and economic interest of the person, such as unlimited generosity with money or foolish economic dealings to the degree of being intrapunitive.
9. Agitated depression, described by Lindemann as showing excessive tension, insomnia, poor self-worth, and negative self-accusations, sometimes with suicidal thoughts and behavior.

Raphael (1984) has identified two patterns—extreme anger and extreme guilt—that are found in distorted reactions. Sadness and sorrow are missing in extreme anger and are replaced with protest and furious rage. The anger persists and eventually can disrupt the entire life of the bereaved, destroying support systems and relationships.

Extreme guilt is marked by preoccupation with self-blame and self-punishment. This pattern generally results from a conflicted premorbid relationship with the deceased and lacks any evidence of sorrow or sadness, only guilt. Continued for long periods, this pattern may result in severe depression.

Conflicted Grief

Conflicted grief arises after the loss of a highly troubled, ambivalent relationship (Parkes & Weiss, 1983). Generally, a complexity of emotions arises following the death, including an intensity of guilt and remorse as well as difficulty accepting the feelings and behaviors that the griever would like to forget. In the aftermath of the death is a period of relief and well-being. Yet, the relief is short-lived because of the guilt and self-reproach brought about by the realization that the relationship was never a good one and the knowledge that there will never be a chance for redemption.

Chronic Grief

Chronic grief refers to a situation in which the early grief response is appropriate, but the intensity of reactions continues without subsiding (Parkes, 1971a; Raphael, 1984). As a result, the individual remains in deep, painful grief as a way of life.

Although many variations of grief exist, these three basic forms—delayed, distorted, and chronic—appear to be the major ones that separate normal from complicated grief. Even here, caution should be used by the caregiver not to make hasty judgments before developing a careful and appropriate assessment of moderator variables that may be complicating the response. What may appear to be a distorted reaction on the surface may, in fact, be a very normal response to an extenuating circumstance not initially noted.

Complicated grief is addressed in greater detail in Part Four.

FACTORS AFFECTING OUTCOME

A number of factors have been identified as complicating a significant loss:

- Attachment to and relationship with the deceased.
- Situation surrounding the death.
- Premorbid personality of the bereaved.

- Social support systems.
- Concurrent crises.

Attachment to and relationship with the deceased. The strength of the attachment formed between the bereaved and the deceased significantly affects both the intensity of bereavement and the time it takes for completion of the grief process (Bowlby, 1980; Parkes, 1971a). The loss of an important attachment figure greatly affects the safety and security of the bereaved one. According to Bowlby (1982), the biological function of attachment behavior is that of protection. As such, it becomes a fundamental form of behavior, with survival as the basic motivation. For some, the attachment was so strong that they never fully resolved their loss (Freud, 1960). The relationship between the bereaved and deceased can present other elements that cause problems in resolution of bereavement, such as ambivalence (Raphael, 1984), guilt (Lazare, 1979), hostility (Bowlby, 1980), or excessive dependency (Lopata, 1973; Parkes & Weiss, 1983).

Situation surrounding the death. Whether death happened suddenly or resulted from a chronic illness makes a difference in outcome. Sanders (1982–1983) found that people who experienced a sudden death situation showed more symptoms of shock and consequent somatic problems over time than did those whose family member died of chronic illness. On the other hand, long-term illnesses exhausted the family caregivers, leaving them little energy to complete the necessary grief work. For minimal grief effect, the optimal time of a chronic illness related to outcome of bereavement appears to be around 6 months. Neither physical exhaustion nor diminution of social support systems totally tax the strength of the bereaved.

Premorbid personality of the bereaved. Factors such as excessive neuroticism, early childhood losses, dependency disorders, or antisocial behavior could cause an individual to deal poorly with the added stress of bereavement. Individuals who have dormant negative self-images may find that bereavement activates these thoughts, making them feel more helpless and defective than before (Horowitz, Wilner, Marmar, & Krupnick, 1980).

Social support systems. If the bereaved individual either has little or no support or perceives insufficient support, the abrasion of grief can be deep and pervasive. One of the most important effects of support groups is that of connecting individuals who can share their grief with others who are going through a similiar situation. In grief, there is a need to know that one is not the only person to have experienced a loss. By talking with others, feeling empathy, and understanding, one connects with the outside world once again.

Concurrent crises. Because bereavement itself is a stress of inordinate proportions, when other crises impinge, whether they were preexisting or are new events, the bereaved has little energy left to deal with anything other than the major task of surviving. In crisis overload, the overburdened individual may find it nearly impossible to resolve grief and move through the bereavement process.

The caregiver needs to be alert to these extenuating factors when working with the bereaved and to recognize that any one of them could cause complications and further impede the process. On the other hand, some individuals may experience one or more of these factors without having a negative reaction. Further research is needed before full understanding of these factors and their effect on the bereavement process is attained.

OUTCOME

The question of what constitutes good or bad outcome in bereavement is still equivocal among researchers and clinicians. Because patterns of normal bereavement reactions are still not clearly understood, it remains difficult to determine criteria for abnormal reactions (Osterweis, Solomon, & Green, 1984). Clinical judgment parallels expectations (e.g., if one survives, remarries, attempts new adventures, and forms new relationships, that person is proclaimed by society as having made a healthy adjustment). However, if that individual is using all the preceding variables to *distract* from the work of grief, then the adjustment, which looked so adaptive at the outset, becomes a cover-up and is consequently nonadaptive. For this reason, it has been difficult to gather reliable data to accurately measure outcome of bereavement. Even death, which on the outside appears to be maladaptive, may to some be a blessed relief from their suffering.

Given the preceding qualifiers, three major outcome possibilities of bereavement have been identified, with many variations falling somewhere in between. No value judgments are indicated with any of the potential directions listed. The choice of how an individual determines the course of actions following a significant loss remains always a personal decision:

1. One can determine to let go of the deceased, form new and satisfac-

tory relationships, adopt a new identity structure, and energetically reintegrate back into the mainstream of life.

2. One can continue in the same manner of living as before the death, proceeding in every way *as if* the deceased were just away, and maintaining the same relationships and roles.

3. At some level, either consciously or unconsciously, one can choose not to invest the energy required to begin a new life, but instead to move in the opposite direction, that of seclusion, sickness, or death. This particular outcome is based on the theoretical notion that each individual has control over personal destiny and can choose either health and integration or disease and disintegration.

Secondary Gains of Bereavement

The outcome chosen depends on many factors, such as personality, situational variables, or the suddenness of the death itself. Another, less evident, factor has to do with the secondary gains the bereaved might receive as a result of moving in one direction or another. For example, if one has a support system that applauds independent actions without reinforcing dependent behavior, there is a greater likelihood that the individual will choose a path related to the first choice outlined. If, on the other hand, one is surrounded with helping people, willing to take on tasks and provide excess nurturance for the bereaved, then that individual will find secondary gains in remaining dependent and grief stricken. And finally, if the bereaved person has few supporters, feels that life has been completed, or lacks the energy to devote to reintegration, then the gains will be in the direction of shutting down, with the goal of subsequent rest.

THE DENIAL OF GRIEF

Grief has been compared to both a physical injury (Parkes, 1972) and a physical illness (Engel, 1961). Yet even with the acknowledgment that grief is painful and long lasting, there is a reluctance to give it much medical attention. After all, most people are taught that grief is supposed to be a normal reaction to loss. As such, the reactions themselves should not be excessive. Unfortunately, that stereotype is erroneous. Geoffrey Gorer (1965) writes, "Mourning is treated as if it were a weakness, a self-indulgence, a reprehensible bad habit instead of a psychological necessity" (p. 131). There has been little social adjustment in attitude since 1965.

In order to disguise the pain, then, the bereaved need to hide emotions. In doing this, however, they deny themselves the right to grieve openly and without inhibition (Rosenblatt, Walsh, & Jackson, 1976). They control their behavior—sometimes to the point of seeming nonchalant—hoping that they will not break down and expose themselves.

A 55-year-old widow from the Tampa study described her feelings as she was struggling to get through the graveside ritual:

> I learned, as my mother before me, that you focus on something, and this is how you get through funerals. Like up to the cemetery, they had this artificial grass and I was really concentrating on the tricks the sun was playing on it. When the chaplain called me, he wanted to know if I had wanted some personal things said and I said, "Oh, good Lord no." I said he had better keep it as impersonal as possible, otherwise we would need hip boots to get out of there . . . because his sister, I know, everybody would have started bawling. As so, he read the 23rd Psalm and something else, but it was very lovely.

This short quote illustrates the cultural-social barriers that prohibit full expression of grief. The bereaved wish to maintain the appearance of strength during public rituals—perhaps because Americans place a high value on emotional control. Yet for some, this control is impossible. They break down and, as a result, feel embarassed, even shameful. The underlying message suggests that public displays of emotion are a breach of etiquette, even un-American. Emotional outbursts make everyone uncomfortable: the bereaved because they feel out of control and weak, and the supporters because they feel embarrassed and helpless. It is as though an unwritten dictum states, "Thou shalt not grieve in public places."

Considering that grief is so painful, it is not unthinkable that grief is denied. The very thought of separation fills people with as much dread as it did when they were children. Left alone, children scream and cry until they receive some comfort. As adults, however, defenses are supposed to be stronger. Negative feelings are more easily repressed and pushed out of conscious awareness. Death and loss have too many negative connotations to merit much concern (Weisman, 1972). After all, who wants to ponder a topic that represents such destructive objectives? So denial is used both to avoid a shameful and embarrassing situation and as a respite or retreat from reality. At the same time, bereaved individuals are aided in their attempts at denial by a public all too willing to go along with their wishes.

For most, grief is a private matter. Not only must one grieve alone, without support, but without ritual as well, for the necessary rituals that have historically bridged psychosocial transitions are greatly diminished in the modern age. Although funerals provide a certain degree of ritual, they have nevertheless diminished in value compared to the rituals of the past (Hinton, 1967). Once burial is completed, much of the community's support falls away. Things move all too quickly back to normal for everyone except the bereaved, who must now mourn alone.

Denial of grief surfaces too in the lack of traditional mourning clothing or accessories (Gorer, 1965). Black may seem drab, but in the past it carried the message of personal sorrow as well as the unspoken request for personal consideration. The significance seemed to work both ways. Just as the comforters were alerted to show proper consideration, so the bereaved were comforted themselves by demonstrating proper respect for the deceased (Gorer, 1965). Recently, a man was sitting in my office talking with me about his grief for his deceased mother. She had been 84 when she suffered a stroke that left her unable to respond to anything. The horror of her paralysis for the family was that she had been such an active, vital woman before the stroke. One would think this man's grief would have been resolved during the year that his mother was unresponsive. Perhaps some of it had. He said that his friends had stopped saying anything to him about her. He feared they had forgotten her. Then he added poignantly, "I wish it were appropriate for me to wear an armband. At least that would be something I could do." Indeed, the ashes and sackcloth of the past had their value.

Grief conduct is a self-perpetuating dilemma. People are self-conscious and ill at ease in the presence of newly bereaved persons because they have had so little contact with other bereaved. In turn, people have little contact with bereaved people because they are self-conscious and ill at ease in their presence. In order to break this cycle, we must begin at the beginning and remove the self-consciousness surrounding the bereaved. An excellent place to start is with children.

In the past, when death and grief occurred at home, children received their death education quite naturally. They learned that mourners were in a special state of mind and required more consideration and more respect. But most importantly, they were able to observe grown-ups as they interacted with the bereaved. Today, children have few role models to imitate. Even worse, they are generally excluded (protected, really) from the rituals of mourning. As a result, we have produced a self-conscious generation unable to support the bereaved. The art of condolence takes a special attention that most do not know how to give.

STIGMA OF BEREAVEMENT

Another problem is that bereavement itself carries a peculiar stigma having to do with the shame of death as punishment (Parkes, 1971a). In our society, most people die after having lived long lives; premature death occurs relatively infrequently. Thus social expectations of life assume longevity. When death interrupts, the survivors feel as though some cosmic force singled them out for this painful, catastrophic event. One widow explained that she felt God had turned his back for a moment when the accident that killed her husband happened. Implicitly, the message was that if God were loving and protective, he would never have allowed this heartbreaking situation to occur. On the other hand, there is often such a strong fear of blaming God that the bereaved will invent rationalizations in order not to incur his terrible wrath.

No situation in life is exactly like another. Besides the fact that situations differ—who has died; when and where they died—the important fact remains that each person is a unique human being expressing a unique personality. Some people have greater coping skills, others have lower frustration tolerance, while still others may be so independent and self-reliant that they repel others' support. Thus, all aspects of an individual's life will have a bearing on the way the person deals with grief. Even the physical condition of the bereaved at the time of the loss will be reflected in the energy available to invest in bereavement resolution.

As caregivers, we need to take a more tolerant view of people in bereavement. We tend to stereotype grief responses, forcing them into a single general pattern. Grief that lasts too long or too intensely may be called "pathological." Grief that is too short or too painless draws suspicion of not caring enough for the deceased. There is too strong a tendency to think in such terms as "good grief" or "bad grief"—even "sick grief." The use of these expressions places qualifications on the bereaved, suggesting that grief is an impairment. Actually, there appears to be no shortcut to surviving a significant loss. As stated earlier, I initially focused on reducing or alleviating the pain of grief. However, after talking with hundreds of bereaved people and after carefully studying the grief process, I have realized that it is detrimental to try to quell the pain of grief. Only through facing grief, openly dealing with the guilt, shame, and hostility, can one rid oneself of the negative reactions associated with grief and get on with the business of living.

CHAPTER 2

Theoretical Foundations: The Evolution of Bereavement Theories

RARELY DOES A new theory take root in isolation. New theories, ideas, and hypotheses often spring from several sources at once or at least emerge in fairly close chronological order. Though Freud proposed the first psychodynamic explanation of the grief process, important input from writers of other disciplines were offered both before and after he formulated his theory. Because of this overlap, I have included here only those theorists whose contributions laid the groundwork for the continuously growing body of literature on bereavement. I recognize that many others have written on the subject of grief and loss, and my exclusion of their contributions does not mean that they are less qualified—just that the writers selected made their statements more clearly and emphatically.

To discuss these theories, I have first presented in considerable detail a case study so that we can see how it could be interpreted in light of a particular theory. It is interesting to note that as each theory was developed, the grief process became better understood. Freud furthered insight into the need for *decathexis*, or releasing the tie between an individual and the objects (including other people) in the environment into which the person invests emotional significance, particularly other persons (Peretz, 1970). Other writers added further dimensions such as introjection, identification, and ambivalence, which better explained the underpinnings of the pain and resistance of grief.

CASE STUDY: HEIDI NORWALK

Heidi, 44, was the divorced mother of three children. She was also an adjunct professor of biology at a large university and was struggling to complete her doctoral dissertation. Until the dissertation was finished, however, she remained in the tenuous position of having only a yearly contract with the university. Naturally, with the responsibility of the children, she did not want to risk that kind of unpredictability. She needed tenure, especially because her middle daughter, age 11, was developmentally handicapped and would require special attention and schooling. Her youngest son, age 8, and oldest daughter, age 15, were a big help to her, particularly her daughter, who was also a best friend and confidant.

Heidi's life with her husband, Jon, had not been easy. They met in college—he, an art major, and Heidi, a natural science student. Heidi was the oldest of six children, so living away from home offered her a wonderful opportunity to be free of some responsibility. Jon, being an only child, missed the pampering he had gotten from his mother. He was extremely talented, but also demanding and at times inconsiderate. Even though they were both students, he expected her to take care of the apartment, shop, prepare meals, and have extra time to help him in some of his more difficult courses. When he and Heidi were married, he had completed a master's degree in fine arts and she had a master's degree in biology. They moved to New York City, where Jon accepted a position in a large advertising firm. In a few months, Heidi became pregnant but continued course work toward her Ph.D. Even then, she still managed to do all the housework as well as support Jon emotionally in his new job.

Despite the fact that they had some good times together, the marriage had been rocky from the beginning. Jon had several affairs. He and Heidi had had three trial separations before the final one, 4 years before I saw her. Before he left, however, she had two more children and finished the coursework on her Ph.D. She took a position at the university with the idea that she would complete the dissertation within a certain period. A year and a half later, Heidi learned that her oldest daughter, Alicen, had bone cancer.

Heidi managed to continue teaching but all her thoughts and effort went into Alicen's treatment. In the meantime, Jon remarried, which further alienated him from Heidi and the children. Heidi had never felt so alone and helpless in her life, but she had no choice but to continue being the sole caregiver to her family.

Alicen died $2\frac{1}{2}$ years later after a painful and debilitating illness. Heidi admitted, with some shame, that there had been times toward the end that she actually wished for Alicen's death. Pain on both sides—hers and Alicen's—was almost too much to bear. The final days were a nightmare to Heidi because Alicen, in a half-crazed state, fought to get out of her hospital bed and go home. She professed loudly that she hated her dad, partly as a result of her real feelings, but also partly because she was so heavily medicated. Alicen's thin little body and sunken eyes were agonizing for Heidi to see; she said she would have given anything to have taken her place. Those terrible memories were burned indelibly on Heidi's mind and she could not escape them in the months to follow.

Shortly after Alicen's death, the university set a deadline for the completion of her dissertation. She had no recourse but to frantically try to finish that project. Heidi was close to a breakdown 4 years later. She had been ill off and on with bouts of flu and severe colds. Both younger children had emotional problems, which further drained her physical and financial resources. It was the ripple effect of tragedy continuing to play itself out for a long time.

Grief was a tormenting nightmare that went on for years. Unresolved anger for her husband, frustration at the university for not giving her more time, but most of all the loss of her daughter all produced a complicated bereavement. Alicen had actually been more than a daughter—more like a close friend who also shared in the care of the two younger children. These factors all contributed to Heidi's unremitting grief.

Some theorists would say that Heidi's grief was pathological because of its severity and longevity. Others would contend that the situations in her life intensified a normal grief reaction. Still others would feel that the adjustment bonds between mother and child are such that when they are broken, the parent is left with a severe narcissistic injury that is never fully healed. All theories may be correct.

The theories explaining grief are scattered throughout the psychological literature. Although the theories differ in degree, each bereavement theory adds to the work of the previous theorist while maintaining an individual approach. Thus, the analytic theorists would argue that Heidi's grief was based on the need to *decathect*—to retrieve the invested energy that she had given Alicen and eventually give up all her ties with her. The psychosocial approach would look at the social intradynamics that arise from the many losses Heidi suffered. The general systems theorists would argue for a biological component that would employ a homeostatic model indicating Heidi's need to regain a healthy inner balance, both emotionally and physically.

SIGMUND FREUD

The first intrapsychic theory of grief was proposed by Freud in his treatise *Mourning and Melancholia* (1917) and has stood as a precedent for scientific investigation and treatment of depression to this day. Although he includes mourning in his discussion, Freud was not particularly interested in this phenomenon itself because it was considered such a normal response in the course of everyday life. We all have losses; we all grieve; we all survive. Rather, it was depression that Freud was primarily interested in. Little had been written about depression before Freud's treatise, but many symptoms appear to be the same as those seen in the grief process. To get to depression, then, it seemed appropriate to Freud first to discuss the observed reactions to grief, then to set up a comparison of this process to the more mysterious aspects of depression, or *melancholia* as he termed it. In this way, he could show the differences seen in grief and evaluate the pathological component of melancholia.

Freud writes (1917) that *grief* is the normal reaction to the loss of a loved person or "to the loss of some abstraction which has taken the place of one, such as fatherland, liberty, or an ideal and so on" (p. 125). Freud believed that although bereavement is a special period in one's life, it should never be regarded as a morbid condition necessitating medical treatment. Further, interference with the process may even be harmful to the griever. Actually, time is what makes the difference—time both to perform the work of mourning and to sever the attachment so that one is free to attach again to someone or something else.

Freud felt that mourning and melancholia are similar in that both are involved in object loss, but he concluded that a large difference lay in the fact that the melancholiac feels a lowering of self-esteem in self-reproach and self-revilement to a masochistic degree. The ego becomes poor and empty. But normal mourning, he said, contains no loss of self-esteem because there are no ambivalent feelings toward the deceased. This statement is true of normal mourning only, he cautioned.

If the bereaved had ambivalent feelings, grief results in a pathological form that Freud called "obsessive reproaches," or obsessional states of self-denigration caused by the conflict of ambivalence. These reproaches are represented in the bereaved by expressions of such things as feeling wounded, hurt, neglected, disappointed, and so forth, culminating in a delusional expectation of punishment. Yet, from what we now know of normal grief, these feelings are the rule rather than the exception. Freud (1917) proposed his theory this way:

> The testing of reality, having shown that the loved object no longer exists, requires that all libido shall be withdrawn from its attachments to this object. Against this demand a struggle of course arises—it may be universally observed that many never willingly abandon a libido-position not even when a substitute is already beckoning to him. This struggle can be so intense that a turning away from reality ensues, the object being clung to through the medium of hallucinatory wish-psychosis. The normal outcome is that defer-

ence for reality gains the day. . . . The fact is, however, that when the work of mourning is completed the ego becomes free and uninhibited again. (p. 126)

Freud's theory implies that a fixed amount of energy that was once invested (cathected) in the loved person must be retrieved (decathected) before the bereaved can become free again to reinvest in another. Yet, because of the reluctance to give up a love-object, this process must be carried through slowly, a little at a time. During this period when the work of mourning is carried through, the grieving person loses interest in everything, cannot experience love. In short, "the world becomes poor and empty" (Freud, 1917, p. 127). But when the work of mourning is finally completed, when all ties with the loved person have been given up, the survivor is once again liberated to reinvest in another person. At this point, Freud felt, grief was completed.

Quite obviously, Freud was not describing an actual situation but rather a general course by which the process of mourning takes place and is resolved.

When losses began to take place in Freud's life, he seemed to modify his earlier thinking on the resolution of grief. In the initial theory, he had spoken hopefully about the possibility of a final detachment from the loved person, but near the end of his life his thoughts changed. In a letter to Binswanger 6 years after the death of his beloved grandson, Heinle, and on the anniversary of his daughter's death, he wrote,

Although we know that after such a loss the acute stage of mourning will subside, we also know we shall remain inconsolable and will never find a substitute. No matter what may fill the gap, if it can be filled completely, it nevertheless remains something else. And actually, this is how it should be; it is the only way of perpetuating that love which we do not want to relinquish. (1929, p. 386)

An avid observer and recorder of human interaction, Freud (like the rest of us) learned best what he allowed himself to experience fully. Although he never modified his theory in writing, his attitudinal shift was substantial. He finally recognized that some losses are irreconcilable and are never full resolved.

In his stated theory, Freud would see Heidi's long-term grief as a sign of her refusal to release her attachment to Alicen. Until she can accept the reality of the death, Heidi will be locked into constant yearning for Alicen, perpetuating the pain and frustration of grief. Yet, because of the ambivalence shown toward the end of Alicen's life, the wish for her death versus the hope for her survival, Heidi is open to obsessive reproaches resulting in lowering of self-esteem and consequent long-term pathological grief.

OTTO FENICHEL

Fenichel (1945) goes a step beyond Freud in establishing two critical points: (1) that an ambivalent introjection in grief is an adaptive response, and (2) that guilt is evident to some degree in all grief.

He writes, "Mourning is characterized by an ambivalent introjection of the lost object, a continuation of feelings toward the introject that once had been directed toward the object, and the participation of guilt feelings throughout the process" (Fenichel, 1945, p. 395).

Fenichel sees bereavement as consisting of two steps, the first of which is an establishment of an introject (of taking the deceased into one's self) and the second, releasing the introjected object (1945). As such, introjection acts as a buffer by preserving the relationship while the process of relinquishment is taking place. This approach is often seen when funerals are planned. Services are carried out as if the deceased were there: Would he want flowers, what type of service would she prefer, and so on.

For example, a mother whose son was accidentally killed while on an outing with a number of friends totally disregarded the needs of her son's friends by having a private funeral. She did this because her son had hated formal social gatherings and she could not see exposing him to that kind of situation now that he could not make the decision himself. Her introject caused her to incorporate the feelings of her dead son and make decisions as though they had been his own.

AMBIVALENCE

When an ambivalent introject is formed, however, grief can immobilize the bereaved. For example, if one had secretly wished for the death of another, consciously or not, that death could be viewed as a wish fulfillment. This ambivalence is particularly evident in sibling death. There is hardly a child raised in a large family who has not at one time or another wished to be the only child—the center of parental love and affection. Implicit in this wish is the unconscious wish for the death of other siblings. Sometimes it is even a conscious wish. In anger and resentment the child may say, "Drop dead." If death occurs at some later time, the surviving sibling is at enormous risk of inordinate guilt and may even wish to die as a just consequence.

Fenichel also points out that ambivalent introjection can sometimes have dire consequences (1945). Some people who have wished another person to die may feel that they themselves have to die. This situation occurred in a case in which a couple lived for 10 years with knowledge of the wife's cancer. The couple had no children; each lived for the other. But during the latter part of the illness, when physical debilitation took its toll, ambivalent feelings arose in the husband over several things: (a) the disfigurement of his wife's massive mastectomy became repulsive to him so that sex was impossible; (b) he often had fantasies of being with other women, which shamed him terribly; (c) when many hospitalizations began to wipe out their small savings, he worried that they would have nothing left at all. Implicit was the wish that she would die, that because death was inevitable anyhow, it would be better to get it over with. When her pain grew even more intense, he became remorseful but also wished for her suffering to cease through a quiet death. Yet, when death came, all these thoughts tormented him beyond belief. He was inconsolable. He felt that he was to blame—that his wife knew of his secret thoughts and that she could never forgive him. Within 4 months, he died of pneumonia.

Fenichel (1945) believes that the greater the love-hate relationship and the greater the self-reproach, the greater the grief. Most often, however, hate is finally resolved in time by positive feelings toward the deceased. According to Fenichel, this resolution is the only way in which we can mitigate the intrapsychic dissonance and escape the punishment of profound guilt.

But even when ambivalence is resolved, Fenichel says, guilt is always present in mourning to some degree. Even in the most benign cases, there is a certain bittersweet knowledge that death has occurred to someone else rather than oneself or another family member. Lifton (1968) describes the guilt seen in survivors of Hiroshima, in which those individuals felt that they should have been the ones to die instead of other family members but at the same time suffered guilt because they were, in some deep way, relieved to have been spared.

In the Tampa study, a bereaved parent was outraged when another mother came to her after the death of her young daughter saying that when she heard the tragic news, she rushed home to gather her own children about her and hold them close. She was relieved that death had not come to her own children. After this, the visitor felt enormous guilt and was unable to visit the bereaved mother again. Guilt from a variety of sources can imperceptibly find its way into the grieving situation, blocking our ability to forgive ourselves.

IDENTIFICATION

For many persons, identification with the deceased has been carried on for some time before the death. This situation is seen in marriages in which the wife has identified with her husband by taking on his achievements as her own. Physicians' wives, ministers' wives, and corporate wives sometimes become an extension of these positions in the community. If the husband dies, the wife is more deprived through role loss than are others who have not established strong role connections.

Thus Heidi's grief, using Fenichel's theory, takes on added dimensions in terms of her close identification with her child. Shame and guilt over wishing for an early death would be a modifying factor as well. Anger toward her husband and toward the university for its poor support and betrayal would add to situational stress. All these elements working together could produce an intense and severe bereavement that would last a long time but would also be seen as normal.

HARRY STACK SULLIVAN

Harry Stack Sullivan, while psychoanalytically trained, developed a theory of grief based on an interpersonal concept of relationships (1956). He feels that it is a waste of time to speak of the individual as the object of the study because the individual does not and cannot exist apart from personal relations with others. The focus of Sullivan's theory, then, is the interpersonal situation and not the person. This approach lends a social dimension to grief theory in that Sullivan is not interested in the personal intradynamics of the grief process but rather in the social interdynamics that arise from various loss situations.

Sullivan sees grief as "an extremely valuable and protective device" (1956, p. 105). This is not to say that he does not admit to its pain or unpleasantness. Sullivan is well aware of the torture people endure as a result of loss. Rather, because grief is dependent on attachment behavior, or as he put it, "the integrative tendency which I call love" (p. 105), grief offers the bereaved survivor opportunity to extricate from the attachment bond. Sullivan feels that the value of grief is that it erases these attachments that threaten to maintain the illusions of love forever.

Sullivan's theory relies heavily on the process of early socialization. If the mother transmits feelings of safety and security to the infant, then the child develops with minimal need to defend against the environment. If, on the other hand, fear and anxiety are transmitted to the infant, the child feels a need to adopt various types of protective measures, such as acute separation anxiety. But Sullivan does not believe that personality is set in concrete at an early age. Changes will take place any time new interpersonal situations occur to warrant growth or regression. Therefore, all experiences have the potential for education; we can learn and grow or defend and regress. Through this approach, Sullivan provides a more optimistic view than other analytic writers in that, even though we may have had a difficult beginning, subsequent positive interpersonal relationships reshape our perceptions and alter our trust in others as well as enhance our own feelings of personal security.

The dynamism of grief (*dynamisms* are what Sullivan calls the recurrent patterns of behavior that typify an individual in relationship to others— emotional responses such as guilt, pride, conceit, etc.), according to Sullivan, represents an obsessional device that, by repetition of acknowledging the death, obliterates the object of the obsession (1956). In other words, by repeating over and over to oneself, "She is gone; she is dead," one is neutralizing the tendency to cling to the lost person by strengthening the hold on reality. Gradually, associations with the deceased are erased.

There are times when the erasing action will not function. Sullivan (1956) says that these situations are ones in which grief becomes a secondary reinforcer, maintaining in some fashion the security of the bereaved person. If the relationship was based on some overcomplex neurotic pattern, if security systems were based solely on an investment in the other, then the threat of losing the entire security system throws the bereaved person open to too much anxiety. Grief then becomes a way of life and is used for the maintenance of security. In these cases, grief is used as a barrier to life, a barrier to change, a barrier to reality. Regressive behavior causes deterioration and disintegration of the personality.

The importance of Sullivan's theory is that it is grounded in a psychosocial approach. Importance is given to the nature of (a) the relationship between the bereaved and the deceased and (b) the depth of the attachment bond. Early socialization also colors the relationship, giving credence to the contributory effect of personality variables on the grieving process.

How could Heidi's grief be interpreted using Sullivan's theory? First, Sullivan would note the significance of the strong attachment between Heidi and Alicen and would recognize the need to erase those ties. In Heidi's case, however, it is apparent that the intense feelings of responsibility that she has learned throughout her life would interfere with the erasing procedure and produce a barrier to change. It could also be argued that the loss of Heidi's husband had not been fully erased so that the new grief accommodated two people rather than one, causing double indemnity. But Heidi's own sense of security, learned from her mother, created an adaptive "set" that provided the fuel for her to continue in a positive manner with her academic work. So, within this theoretical framework, Heidi's response was a product of her relationships with others during her life, whether they were positive or negative.

GEORGE POLLOCK

As an ego psychologist, Pollock's (1961) theory of bereavement is based on an ego-adaptive process that sees the disrupted mourner struggling to renew an internal balance while readjusting to a threatening external environment.

Pollock's theory is closely tied to Cannon's (1929) model of stability through homeostasis. In this model, the internal environment balances the external one so that a positive equilibrium is maintained throughout. If the body develops an infection, the system quickly goes into action to restore health to the organism. Similarly, if other disruptive states occur, such as the termination of a close relationship or loss of something held dear, psychological lesions result. A basic element of every living organism, at any point in life, is the capacity for adaptive responses to the external milieu, which in turn produces a state of balance in the internal environment. Grief is seen as adaptive, in that from the moment of awareness of loss, one is constantly striving to regain balance and reestablish an intrapsychic homeostatic state.

Based on this notion, Pollock presents the following components that make up his theory of the grieving process.

ACUTE STATE

Shock
Immediately upon learning of the death, a person experiences an initial overturn of ego equilibrium. There may be panic, moaning, wailing, and even fainting. This stage is usually short-lived and is followed closely by the grief phase.

Grief
Realizing (though not necessarily accepting) that death is an actuality, a person suffers intense psychic pain created by deep despair and sorrow. The deep suffering of this phase is explained by two theories, one from Freud (1941) and one from Federn (1952). These theories are the "swelling hypothesis" and the "avulsion hypothesis." In the swelling hypothesis, pain is caused by swelling of the ego, which creates excitation without the ability to discharge the energy because the object is missing. The avulsion hypothesis refers to ego impoverishment: The object is gone, and libido (energy) may temporarily be avulsed with it. When this avulsion happens, the only avenue is to withdraw and conserve energy.

Separation

If a person previously had a healthy relationship, the task of internal object decathexis is less difficult. The person is able finally to relinquish the deceased. However, if the bereaved continues to maintain the introject (keep a secret internal communication with the deceased), grief resolution will be delayed.

CHRONIC STATE (REPARATION)

This period marks a step toward a lasting adaption without the loved person. Pollock feels that because the griever faces many secondary losses as a result of the death—such as the need to give up home, social group, possessions, and so on—new griefs are often added. These new griefs cause overload for the bereaved, making reparation even more difficult.

Pollock sees bereavement as a process through which an attempt is made to maintain the constancy of the internal psychic equilibrium. He views grief as a process of adaption that provides the griever with the possibility of growth and positive change.

How would Pollock view Heidi's grief? As an ego psychologist, he might begin by noting the many disruptions in Heidi's life prior to Alicen's death. Realizing the need to regain both external and internal balance, she would be constantly striving to recover from one situation while she was plunged into yet another. Heidi reacts well, with adaptive responses, but she is physically worn down with sheer numbers. Both the swelling hypothesis (which explains the agony of the loss) and the avulsion hypothesis (which speaks to her emptiness later on) offer interesting interpretations. But because of the discord, not only in her own life but in her daughter's as well, excess guilt and anger are evident. These excess emotions make grief resolution slow and even more difficult. Even so, Pollock (1961) states that "the loss of a child can never be fully integrated and totally accepted by the mother or the father" (p. 353).

JOHN BOWLBY

The conceptual framework that John Bowlby has adopted to explain loss and bereavement uses a combination of both attachment theory and human information processing (1980, chap. 3). *Attachment theory* refers to the affectional bonds that are created by familiarity with and closeness to parent figures early in life. They come from a need to feel safe and secure. *Human information processing* relates to the central control of sensory inflow, much of which is outside conscious awareness. Bowlby also describes "defensive exclusion," which is used when the system is in danger of trying to process difficult information. The result is often a type of denial or repression used to block out unwanted information. If defensive exclusion continues to be used, reality is masked, leaving the bereaved person unable to relate to others.

Bowlby (1980) divides bereavement into four phases, as follows:

1. *Numbing.* Initially, the griever feels stunned, unable to process the information. However, as reality impinges, numbing gives way to the second phase.
2. *Yearning and Searching.* This phase is a combination of intense separation anxiety and defensive exclusion, which triggers the desire to search for and recover the lost person. Failure to recover the deceased brings repeated frustrations and disappointments until the bereaved reaches the next phase.
3. *Disorganization and Despair.*
4. *Reorganization.* The phases of disorganization and reorganization are set forth without clear-cut division.

Bowlby states that the central task of these last two phases is to reconcile the double-edged quality of belief and disbelief; strong emotions must be borne, along with endless questions dealing with the how and why of the loss. There is also a need for redefinition of self. New skills must be acquired, old ones discarded. It is a process, Bowlby says, of "reshaping internal representational models so as to align them with the changes that have occurred in the bereaved's life situation" (1980, p. 94).

The immense value of Bowlby's work lies in his ability to examine grief as a characteristic that is adaptive both in animals and humans and is therefore universal. In citing Darwin's (1872) and Lorenz's (1952) descriptions of sorrow seen in animals, Bowlby concludes that searching and crying are adaptive mechanisms designed to retrieve the lost attachment figure. Because these behaviors are often successful in reuniting loved ones, they have continued on as an automatic, intrinsic response to loss. Thus, Bowlby posits a biological basis for the grief response that is seen across cultures and species.

Back to Heidi's situation: How might Bowlby view her grief? Based on his approach of attachment theory, he would focus on her continuous separation anxiety as a factor that kept her in a dysfunctional state. Because loss followed upon loss with little respite, she was unable to get past the stage of disorganization and to begin the restorative process of reorganization. With the tasks of not only nurturing her remaining children but also providing for them financially, she was forced to deny her own emotional needs, keeping herself locked into old patterns of responding.

GEORGE ENGEL

George Engel (1961) raises the question, "Is grief a disease?" He makes an important addition to the bereavement literature by making use of two primary biological modes of response to danger and associating them with object loss (1962). Engel proposes that the central nervous system is organized to mediate two opposite patterns of response. The first, the fight-flight reaction, is considered to be the biological anlage of anxiety. This reaction serves both to prepare the organism for vigorous physical effort and to cushion against physical trauma.

The second, the conservation-withdrawal system, comes into play when the first system threatens exhaustion. This system is considered to be the biological anlage of depression-withdrawal. This state is adaptive in that it encourages rest in the physically sick organism and permits subsequent recovery and survival. Conservation-withdrawal in bereft individuals allows and facilitates the recouping of extended internal resources and the recognition that recovery and survival is possible through gradual identification of other sources of comfort.

This process is not a depletion of energy, as would be seen in massive fatigue, but instead is a move toward withdrawal, often marked by the requirement of more sleep than usual (Kaufman & Rosenblum, 1967). This system is usually expressed in the daily pattern of fatigue and the need for more rest. Engel states that conservation-withdrawal contributes more consistently to the common symptomatology of physical illness than does anxiety (Engel, 1962). This belief supports Engel's earlier proposal (1961) that grief should be considered a disease from the viewpoint that "pathological" refers to a changed state and not to the fact of the response. As Engel (1962) states, "It is a 'holding action' until the arrival of external supplies helps in the form of a supporting object" (p. 95).

Engel (1972) divided the sequence of events that characterize the grieving process into six stages:

Shock and disbelief.   Stunned in the beginning, the mourner needs time to process the event of death.
Developing awareness.   The fight-flight pattern is activated in terms of emotional acting out. Crying, anger and irritability, and guilt are common forms of anguish.

Restitution.   The ritualization of mourning acts to draw family and friends together in a supportive endeavor. The recovery process is initiated as the reality of death is acknowledged. Religious and spiritual beliefs may provide a sense of peace as expectations for reunion after death are emphasized.

Resolving the loss.   Withdrawing from others allows grief work to take place and, at the same time, conserves valuable energy. By utilization of rest, one is able to recoup strength and move on to successful healing.

Idealization.   The process of idealization works initially to help quell negative feelings toward the deceased. However, as memories are dealt with, two important changes are taking place. Recurring reminiscences about the lost person begin to bring into focus the more positive qualities of the deceased, and at the same time, the bereaved begins to take in admired qualities and attributes of the deceased. As this idealization takes place, the griever's preoccupation with the deceased lessens and he or she is able to reinvest feelings in other projects.

The outcome.   Successful completion of mourning takes a year or more but with it comes the ability to remember both the pleasures and disappointments of the lost relationship without pain. Many factors, such as degree of guilt, ambivalence, dependency, age, and number of prior losses, affect the outcome and have bearing on the length of time for full resolution (pp. 379–383).

COLIN MURRAY PARKES

Based on his study of 22 London widows, Parkes (1972) concluded that grief resembles a physical injury more than any other type of illness (p. 5). He feels (along with Engel) that the loss can readily be spoken of as a "blow," just as in the case of a physical injury. When complications occasionally arise, the outcome may be fatal. Grief is seen as a major stressor having profound implications for health. As such, Parkes can be seen advocating a biological theory of grief.

Like Engel, Parkes feels that the stress of bereavement is closely aligned to Cannon's fight-flight theory, which was important in demonstrating that whether an animal is preparing to fight or flee, a single physiological response will be made (Cannon, 1929). This response includes changes in body function.

NUMBNESS

The first stage, that of numbness, can occur immediately upon hearing of the loss or even some minutes later, but will last anywhere from a few hours to a few days. Numbness is seen as adaptive in that it acts as a psychological and physical barrier to immediate pain, enabling the griever to carry out the duties of the ritual.

SEARCHING AND PINING

Numbness gives way gradually to the second state, that of searching and pining. Characteristic of searching behavior is restless hyperactivity, inability to concentrate on anything but the lost person, and ruminations surrounding the death together with a loss of interest in things and people other than the deceased (Parkes, 1971a).

Pining, a term reminiscent of Melanie Klein (1940), is the emotional counterpart of searching behavior. Parkes also speaks of "pangs" of grief as episodes of severe anxiety and psychological pain.

DEPRESSION

Once the intense pangs of grief subside, as one realizes that searching is fruitless and as anger loses its potency, feelings of apathy and despair predominate. This stage is primarily the period of being forced to accept a changing assumptive world or of being made to realize the alterations that must be made in order to survive.

RECOVERY

Recovery comes about when old assumptions and modes of thinking are relinquished. Not until then is the individual free to begin again.

Using Parkes's theoretical approach, we would need to look at what Heidi has lost in her daughter's death. We see that Alicen had been her closest friend, confidant, and helper. In addition, Alicen, as her offspring, represented an extension of Heidi herself. Part of Heidi died when Alicen died. Parkes might take into account the stress experienced by Heidi at all levels. Searching and pining act to interfere with the work she must accomplish, creating even greater stress. From this, her symptoms of nervous exhaustion could be interpreted as the depressive stage, with recovery not actualized until stabilization occurs.

MARDI HOROWITZ

By examining a wide range of individuals undergoing serious life events, Mardi Horowitz has identified a predictable pattern of responses labeled the Stress Response Syndrome. These responses were determined from a wide variety of events, such as military combat, concentration camp internment, personal illness, dying, rape, and mental illness. The response pattern holds true across all events in spite of personality differences and individual capacities for coping. Based on an in-depth study of clinical and experimental studies, Horowitz conceptualizes a phase-oriented theory of four coping patterns beginning with the event itself.

OUTCRY

An initial reaction is accompanied by strong emotions such as fear, sadness, or rage. The outcry can be either silenced or bombastic. Much of the reaction will depend on the coping styles of the individual.

DENIAL AND NUMBING

Two predominant phases form the nucleus of Horowitz's theory, the first of which is denial and numbing. Here the bereaved attempt to avoid facing the memory of the traumatic event by utilizing numbness and denial; they avoid the implications of the threat of the losses. These symptoms offer the opportunity to balance the threat of loss by containing them within limited constraints.

INTRUSION

In the second predominant phase of Horowitz's theory, the bereaved experience sudden intrusive repetitions of unwanted thoughts, feelings, and behaviors. Hypervigilance and stress create added confusion as the bereaved attempt to make sense out of their current situation. Emotional attacks of shame, rage, and guilt continue to inhibit their ability to curtail the trauma-related images and thoughts. These attacks, however, are seen as catalysts for the individual to do the work of integrating the trauma.

WORKING THROUGH

Following the period of denial and the intrusive state, bereaved individuals alternate between the two states until a working through begins to manifest itself. Facing the reality of the traumatic event and then integrating it with the remainder of life culminates in the stress response reaction. Working through the Stress Response Syndrome to final completion requires that individuals process the emotional and ideational aspects of the trauma before they are fully able to remove old aspects of their assumptive world. Revision of these old assumptions into an acceptable balance (fitting the old with the new) will place the bereaved on the right path to what Horowitz calls "the completion tendency."

COMPLETION

This phase occurs when the new information initiated by the trauma has been balanced with the existing memories, feelings, and perceptions, and all are molded into an organized unit. Completion requires the resolution of those old assumptive mental models and the new information that the bereaved are learning to live with (Horowitz, 1985).

Using Horowitz's Stress Response Syndrome, it is easy to see that Heidi appeared to have remained in the Outcry mode an exorbitant period of time. She seemed to have spent little time in the Denial and Numbing phase, which put added stress on the grieving period. The exhaustive dissertation work was not a distraction but an added stress physically, mentally, and emotionally.

THERESE RANDO

Therese Rando has carefully outlined three basic phases of grief and mourning characterized by a major response toward the loss: avoidance, confrontation, and accommodation. Rando feels that the items represented cover all the different loss reactions regardless of number, type, or source found in acknowledged theories. She points out that the three phases are not discrete but will oscillate among themselves depending on situational or personal issues of each case.

AVOIDANCE PHASE

The avoidance phase is a shortened phase covering the acknowledgment of the death and for a short period following. As Rando states:

> Like the physical shock that occurs with trauma to the body, the human psyche goes into shock with the traumatic assault of the death of the loved one. (1993, p. 33)

As such, this period serves as a buffer, acting as an emotional anesthesia to the bereaved while allowing the griever a period in which to absorb the terrible awareness of the death.

CONFRONTATION PHASE

The confrontation phase is a time of coming to grips with the loss, of grappling with and acknowledging the pain of separation, and of dealing with the vacillations of emotions that often fluctuate between anger and deep sadness. During this period there is a gradual decline of the symptoms of acute grief as well as a gradual emergence into the everyday world. Even though their world is being reconstructed slowly, the bereaved are struggling to live without the deceased yet at the same time to keep the new relationship with the deceased appropriately alive.

ACCOMMODATION PHASE

The goal of the accommodation phase is to learn to live with the loss and to readjust one's new life accordingly. The bereaved need to adapt and adjust to the many changes that loss brings about. Accommodation doesn't mean that one no longer mourns, but that one manages and continues a new life without the loved one.

Along with her three phases of grief, Rando has posited what she has termed the six "R" processes of mourning. Those processes, she feels, must be undertaken in order for a loss to be resolved in a healthy way. The bereaved individual does not necessarily need to complete the processes in sequence but can move back and forth among them. These processes are as follows:

1. Recognize the loss.
2. React to the separation.
3. Recollect and reexperience the deceased and the relationship.
4. Relinquish the old attachments to the deceased and the old assumptive world.
5. Readjust to move adaptively into the new world without forgetting the old.
6. Reinvest.

In using Rando's theory, we can see that Heidi was in the avoidance phase even before the death occurred; the psychic shock left her physically depleted, unable to deal with the important issues confronting her. Heidi's was a complicated grief of enormous proportions.

CHAPTER 3

Sanders' Integrative Theory of Bereavement

BY BUILDING ON the preceding theories and by use of empirical research, I have been able to move a step closer toward developing a
workable theory of bereavement. It is my contention that an individual moves through five phases of bereavement: (1) shock, (2) awareness of
loss, (3) conservation-withdrawal, (4) healing, and (5) renewal. The central
element of the integrative theory of bereavement described in this volume
is that each of the psychological forces that operate during the process of
grief also has a biological anlage that determines the physical well-being of
the individual. Each level of change and awareness in the course of grief
can be seen as a progression toward resolution and homeostasis, and bereavement can be seen as adaptive rather than debilitative, as growth rather
than regression.

My theory ties into Cannon's fight-flight theory, which was important in
demonstrating that whether an animal is preparing to fight or flee, a single
psychological response will be made (Cannon, 1929). This response includes changes in body function under the control of the sympathetic part
of the autonomic nervous system. The changes have the effect of putting an
individual into a state of readiness for whatever action is needed. Reserves
of energy are mobilized, muscular performance is enhanced, and sweating
and heart rate increase. As G. L. Freeman (1948) writes:

> Theoretically at least, both anabolic and catabolic processes are at work in
> every reaction to stimulation. At first the anabolic processes predominate,
> with the result that a measure of general energy expenditure shows incre-

ment. Later the anabolic processes begin to subside, catabolic processes begin to catch up, and the measure of energy expenditure shows decrement. (p. 77)

This logical explanation helps us understand the biological concomitants to psychological and behavioral responses shown in grief. Tying the structure of Cannon's theory to the first phase of Sanders's theory provides an underlying basis for the characteristic, initial, overt response of bereavement—that of shock.

Neuroendocrine changes do indeed occur following a bereavement (Kim & Jacobs, 1993). And although the majority of individuals do not suffer terminal effects following a major loss, a small number do. Many of these individuals suffer what is known as complicated bereavement. However, given the practical problem of studying individuals who are suffering deep grief, only a few studies have followed that path. As far back as 1964, Wolff, Friedman, Hofer, & Mason studied parents of fatally ill children. By studying urinary 17-hydroxycorticosteroid excretion rate (17-OHCS is a cortisol metabolite reflecting adrenocortical activity), the researchers found that fathers were more effective than were mothers in defending against the impact of threatened loss. Data that uncovers physiological responses remains scarce because they must be obtained by intrusive measures.

SHOCK—PHASE 1

One can follow the course of grief through the five phases just listed and understand the biological basis. In the initial phase, shock, the bereaved moves in a confused state of disbelief and is in an intense state of alarm. Adrenalin outpourings provide the physical stamina needed to carry through with the ritual requirements. However, this phase also provides a numbness that protects the bereaved from experiencing the intense pain that is to follow. In this phase the fight-flight phenomenon as outlined by Cannon comes into play. Adrenalin acts like a self-induced drug, giving the bereaved the fuel to carry through the difficult initial period of painful loss and agonizing acknowledgment of the death.

Unless the excitation aroused by the stimulus is allowed to abate, the individual will continue to be aroused and hence to maintain a state of total disequilibrium. This problem can be observed in cases of multiple deaths in which the survivor manages to get through the initial phases of grief but, when confronted with a new loss, is thrown back into this first phase of grief (shock). The bereaved person never reaches the optimal level of homeostatis but instead maintains the initial exhaustive phase. The problems facing survivors of AIDS patients are a good example. A person may manage to deal with one death, only to have that death be followed shortly afterward with another death, whether friend or family member. The energy mobilization occurs repeatedly until the individual reaches total exhaustion. At this point the bereaved may show the debilitating effects of somatic decline and subsequent physical illness.

AWARENESS OF LOSS—PHASE 2

The realization of reality must be faced, and as the numbness begins to wear off, the bereaved must come to grips with the loss that has taken place. The novocaine has abated, and with it, the temporary buffer. As the buffer of loss recedes, the bereaved must face the physical and mental agony without the added support of a numbing agent. Separation anxiety becomes rampant as the bereaved gears up for what feels like a nervous breakdown. Feelings of danger predominate. There is no safe place. The bereaved uses enormous quantities of physic energy, which further creates undue stress. Substantial evidence connects long-lasting stress to a weakening of that part of the immune system responsible for maintaining resistance to various types of infectious diseases (Irwin & Pike, 1993). The seesaw of emotional outbursts during this phase creates the largest drain on energy supply. Yearning, crying, angry outbursts, guilt, shame, and sleep disturbance all contribute to the stress and confusion.

CONSERVATION-WITHDRAWAL—PHASE 3

Engel has described a period of necessary withdrawal, a time to conserve energy (1962), and indeed the grieving person must finally pull back to save what little energy remains after the tremendous outpouring of the previous phase. This system is considered by Engel to be the biological anlage of depression-withdrawal. The constant battle of overflowing emotions takes its toll on the grieving person, who feels a need to rest (the body's natural response to overexertion). However, for the bereaved this period can be a frightening time because it feels so much like depression. A fatigue overwhelms grievers, and they have difficulty carrying on even the simplest of tasks. People have told me that it took enormous effort to even get out of bed in the morning. This fatigue is hard for the bereaved to understand when before (during Phase 2), they seemed to have energy enough to take care of all the necessary duties. This phase is filled with a sense of despair. All the crying, yearning, and searching of the previous period have failed to bring about the results they were hoping for—namely, to regain the lost one. The feelings of helplessness pervade and with them a sense that they have lost control of everything, their life, desires, hopes, or dreams. Grievers feel that they can do nothing more and that nothing will ever matter again anyhow. The first two phases of grief have been intense, leaving the individual open to infections and autoimmune diseases. The immune system has been badly compromised.

Although this period may appear to be debilitative, it nevertheless has redemptive value. During this period, away from others, the bereaved has the opportunity to do the necessary grief work—the ruminating and preoccupation with the deceased. Old conditions can never return. The deceased is gone; no amount of wishing or concentrating can return the dead. Grievers begin to see that new approaches must be made, new relationships established, a new life built. In the final analysis, grief work depends on accepting the loss and consequent changes in one's life. But in shutting down for this third phase, the mind and body have had time to begin healing. Strength begins to return.

The turning point has been reached.

This turning point is marked by a decision either to move forward and let go of the past or to remain in a status quo position, behaving much as if the deceased were just away and might possibly return at some later date. A third choice is possible, but it is seldom discussed as an alternative. This choice is a decision to die, to give up. Usually this choice is not a conscious decision but is more of an unconscious desire, and death results from illness or unconscious accident.

Up to this point, biological mechanisms have been the primary motivating forces that move an individual from one phase to another. Impact (shock) led to anxiety (arousal), which eventually caused exhaustion (withdrawal). Hibernation is necessary if one is to regain strength lost in the earlier phases of grief. Through rest, strength is regained, and one discovers the motivation to move on to the next phase. One can then invite a healing. In most cases, the turning point depends on the determination to survive and change.

When one has gathered enough strength to face a future or to simply plan one day ahead, then a step has been taken to move to the next phase. Healing has begun.

HEALING, THE TURNING POINT—PHASE 4

Gathering strength gives the bereaved the impetus to go forward with a new life. The process does not consist of sudden jumps but instead of a gradual change in attitude. There is a growing recognition of the possibility of a new life. Making decisions about future life changes can be fearful at any time, but during a period of grief such decision making can have double ramifications. Grievers experience a fear of making a mistake that will make the future even more frightening. But doing nothing only leads to feelings of helplessness. Gaining control comes in bits and pieces. By assuming control even on a small level, things slowly begin to take a new shape. The return of confidence is gradual and erratic. An identity that had been based on life with the deceased must now be replaced with a new identity. However, developing a new identity is difficult because while in the process of relinquishing old roles, one must build new ones. The process is essentially one of death and rebirth.

This phase is also a period of forgiving and forgetting. Forgiving oneself can be a difficult task as one tries to deal with the self-effacement of survival guilt, shame, and rage at having been left alone. On the other hand, forgetting implies "letting go." But forgetting in no way suggests that memories will be erased or that anniversary reactions will not be felt. Rather, it means that thoughts and feelings will be held appropriately in one's heart. However, the circle is gradually closing as the bereaved gains motivation to form new ties. Trying out new friends and lifestyles can be treacherous and disappointing with many discouraging starts and stops. Yet the motivation to go forward makes the difference. This progress is borne when the bereaved person can look back past the events of the death and see happy memories, joyful times. Hope emanates from every small success and with that hope is the entry into the final phase of grief—renewal.

RENEWAL—PHASE 5

For the most part, the pain has subsided. Of course, anniversaries will still be difficult. Yet the bereaved is not the same person as before the loss. A sense of competency derived from accepting responsibility for oneself lends the strength necessary to try new things, meet new friends, and begin creating a lifestyle in which emotional needs are met. This phase is as long and arduous as the ones before, perhaps longer, and often more difficult. As the bereaved, with an uncertain foothold on a frightening future, carve new persons out of the old, they find that it is not always easy to accept responsibility for their lives, especially when they have relied on others for this task. Yet, when they see little choice but to take matters into their own hands, learning by this experience will be the best teacher around. And from these experiences they find a new sense of vitality. The bereaved have the potential of developing into stronger, more confident persons than they were before. The despair that was felt in the third phase has lifted, providing a renewed feeling of functional stability.

How can this integrative theory be applied to the Chapter 2 example of Heidi and her struggle with grief? Heidi went into her loss having suffered a strong compromise of the sympathetic nervous system. Her struggle to keep Alicen alive, her ambivalence about Alicen's death as well as the terrible memories of Alicen's frail little body sapped what strength Heidi had left to deal with the enormous responsibilities of her two children, her dissertation, her classes to teach, and her own tenuous health. Every phase that Heidi dealt with was met with diminishing energy. Her anabolic processes never had time to subside because every challenge drained her even further. The conservation-withdrawal phase, which would normally allow her time to regroup and gather strength, was bypassed so that Heidi could tackle her duties. As a result, Heidi would be trapped in the center of a huge dilemma for a long time, not able to reach a quiet time of healing or an emotional reconciliation.

The integrative theory of grief also takes into account the effect of personality correlates in connection with bereavement patterns. Bereavement has primarily been examined as a unidimensional process, with little latitude allowed for individual differences. Theorists, for the most part, have used anecdotal incidents from which to generalize bereavement processes, thereby promoting subjectively derived options of what is pathological and what is normal. The continuum of grief ranges from "too much, too long" to "too little, too short." Thus, the parameters for what have been considered acceptable grieving have become narrowly focused on the mean of an imagined population that shifts in degree from one theorist to another. Few writers have taken into consideration premorbid characteristics of the bereaved when explaining their behaviors. Yet, few would deny that persons do exhibit characteristic idiosyncratic responses to stress. By using the MMPI (Minnesota Multiphasic Personality Inventory, a well-validated personality inventory), and the GEI, Grief Experience Inventory (Sanders, Mauger, & Strong, 1977), a standardized grief inventory, as objective research tools, researchers showed that premorbid adjustment strategies did contribute to the outcome of bereavement (see Chapter 9). An individual's inner strength or psychological good health will be a mitigating influence on the ability to cope.

The integrative theory considers both internal and external moderator variables. External moderators include such factors as social support systems, how the deceased died, who died, socioeconomic status, and so on.

Table 3.1   Integrative Theory of Grief

The first phase: Shock—the impact of grief

General Description of Phase 1
  Disbelief
  Confusion
  Restlessness
  Feelings of unreality
  Regression and helplessness
  State of alarm
Physical Symptoms of Phase 1
  Dryness of the mouth and throat
  Need for sighing
  Loss of muscular power
  Weeping
  Uncontrolled trembling
  Startle response
  Sleep disturbance
  Loss of appetite
Psychological Aspects of Phase 1
  Egocentric phenomenon
  Preoccupations with thoughts of the deceased
  Psychological distancing

The second phase: Awareness of loss

General Description of Phase 2
  Separation anxiety
  Conflicts
  Acting out of emotional expectations
  Prolonged stress
Physical Symptoms of Phase 2
  Yearning
  Crying
  Anger
  Guilt
  Frustration
  Shame
  Sleep disturbance
  Fear of death
Psychological Aspects of Phase 2
  Oversensitivity
  Searching
  Disbelief and denial
  Sensing of the presence
  Dreaming

(continued)

Table 3.1   *(continued)*

The third phase: Conservation-withdrawal

General Description of Phase 3
  Withdrawal
  Despair
  Diminished social support
  Helplessness
Physical Symptoms of Phase 3
  Weakness
  Fatigue
  Need for more sleep
  Weakened immune system
Psychological Aspects of Phase 3
  Hibernation or holding pattern
  Obsessional review
  Grief work
  Turning point

The fourth phase: Healing—the turning point

General Description of Phase 4
  Turning point
  Assumption of control
  Identity restructuring
  Relinquishing of roles
Physical Symptoms of Phase 4
  Physical healing
  Increase in energy
  Sleep restoration
  Immune system restoration
Psychological Aspects of Phase 4
  Forgiving
  Forgetting
  Search for meaning
  Closing of the circle
  Hope

The fifth phase: Renewal

General Description of Phase 5
  New self-awareness
  Acceptance of responsibility
  Process of learning to live without
Physical Symptoms of Phase 5
  Revitalization

(continued)

Table 3.1 *(continued)*

Functional stability
Caring for physical needs
Psychological Aspects of Phase 5
  Living for oneself
  Anniversary reactions
  Loneliness
  Reaching out
  Time for the process of bereavement

Internal moderators describe elements that are endemic to covert personal state, such as age, gender, ego strength and personality, attachment to the deceased, current physical functioning, and so on. How these moderator variables interact during the process of bereavement will have a significant effect on the outcome (see Figure 3.1). Three general possibilities result: The bereaved can (1) determine to go on with life in a new way, (2) decide not to make changes and to live as if the deceased were simply away for the moment, or (3) submit to the complications that arise and become ill or die. The third outcome usually results from an unconscious decision.

What separates this integrative theory from preceding ones is the inclusion of the notion of motivation. What actually encourages a person to even want to get through the phases of grief when life is so painful and bleak? In the first three phases, motivation is based primarily on biological needs. Shock, the impact of loss, protects the griever initially from being overcome by the pain of separation. However, emotions that are dammed up during this period will finally erupt and spill over. Gradually, shock wears off and the reality of death forces the fight-flight response, or the alarm reaction. Even here, the griever tends to gain respite through occasional denial. Yet the individual can tolerate only so much stress before compete exhaustion threatens. In this phase the bereaved must pull back and conserve energy in order to survive physically and begin a healing process. At the end of the third phase the griever makes a decision, conscious or unconscious, to survive and begin a new life or to remain in perpetual bereavement and, perhaps, die. If either of the latter decisions is made, bereavement becomes fixed in the third phase.

A decision to survive, however, is not the end of the bereavement process, for the hardest part of grief resolution rests in the enormous changes that must be implemented and carried out. Not until one has reached a new level of functioning, incorporating the necessary changes, can one feel ready to begin again, to be a new person in a new life.

The theory can be broken down not only into five phases of the bereavement process but also into three levels represented by the emotional, bio-

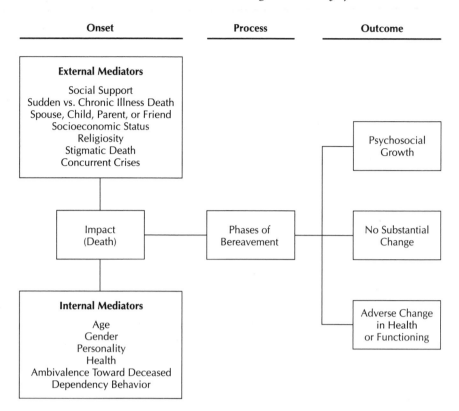

Figure 3.1   Integrative theory of bereavement.

logical, and social components of functioning. Table 3.2 illustrates this breakdown.

I must point out that the use of the phrase *stages of bereavement* may unintentionally imply an invariant process that "fixes" the individual at a particular place on the stage continuum despite intervening variables. An example of this unintentional implication is the model set forth by Elisabeth Kübler-Ross (1969) in determining the stages of dying. Although Kübler-Ross's theory has been open to much controversy (Schutz & Aderman, 1974), it has nevertheless been supported by many caregivers who are still forcing individuals to rigidly fit the schema rather than using it as only a general guideline. The bereavement process does not have clear-cut stopping and starting points, but rather it implies a free-flowing process; symptoms of one phase often overlap the symptoms of the next—or even of the previous phase during temporary regression. Because of this overlap, I have chosen the term *phase* rather than the more rigid term *stage*.

The following five chapters address each phase individually, delineating the symptoms that are most evident for that particular phase. Not every

Table 3.2   Tripartite Levels in the Phases of Bereavement

Phases	Levels		
	Emotional	Biological	Social
1. Shock	Impact	Trauma	Egocentrism
2. Awareness of loss	Anxiety	Acute stress	Regression
3. Conservation-withdrawal	Despair	Chronic stress	Withdrawal
4. Healing	Gaining control	Healing	Restructuring of identity
5. Renewal	New level of functioning	Recovery	Renewal

person will experience every symptom presented, but the grouping of symptoms will alert the caregiver to the possibilities that could be operating during that particular phase.

As mentioned earlier, the experience of loss is affected by many moderator variables, both situational and personal. Although the phases of bereavement are set forth in a particular order, they do not represent an inflexible pattern. The griever unquestionably moves forward and backward as circumstance or need requires, occasionally becoming stuck in one phase or another for some time.

Just as symptoms vary, so also does the length of time that it takes to complete the bereavement process. For example, a bereaved parent may be in shock for weeks or months, whereas shock over the loss of an elderly parent may last only a few hours. Similarly, if the resistance to accept change in one's life is rigid, one could become fixated in the third phase of bereavement for several years.

Time limits placed on grieving individuals can cause enormous problems with grief resolution. If grief continues beyond the proscribed period of time established by the caregiver, the bereaved person becomes unduly frustrated, which could develop into feelings of hopelessness and helplessness. The caregiver must be patient. The caregiver also should be cautious is using such terms as *pathological grief*. Recognizing that each individual is unique and that the course of bereavement is affected by many moderator variables, the caregiver needs to be sympathetic to and understanding of the differences among the situations surrounding the bereaved, but just as important, the caregiver needs to know that there are wide differences among grieving people themselves.

PART TWO

PHASES OF BEREAVEMENT

CHAPTER 4

The First Phase:
Shock—The Impact of Grief

When she died, I just absolutely went to pieces. I went into, I guess, shock. She died in December. In April the doctor had told me she couldn't live. But you live with death and you still refuse to accept it. I just went to pieces, and I gradually pulled myself together, at least I thought I did. I was working. I went back to work, oh, within a week, I guess, and thought I had pulled things together and thought I was acting rationally, but I lost my job. So obviously I wasn't.

Widower, age 46

A NUMBER OF THEORIES concur that the initial reaction to a significant loss is shock (Averill, 1968; Engel, 1972; Rando, 1984; Raphael, 1984). Shock and disbelief express the impossibility of death. Sudden unexpected death has been found to cause a greater degree of shock in the bereaved than does grief in which there is a long preparatory period (Lundin, 1984; Parkes & Weiss, 1983; Sanders, 1982–1983). Yet, even when death had been mentally rehearsed over and over, even when death had been anticipated, some degree of shock and disbelief is still present.

People have said to me, "I knew it was coming. I thought I was prepared, but I didn't know it would be like this, so final, so silent, so irrevocable." In the Tampa study, some patients had even been comatose; the family had been able only to visit and carry on one-way conversations. But this half-life was vastly different from death. The unconscious person was still in this world; at least he or she could be seen and touched.

GENERAL DESCRIPTION OF PHASE 1—SHOCK

Shock is a general term used to describe the degree of trauma. The degree of trauma depends not only on the level of attachment to the deceased but also on such things as how, where, or when the death occurred. Was it noon or 3:00 A.M.? Were there others around, or was the bereaved alone with the person when death occurred? How many people nearby could really be counted on? These elements all have an effect on the intensity and length of the shock reaction.

How people think they will react to the death of others may differ sharply from how they actually do. The impact of death produces a physical shock that lasts much longer than is ever anticipated. How persons deal with shock—or more important, how they allow others to help them through the early period of shock—often determines the course of grief. For it is during this phase that the bereaved need the greatest physical support. The confusion, the feelings of unreality, the sheer disbelief that such an event has occurred, leaves survivors unable to process normal sequences of thought. The survivors feel that they need to be held up by the armpits just to get through the rituals of death.

CHARACTERISTICS OF PHASE 1

Disbelief • Confusion • Restlessness • Feelings of unreality
• Regression and helplessness • State of alarm

DISBELIEF

Disbelief functions as a buffer that permits the bereaved to process the reality of the loss gradually. As such, it is adaptive (Averill, 1968). Without this protection, the emotional assault experienced in early bereavement would be too intense to bear. Grievers would be overwhelmed. While the bereaved are not thinking of anything but how and why the death happened, denial and disbelief offer natural respite—short temporary retreats from the awful reality of the loss.

CONFUSION

The shock of final separation from a loved one leaves the bereaved confused and off balance—unable to conceive of a world without that person.

Once the loved one is gone, the bereaved's world view is shattered. What was constant and dependable in the past no longer exists. Though the bereaved can recognize the reality intellectually, it takes time to process the actuality of the loss. Bereaved people express such things as "I feel so vague. I can't keep my mind on anything for long" or "I'm afraid I'm losing my mind. I can't seem to think clearly."

Crises upset the usual habits of behavior. The bereaved have temporarily lost the feelings of safety on which customary reactions are based. Instead, the bereaved need to realign their behavior to fit the new situation. The major problem, however, is that this loss is a novel circumstance, about which the individual has had little or no experience. Each step or decision requires attention that heretofore was handled by habitual responses. The bereaved must now attend to each response made. With so much information input, the bereaved become confused. The paradox of this confusion is that just when the bereaved must make weighty decisions (funeral, pallbearers, obituary, wake, etc.), the mind is reeling with the shock of death. The head has become a speeding roller coaster, and the body has trouble catching up. The world has been turned upside down, and nothing seems to make sense.

RESTLESSNESS

Part of the confusion of this stage is acted out in restless behavior. Because the world has become a threatening and unsafe place, defensive systems keep the bereaved in a constant state of alert. This state of alert continues even though the body is exhausted. The bereaved may start to do something only to forget what needed doing. The new experience of restlessness may be felt as a "flightiness" or as shortened attention span. Parkes (1972) noted that the majority of widows in the London study experienced restless behavior that decreased gradually in the first year. This restlessness can be explained in terms of increased muscle tension brought about by activation of the sympathetic nervous system (SNS). This activation serves to gear the animal for alert behavior and quick movement. It has been described as a "fight or flight" reaction—adaptive in the wild but of little use in this situation (Cannon, 1929).

FEELINGS OF UNREALITY

How death happens makes a difference in how one can process the reality of the event. How could an automobile accident be described without discussing the crash—the moment of impact? The harshness of the impact determines the degree of damage to the automobile as well as to the passengers. So it follows that the way in which death occurs—whether it is sudden or expected, whether the bereaved person is told in a gentle and understanding manner or jarred abruptly into the knowledge of death—all these things make a difference in how the death is processed and the grief survived.

I remember a widow who had come to this country with her husband. Her husband was a military officer stationed in Germany when they met. They had married there and she had returned with him to the States. Her family were all in Germany, and the couple had not had time to make new friends in this country. The husband had a flare-up of an old abdominal problem that required exploratory surgery. The physician assured them both that it was a routine case. Yet, during the operation, something went wrong, and the husband died.

The physician sat down immediately to try to explain the entire procedure to the widow. He went slowly so that she could understand. But when he had finished, thinking perhaps that he had followed all the rules by appropriately informing the survivor, he abruptly asked, "Now would you like to see the cadaver?" Jolted into abrupt reality, her reaction was one of shock, anxiety, fear, and horror. Parkes (1985) states, "Such moments will be vividly remembered for the rest of the recipient's life, and they constitute a trauma as real as any surgical operation" (p. 15).

Everyone needs to recognize that conveying information about death is a difficult moment for the bearer of such disastrous news, but caution should still be used in not making too abrupt an announcement. To the bereaved, it will be an added abrasion. As Dubin and Sarnoff (1986) write, "A staff that is aware of the needs of the grieving person and can facilitate this process will help cushion the trauma of loss and set the basis for a healthy grieving process" (p. 57).

REGRESSION AND HELPLESSNESS

Shock brings about feelings of helplessness. After her husband died, a Tampa widow said

> You're just helpless you know. You just keep saying, "Help me, somebody help me." There was just nothing anyone could do. Yet he really got sick on Thursday night and he died on Monday. But to stay there those 4 days just watching him around the clock ... the doctor finally told us that he was

dying. He said that there was just nothing he could do, but it was awful to watch him suffer and he could not close his eyes. I remember saying, just please close your eyes and rest, but I guess at that point he was just semiconscious or whatever and he didn't close his eyes for 4 days.

This woman carried that visual impression for months. It plagued her as she ruminated on the events before the death. She could not get past the memory of her own helplessness in the face of her husband's battle.

The uncontrollable events of bereavement lead to feelings of helplessness. Nothing can be done to bring back the deceased. From this, the bereaved are catapulted back to childhood feelings of helplessness and little control over the world (Rochlin, 1965; Seligman, 1975). As a result of this loss of control, the bereaved feel that the world has become an unsafe place. This feeling initiates a regressive reaction, which, for a time, makes the bereaved feel weak and dependent on others.

STATE OF ALARM

During this phase of grief, the bereaved person is in a state of intense physiological alarm (Parkes, 1972). As stated previously, this response is governed by the sympathetic part of the autonomic nervous system, causing physical changes that mobilize the energy resources for action. When energized, this system acts to move blood away from the hands and feet toward the head and trunk, causing icy fingers, sweaty palms, and even some trembling in the entire body. Blood is also moved away from the gastrointestinal tract, reducing appetite and often causing nausea (Pelletier, 1977).

Along with these symptoms, excessive quantities of hormones are pumped through the bloodstream to prepare the individual for escape or combat. Messages are transmitted throughout the neuroendocrine system, causing significant changes in the body's biochemistry. It has been proposed that these changes, if allowed to continue over a period of time, could inhibit the body's immune system, which in turn would reduce the capacity to resist infection and disease (Fredrick, 1982–1983). It is easy to see why a bereaved person is at risk of illness and even death when a prolonged period of stress continues unabated. This proposal could explain, in part, the high rate of mortality and morbidity following a significant loss. People get sick more often during bereavement.

The state of alarm is a natural reaction to a threat to security. The bereaved is experiencing the loss of a beloved person who, only shortly before, had supplied some degree of protection and security (however minimal). This loss can throw the bereaved into a state of anxiety and even panic. The world is no longer perceived as a safe place, and this perception can set up a defensive posture and cause the bereaved to become fearful and to recoil.

Grief's role as a major stressor is clearly depicted in the case of a bereaved Tampa parent, Mrs. Smith. She was a single parent with a 21-year-old son, John, living at home. Two months after John's death, she was so crippled with arthritis that she had to use a walker for ambulation. The acute arthritis symptoms had come on only 2 weeks after his death. But prior to this time, Mrs. Smith had been healthy and active.

John had had a long history of diabetes, which increasingly had caused him difficulty in maintaining a proper blood-sugar balance—it was either too high or too low. He was on medication and seeing a physician. Several things had happened to warn Mrs. Smith of John's imminent death. First, about 3 weeks before John's death, she dreamed that she saw her son laid out at a wake. She kept quiet about it, but she felt apprehensive and frightened.

Then her brother, who lived in another part of the country, called to tell her that he had seen her in his home two nights before. He said that he had not been able to sleep and had gotten up around 11:30 P.M. to read in the kitchen. Suddenly, he said, she had appeared to him, telling him that her son was going to die soon. He said that he even had a short conversation with her. His wife had called to him from the bedroom to inquire whom he was talking to. He had not intended to tell Mrs. Smith about this incident, but he had become increasingly worried 2 nights later and called to see how John was feeling. Mrs. Smith did not tell her son about the phone call.

Three days later, John was working on the engine of his car in the side yard. He had been bending over the fender for a long time and his position had not changed. Mrs. Smith said she suddenly felt a cold chill settle over her, and she immediately went to check on him. He was lifeless. Blood was streaming from the corner of his mouth. All she could do was scream. When neighbors raced over, she ran back into the kitchen, continuing to scream. She could not go back outside until the ambulance arrived and drove away with her son.

While the medical personnel worked on John (about 45 minutes), Mrs. Smith sat in the waiting room, immobile. She could not move her legs. Her hands and fingers were set in a peculiar fixed position. Her heart rate and pulse were barely noticeable. Her family physician was called to the hospital, where he talked to her gently and calmly. Two Valiums were prescribed. Eventually, some feeling returned to her limbs.

Prior to the death, she had had only minor touches of arthritis in her fingers, but 2 weeks after the death, she became crippled again—this time with arthritis in her legs. During the interview, she was emotionally frail, crying each time we came close to personal feelings. She could describe the events surrounding the death, but that was as far as she could go. Shock and disbelief still pervaded her thinking. Hers was a deep, profound grief that consumed her. When asked what her immediate reactions to the death had been, she said that she had thought of the dream and of her brother's precognitive experience, feeling guilty that she had not warned her son. She felt that she was in some way responsible for the death.

When I saw her 1 year later, she told me that she was suffering from symptoms of a cardiovascular nature that would probably require surgery. Her son had died of a heart attack. She said that she had been sick constantly since John had died. Other grievers have reported this same type of identification phenomenon (Krupp, 1965; Lindemann, 1944; Parkes, 1971a; Zisook, Devaul, & Click, 1982). These researchers noted that a number of individuals felt that they had contracted the same illness or expressed symptoms of pain in the same area of their bodies as did the one who had died.

Shock may be experienced in many different ways. Some persons are unable to feel—they are numb and unresponding. Some scream, some faint, some rant and rave. Some go on as before, acting as though no change has taken place. Generally, persons respond to shock in much the same way as they have responded to other stressful situations in life. Each individual responds to stress uniquely. Caregivers should be alert to various reactions, treating each of the symptoms as they arise. If the bereaved individual is nurtured and tended to as one would tend any shock victim, chances for a less abrasive bereavement are strengthened.

PHYSICAL SYMPTOMS OF PHASE 1

Dryness of the mouth and throat • Need for sighing •
Loss of muscular power • Weeping • Uncontrolled trembling
• Startle response • Sleep disturbance • Loss of appetite

A variety of symptoms are experienced during the shock phase: a need to yawn and to sigh, dryness of the mouth and throat, loss of muscular power, weeping, and sometimes uncontrollable trembling, especially while speaking about the events surrounding the death (Lindemann, 1944).

A startle response is often evident after an accidental death, similar to a knee jerk but involving the entire body (Sanders, 1979–1980). One father told me of reliving over and over the car accident that killed his son. Every time he visualized the impact of the crash he would have a startle response as though he himself were receiving the blow. He identified so closely with his son that he felt the collision himself.

A loss of appetite and an inability to sleep also accompany the shock phase. Because the body is in a constant state of alarm, the bereaved may find it helpful to take a mild antianxiety agent to slow down the racing central nervous system. It is important for the grieving person to have whatever rest can be obtained. The effects of prolonged physiological stress can be damaging to the system (Pelletier, 1977). The aforementioned symptoms are reactions characteristic of systemic stress, giving an indication of the amount of strain being placed on the bereaved individual.

PSYCHOLOGICAL ASPECTS OF PHASE 1

Egocentric phenomenon • Preoccupations with
thoughts of the deceased • Psychological distancing

EGOCENTRIC PHENOMENON

Shock is an egocentric phenomenon: Cognitive awareness is narrowed, and attention is drawn to personal needs. Loss of a dearly loved person implies both a loss of that person and a loss of that part of ourselves that was intimately intertwined with that person (Bugen, 1977). Because of this loss, in order to survive, our bodies set up defenses that provide greater protection against overwhelming assault. A general sense of vagueness pervades perceptions of external events while the mind is bombarded with racing thoughts and feelings. One widow said that it was like being encapsulated in an opaque shell with her deceased husband: Her thoughts were solely of him, and everything else was outside the shell. She described her feelings this way:

> I was crying lightly at the funeral. But I don't know, I felt like I was inside of something, way down deep. You know, like I was . . . like I was there in some place all by myself, and something was happening that really wasn't happening. I don't know how to say it. I was unaware of everybody else except myself and my husband. I don't remember. . . . I can hardly remember anything that anybody was saying. I don't even remember his people being in my home except the day they left. I don't even know where they slept, I don't even know if they ate. I don't even know if I ate.

Another widow spoke of "being behind a wall," still another of being "wrapped in a blanket." All thoughts and feelings are concentrated on the lost person. Conversations about subjects other than the one who has died are meaningless and boring. C. S. Lewis (1961) wrote after the death of his wife:

> There is a sort of invisible blanket between the world and me. I find it hard to take in what anyone says. Or perhaps, hard to want to take it in. It is so uninteresting. Yet I want the others to be about me. I dread the moments when the house is empty. If only they would talk to one another and not to me. (p. 7)

Preoccupations with Thoughts of the Deceased

Starting in the shock phase and continuing through much of the first three phases of bereavement, attention constantly focuses on thoughts of the lost person. The bereaved ruminate on events leading up to the loss and to the death itself (Parkes, 1972). In the Tampa study, bereaved individuals reported that thoughts of the deceased never left their minds. They sometimes felt that the deceased was nearby, which usually brought a momentary sense of peace. Then full knowledge of the death returned, and the agony of loss was experienced again.

The rituals of death must be handled during this phase. While the bereaved is inwardly screaming, "No, no, it can't be," the bereaved is outwardly moving through the paces of the funeral preparation and burial. The cadence is slow but relentless. Yet, the rituals of death become the glue that holds the bereaved together during this first phase.

In the Tampa study, getting through the funeral took all the will and attention the bereaved could muster. This period was marked with several wrenching events such as the first trip to the funeral home to make the arrangements. Few people had made prior arrangements, so multiple decisions were required shortly after the death. What type of funeral? What type of casket? What clothing should be worn? Each decision can require much deliberation, especially if there are family differences. Usually, one person made most of the decisions and took responsibility for the arrangements.

One widow described going with her brother-in-law to the funeral home after they left the hospital, even though she did not plan to make the arrangements.

> So I came home, and it was just a numb feeling. I just went through all the motions, and I went down with his brother to make the funeral arrangements. He made most of them for me but I went down with him anyway, and that was it. I just really didn't have any feeling, just numb. I was in shock really. And I

think looking back on it that I was actually in shock the whole time he was in the hospital the last time.

For some, the first visit to the funeral home to view their beloved family member was the hardest thing they had to do. Getting the nerve to walk up to the casket and to see the person lying there seemed to be a frightening task for many. But often the experience was rewarding. One adult son said of his father:

> I didn't know how he would look. I was afraid that they would have made him look unnatural or strange. Dad lost so much weight during his illness . . . he went from 210 to 110, just skin and bones. It had hurt me so much to see him go down like that. He was always so big and strong to me and to see him so frail broke my heart. But when I saw him in the casket, I was surprised. He looked so peaceful and not nearly so thin as he had before. I must say, I was really comforted to see him like that. It was just as though he were sleeping. I actually looked to see if he was breathing.

Another family solved a standoff about how to dress their loved one by buying a new pair of pajamas for their elderly father. "If he looked like he was asleep," they asked, "why not dress him in the clothing of sleep?"

For many in the study, it was a relief to view the family member at the funeral home after a debilitating illness. A mother of a teenage son who had died of leukemia, distraught after the long terminal illness, told about going to the funeral home.

> Well, we went, you know how they let you come and check everything out, and the funeral director was a friend of ours—well not a close friend. He is a neighbor down the street from us, and he told us to come in and look and see if everything was to our specifications. I sensed relief when I looked at him, at being so restful and beautiful and at peace and I couldn't shed a tear because for once he was not hurting and nobody was bothering him.

The second wrenching event experienced during this period is the visitation, or wake. This event is when the bereaved has to face friends and maintain some semblance of composure. In our society, in which an open display of emotion is practically taboo, an added burden is placed on bereaved individuals. They must make themselves walk through the funeral rituals, all the while feeling as if they might break down but never allowing themselves to. The strain is more strenuous than a full day of physical work. The feeling of vagueness and numbness that accompanies the shock reaction helps many bereaved persons survive this difficult experience.

Most of the respondents in the study felt that the funeral home had done a good job and had met their needs during a time of immense confusion. When asked if they would have changed anything, the majority answered no. Yet, a number admitted that they had not really noticed what had gone on.

One widow had promised her husband that she wouldn't cry until the funeral was over and was proud of the fact that she had been able to carry it off. During this period, feelings of unreality prevailed. Another person said,

> Like I remember putting on my hose, and I thought to myself, "I am putting on my hose to go somewhere I really . . . I don't want to go. And how terrible that I'm going to my child's funeral. It's not true. I'm not going." And then I continued to go like a robot. I went but I didn't seem to know I was going. . . . It was just like I was wrapped in a veil or something. . . . I guess we can be thankful that the Lord does that. I had no feeling. I had no feeling.

As impossible and painful as this period was for most people, they usually held themselves together, even feeling a sense of pride that they were able to control their emotions so well. Several found extra readings to include in the funeral service, readings that were favorites of the deceased. In one case in Tampa, at the funeral of their mother, four of her children sang a favorite hymn even though tears were streaming down their faces as they did it. One young mother was encouraged to dress her dead child. Feeling at first that she could not do it, she gradually prepared herself and found enormous comfort later in the knowledge that she had done something that was difficult. Of course, taking on difficult tasks is not for everyone, but those who could seemed to experience less guilt during the bereavement. As a matter of fact, it seemed that those who put themselves out, who did more during the ritual days, fared better during their bereavement than did those who had little input in the planning. It was as if the extra effort expiated their feelings of guilt somewhat. They could later point with pride to the strength they managed to call forth when it was necessary.

PSYCHOLOGICAL DISTANCING

Psychological distancing is a defense used by individuals to guard against a painful situation by emotionally removing themselves from the situation. This is similar to the psychic numbing that Lifton (1979) spoke of when he observed survivors of the Hiroshima bombing:

> At the heart of the traumatic syndrome—and of the overall human struggle with pain—is the diminished capacity to feel, or psychic numbing. . . . The

survivor undergoes a radical but temporary diminution in his sense of actuality in order to avoid losing this sense completely and permanently. (p. 173)

In other words, to protect themselves from pain, the bereaved gain distance even from themselves, producing an unreal feeling of being apart from themselves. This defense cannot be cognitively willed by an individual, but it occurs at an emotional level. Many bereaved persons, particularly during the first few days of grief, have told me that they felt as though they were standing off to one side watching themselves go through the motions of living. One young widow explained it this way:

> It was so strange. I was putting on my makeup, combing my hair, and all the time it was as if I were standing by the door watching myself go through these motions. How else could I have done these things? It was impossible. I was only 38, and I was getting ready to go to my husband's funeral.

The shock phase is adaptive in that it forms an insulation against the chaotic outside world. This insulation does not mean, however, that pain is not there—far from it. Yet much of the agony of loss is postponed until the bereaved can begin to cognitively process the event of the death or loss itself.

Shock can last from a few minutes to many days, but it usually passes into the next phase of grief when the rituals of death are over and the emotions that have been constricted so tightly begin to release and overflow. At this time, an awareness of a variety of emotions erupt, sometimes with frightening violence. The second phase of grief has begun.

CHAPTER 5

The Second Phase: Awareness of Loss

We had the funeral sooner than we had to because we thought that it would be less painful . . . that if that part was over we would forget sooner. But we were wrong. The worst part was after it was all over and I was left alone. Then I really began to grieve big time. But there was no one with me to share my grief.

Widower, age 58

GENERAL DESCRIPTION OF PHASE 2

Separation anxiety • Conflicts • Acting out of
emotional expectations • Prolonged stress

THE FUNERAL is over. Friends and family have resumed their normal lives. The true significance of the loss hits with full force. Until now, shock has provided a temporary buffer against the emotional turmoil of loss. But now, as the griever enters the second phase of bereavement, the insulation has been stripped away and the bereaved person is left raw and exposed.

SEPARATION ANXIETY

A major component of this phase is that of intense separation anxiety. It is a period marked by acute emotional disorganization, giving the feeling of

61

being on the edge of a nervous breakdown much of the time. The death has been intellectually acknowledged but not emotionally believed.

Research on separation anxiety has been done primarily with children or animals separated from their mothers (Bowlby, 1953; Spitz, 1946). Animal studies have shown the devastation that infant monkeys go through when removed from the mother's cages. The expression on their little faces reveals the anguish of their immense distress (Kaufman & Rosenblum, 1967). Human infants have died from the grief of this loss. The infants give up on life when their mothers are no longer available (Spitz, 1945).

Without a safe, secure haven, separation produces feelings of danger. The bereaved need to be vigilant, to maintain an alert posture; but at the same time, they realize that control is tenuous. This sensation of utter loss of control is probably one of the most shattering and chaotic experiences possible (Seligman, 1975). The bereaved suddenly realize that everything that had been dependable has gone, leaving the bereaved vulnerable and afraid—experiencing profound separation anxiety.

When an emotional attachment is broken irrevocably, the pain is like the pain of losing an arm or leg (Parkes, 1972). Even after learning to live without the needed appendage, the continuing "phantom limb" phenomenon causes pain in the missing body part. Grief results from the sudden wrenching away of an integral part of self, and the actual physical pain is sometimes unbearable. As a matter of fact, one study (Shuchter, Zisook, Kirkorowicy, & Riscj, 1986) indicated that grief "may be more related to separation anxiety than it is to primary affective disorder" (p. 880). In supporting the bereaved, it is well to keep in mind the gross insecurity that is being experienced at this time.

CONFLICTS

This stage also represents a period of many conflicts. Several of the widows in the Tampa study were afraid of living alone but hated to live with anyone else. Barbara, a 58-year-old widow, invited both of her children and their families to move in with her. She was terrified of living by herself. Yet when the two families finally moved into her small home, she was a nervous wreck from the noise and congestion caused by eight extra people. By then, she did not know how to ask them to move or even if she wanted them to. Another widow, who had few friends in Tampa, wanted to make a trip to visit close friends. But her three dogs, two cats, and canary all needed attention, keeping her near her home most of the time. She was extremely lonely, rarely having a visitor. She wondered how she would ever make new friends when being kept so close to home, but she resisted parting with her animals.

These conflicts are hard to resolve because they usually present yet another loss of one kind or another—something too painful to accept when one is experiencing already intolerable hurt.

ACTING OUT OF EMOTIONAL EXPECTATIONS

Emotional acceptance is slow to arrive. Expectations about the presence of the deceased result in disappointment for the bereaved. A widow sets his place at the table before fully realizing that he is not there. A widower thinks of something and begins to say it when he realizes that she is no longer there to hear. Mr. Black, an elderly widower, told me that he worked in his wife's garden after her death, trying to keep it up the way she had. Sometimes, he said, he would come upon an unexpected and beautiful bud and would find himself calling out to her in sudden excitement before he realized she was not there. The awareness of death, of separation, continues to produce a raw pain as each expectation is met with frustration and disappointment.

One widow told me of her grief. She had been happily married for 41 years when her husband became ill with lung cancer. This couple had done everything together and, as is the wish of all happily married people, had hoped to grow old together. She said they lived down the street from an elderly couple who were always seen together. On spring days, they would be sitting together on a little bench on the side of the house where the sun could warm them. They would always be holding hands. Her husband would say as they drove by the couple, "This is how I would like us to be when we grow old." Instead, his wife helplessly had to watch him slowly and painfully die of his disease. She told me of listening to the radio when a favorite song of theirs was played. She said that she began to sob uncontrollably and had to double up with agonizing stomach pains. It was as though her insides were being torn loose, she said. The music had suddenly brought him back, and it took a moment for full realization to hit that she was alone.

Until experiencing it or seeing it, the impact of such loss is difficult to imagine.

PROLONGED STRESS

Grief uses enormous quantities of psychic energy, which in turn creates undue stress. Just maintaining a daily routine can sap the strength of the bereaved. It is the prolonged nature of the stress response that creates the greatest difficulty during this phase. As mentioned in Chapter 2, substantial evidence connects long-lasting stress to a weakening of that part of the immune system responsible for maintaining resistance to various types of infectious diseases (Bartrop, Luckhurst, Lajarus, Kiloh, & Penny, 1977; Morillo & Gardner, 1979; Paulley, 1984). Parkes (1964) reports that consultations for widows increased by nearly half during the early months after a bereavement and that the amount of sedation prescribed to widows under 65 was seven times greater during this period. These facts are borne out by research that indicates a high incidence of illness, accidents, even death among bereaved people (Kaprio, Koskenvico, & Rita, 1987; Stroebe, Stroebe, & Dormittner, 1985).

The physical stress, however, is not the main problem in expenditure of energy. The seesaw effect of emotional outbursts during this phase creates the largest drain on energy supply. It takes a lot of energy to cry or to feel rage, guilt, or frustration—sometimes all at once. Yet it takes even more energy to contain and defend against emotional outbursts when around others. Allowing pent-up emotions to be released is healthier by far than holding them in. In the long run, it is better to give in to one's emotions and ride out this turbulent period of grief, painful as it is.

Some persons attempt to escape this pain by developing a pattern called "flight into activity." This pattern intensifies normal functioning, and the bereaved races through the daily schedule hardly stopping for a breath. For example, after her child's death, a bereaved mother in the Tampa study dove into a whirlwind of activity, doubling up on club work, redecorating her house from top to bottom, and before that activity was finished, she began a real estate course. Eight months after the death, she was completely exhausted. At times, she would maintain a catatonic position for several hours at a time, her body heavy and her mind blank. Her mood dropped dramatically as she thought about taking her own life. Feeling that she was losing her mind, she finally made an appointment with a psychiatrist, who suggested a complete physical as well as psychotherapy. The internist put her to bed for 3 weeks, and between the two physicians, she was made to realize what a strain she had placed on herself, both emotionally and physically. She had grossly underestimated the amount of energy needed for grief as she tried to distract herself from the pain of loss.

PHYSICAL SYMPTOMS OF PHASE 2

Yearning • Crying • Anger • Guilt • Frustration
• Shame • Sleep disturbance • Fear of death

Any one person may not necessarily feel all these symptoms, and a person may also experience a number of unique symptoms that are not noted here.

The important point is that this phase of emotional upheaval involves many different responses, and it is the sheer number of outbursts that overwhelms the bereaved person. One, or even 2, can be managed by most people, but when 5 or 10 emotional outbursts take place in a short time, it becomes next to impossible to cope with anything else.

YEARNING

Yearning describes the terrible longing one feels when separated from a loved one. This has been described by Bowlby (1960a) as the need to attempt to recover the lost person.

> So long as the response systems are focused on the lost object there are strenuous efforts to recover it; and these efforts may continue despite their fruitlessness being painfully evident to others, and sometimes also to the bereaved himself. (p. 319)

Intellectually, one would not wish for the loved one to return if he or she were suffering. But yearning begins at a deeper level. The child in us resists abandonment and seeks reassurance. One is never emotionally ready to part with those whom we love and to whom we are deeply attached (Freud, 1917).

CRYING

Crying is an important method of emotional discharge. Yet many people cannot cry, and it would be unrealistic to assume that they would weep during grief. Some people cry only when they are alone so that the general public does not see their response. For these people, crying is humiliating, so they reserve it for private times. One widow in the Tampa study refused to allow even her children to see her crying. She felt that she should be strong in front of everyone. But there were times, she said, that she would cry all night long.

For most, crying occurs in waves. Crying can signify despair, anger, frustration, helplessness, shame, guilt, even relief. Not all feelings are experienced in every loss, nor are all emotions experienced at the same time. But crying has adaptive value. Not only does it supply a catharsis for the bereaved person, allowing an outlet for pent-up emotions, but also it engages the help of others by eliciting sympathy and offers of help. This reaction is important, for most people need support during bereavement.

ANGER

Six sources of anger have been recognized as causing major despair and discomfort in bereavement: confrontive anger, displaced anger, ambivalent anger, internalized anger, helpless anger, and appropriate anger. Each is addressed individually here.

Confrontive Anger

The loss of a loved person, with its many frustrations and disappointments, leads to feelings of helplessness, so it is only natural that the bereaved long for support from everyone. When this support, for one reason or another, is not forthcoming from family and friends, the bereaved person feels isolated, betrayed, or deserted. The bereaved, as a by-product of their feelings of betrayal, may then confront these persons with irritability and hostility.

Displaced Anger

Anger is considered antisocial in our culture, particularly if the anger is not "justified." But at times the bereaved direct hostility toward persons who are not to blame for the death but who are visible and at hand—the health care system, funeral director, minister, or even God. The bereaved need desperately to blame someone for what happened. This need can result also in blaming the deceased for not taking appropriate health or safety precautions, for abandoning the family, or for causing immediate hardship, such as financial difficulties or social isolation. This action allows the frustration to be taken out on a scapegoat, especially when there is no one else to blame.

Ambivalent Anger

No relationship is pure love. Yet often the bereaved are led to believe that their attitude must be perfectly loving, that to express anger toward anyone, particularly the deceased, is unthinkable. The process of idealizing the deceased leaves the bereaved without an outlet for coping with the ambivalent reality of the relationship.

Internalized Anger

Some bereaved persons try hard not to direct anger outward or to display it in any way, but instead they deal with anger by turning it inward. Anger turned inward is more debilitating than anger turned outward. It can result in psychosomatic problems such as asthma, arthritis, or ulcers. Organic disorders, such as cardiovascular disease or certain types of cancer, have been connected with anger turned toward the self. Repressed anger has also been connected with nightmares, feelings of hopelessness, and depression. Anger that is repressed and turned toward the self rather than being directed outward prevents the resolution of grief work. Internalized anger is most difficult to detect, but professionals should look for it, especially if little or no anger has been observed throughout the course of bereavement.

Helpless Anger
Helpless anger is similar to internalized anger, but it is expressed with more weeping and agitation. The sheer helplessness of frustration and deprivation, coupled with the hopelessness of having to forfeit a beloved relationship, leaves the bereaved feeling powerless and out of control. Helpless anger is often seen in suicide cases.

Appropriate Anger
Appropriate anger is directed toward those who were in some way directly responsible for the death. Murder, manslaughter, or death caused by an drunk driver represent situations associated with appropriate anger. Often the bereaved deal with this type of death by attempting to obtain justice for the person apprehended. Professionals can best help a bereaved person deal with appropriate anger by allowing its proper ventilation within the therapeutic confines or by helping direct the anger toward some purposeful goal.

Anger is a natural by-product of grief. Frustration, helplessness, and deprivation all create feelings of anger and hostility, which are often directed toward others. In many situations, the bereaved person feels anger at being left to handle everything alone.

Mrs. White, a 62-year-old widow whose husband died of cancer, had spent long hours taking care of him, managing to keep him out of the hospital for most of his illness. He was at home and remained conscious until he died.

This marriage had been a second marriage for both, but it had been an extremely happy one for 8 years. During this time, Mrs. White had completed a master's degree, and Mr. White had done all the cooking and housework. Soon after his death, Mrs. White went to work, but she found it hard to manage her job and do the housework. She was exhausted most of the time.

Mrs. White's married daughter lived nearby, and the two provided each other with a great deal of mutual support. Mrs. White babysat for her two grandchildren every Thursday evening, but rarely went out other evenings. She was extremely lonely as well as uncertain about her future. Although her job until retirement was secure, she nevertheless felt isolated by society. She was angry at having been left "with the whole mess." She was financially strapped and had to continue to work until retirement in a position that was boring and dull. She joined a widow-to-widow group 2 months after the death but found that their discussions revolved around practical issues rather than emotional ones for which she felt she needed help. This experience prompted her to go into a group therapy situation, which eventually helped her allay some of the general feelings of anger and frustration.

A Catholic woman said, "I stopped going to church when my mother died. She was such a religious woman and so good. If God would let her suffer so, then I don't believe in all that stuff." Anger is a difficult emotion for many people to express, but it is even more difficult during bereavement when outward behavior is being closely observed. In these cases, anger is usually directed inward. Some people, in an attempt to hide their anger in grief, adopt a wooden expression. However, this response repels anyone who would otherwise want to help. By being so wooden, the bereaved individual relinquishes needed support.

Yet anger is not necessarily present in all bereaved individuals. I have seen many cases in which no anger is evident at all, either initially or at the end of grief. Anger is an individual reaction that depends on the many variables surrounding the bereaved person and the death situation. But it is important that caregivers as well as the bereaved be aware that hostilities may exist and recognize that anger is a natural response in grief. Supportive listeners who are not shocked at angry outbursts can provide an atmosphere of nurturance and healing.

GUILT

Guilt seems to play a large part in most losses. It may be a small nagging remembrance of something that should have been done or a full-blown, persevering guilt stemming from ambivalence associated with a lifetime of rejection or other hurts. Either way, guilt can be one of the most self-disparaging and self-defeating responses in grief.

Causal Guilt

For most of the respondents in the Tampa study, guilt was brought about by things associated with the death itself. One widow anguished over the fact that she had not been firm with her husband when she thought he needed to see a doctor. She said, "I knew he was overweight, had high blood pressure and loads of other physical problems, but he simply would not go near a doctor. I pleaded with him often. Now I wonder if I shouldn't have been firmer and insisted." Even though she knew she could not have made him go, the thought kept cropping up, making her feel somehow responsible for his death.

Another widow berated herself for not sensing that her husband was ill, for not having a keener eye to detect trouble.

> I don't know. How would I know if someone never talked? I feel guilty sometimes that maybe if I had looked at him more and had seen that he was looking tired. . . . But he always said he was tired, you know. And working in the station, he was tired. But then I remind myself; surely I could have seen, but never did I stop to think. . . . I really couldn't have you know. I guess everybody. . . . I guess I am really not to blame because he didn't tell me he felt bad.

Nevertheless, she had a little nagging doubt that needed to be worked through.

Parents of children who have died usually feel a strong sense of guilt for allowing the death to occur whether they could have done anything or not. This is especially true of accidental deaths. So much of this guilt stems from the fact that from the moment of conception, parents feel responsible for their children. When something happens to a child, parents often accept the blame, feeling in some way that they had failed. Even in a death caused by chronic illness, such as leukemia, in which everything possible had been done, parents think that maybe if they had sought this treatment or seen that specialist, things would have been different. In one case in which a teenager had died in a car wreck, the parents berated themselves for allowing him to go out that night.

But parents are not the only bereaved to experience guilt. One adult daughter whose father had died initially felt relief that he was finally out of pain, but she later felt guilty for thinking that way. Another widow was afraid that she would dream of her husband, thinking it would hurt too much. But even as she said this, she immediately felt guilty for her disloyalty.

Guilt stems from a wide variety of sources and can often act to slow down the bereavement process. Guilt can be at the conscious or unconscious level, but either way it can cause unneeded distress and misery.

In the Tampa study, the bereaved persons felt guilt accompanying any pleasure that the deceased also might have enjoyed. One widow said,

> I was eating lunch today and I thought, "How terrible it is that I can enjoy lunch." And he enjoyed things so. I mean he couldn't live long enough to enjoy the things that he worked so hard for, and that crosses my mind. He worked so hard thinking that the day would come when he could retire in just

another 4 years. And I thought how terrible it was to be taken away after working so that he could one day just do what he wanted to do, fish, putter, which he always wanted to do and never had time for. So, I sometimes feel that way. I feel guilty about all of it.

Survivor Guilt

Survivor guilt relates closely to the guilt of enjoying pleasures that the deceased can no longer experience. The survivor feels guilty for still being alive when the loved one is dead (Lifton, 1968). Even in the most benign cases, when a distant relative or casual acquaintance has died, people experience a certain bittersweet realization that death has happened to someone else rather than to them. For example, as mentioned in Chapter 2, after the death of her young daughter, a bereaved mother was outraged by the comments of another mother who visited her. The visiting mother unthinkingly said that when she heard the tragic news she rushed home to gather her own children about her and to hold them close, relieved that death had not come to her own children. Almost immediately, the visitor felt enormous guilt over these feelings and was unable to visit the bereaved mother again.

Survivor guilt was particularly evident in the Tampa study among parents who had lost a child. The impossibility of surviving their child remained foremost in their thoughts. "Why?" was an obsessive rumination. It was incomprehensible to think that they had outlived their child—that somehow the natural order of the universe had been reversed. Several voiced their wishes that they could have exchanged places with their child, and most felt that their lives had been brought to a stop for now if not forever.

Many siblings of children who die experience survivor guilt. Most children raised in a large family have, at one time or another, wished to be the only child—the center of parental love and affection. Implicit in this desire is the unconscious wish for the death of the other siblings. Sometimes the wish is even a conscious one. In anger and resentment, the child may say (or at least think), "I wish you would drop dead." If death occurs at some later time, the surviving sibling is at enormous risk of inordinate guilt and may wish to die as a just consequence.

Guilt can lead to feelings of unworthiness, shame, and self-blame. People may see a need to atone for the death, resulting in a lifetime of unhappiness. Too, when guilt is intense, the bereaved person may reject the help of others, feeling unworthy of the effort and blocking an avenue of possible help and nurturance.

The bereaved can be helped to deal with their guilt if encouraged to express their true feelings in the presence of an accepting, nonjudgmental friend. In expressing these feelings and in discussing the events that underscore the guilt, the bereaved can eradicate their guilt and better resolve their grief.

FRUSTRATION

It is easy to see why frustration would be a dominant characteristic of this stage of grief. When the bereaved is deprived of the things that heretofore have been expected, needed, and cherished, and when there is no hope of retrieving these resources, a sense of immense frustration results. Yet the constant yearning for these things keeps the bereaved person in a state of unresolved irritation. A large study on conjugal bereavement revealed that a high level of irritation was fairly universal among participants (Parkes, 1975). Grievers who are confronted over and over with the expectation of finding the lost person only to face the continuous disappointment of emptiness and failure experience enormous frustration. One widow in the Tampa study said,

> I go to work in the morning and during the day my mind is fairly well occupied and I forget that he is gone. When I come home at night, I rush into the house expecting to find John. It is not until I turn on the hall light that I remember he is not here. Then I die inside all over again. When will I get used to his being gone?

Frustration is a reminder that every individual is still a child at heart, and this regressive phenomenon is nowhere more evident than when one feels abandoned after a significant loss.

SHAME

Grief and shame are closely aligned (Schneider, 1977). Because our society views death as the worst thing that can happen to us, it is often seen as punishment not only for the one who died but also for those who must grieve (N.O. Brown, 1959). The bereaved person feels victimized and penalized, as though a sentence were being handed down by some higher court above which there is no appeal.

One bereaved mother said to me, "I felt as if I were standing on a mountaintop being tossed around by the wind, exposed and vulnerable like the gnarled old trees above the timberline." She said that grief felt like punishment from some cosmic force for a crime against society that she did not commit. The stigma of death generalizes to the survivors, making them feel alienated and stripped. As long as death is viewed by our culture as a failure, the survivors will experience some degree of shame.

Shame differs from guilt in that it results from internalizations of parental and societal values. Self systems are built from the models learned while growing up. Consequently, an individual takes on the values that have been taught by significant others. These values become the myths and values of the society. Acting in accordance with those values results in feeling comfortable and secure. However, acting in ways other than those that have been adopted results in feelings of shame and consequent loss of self-esteem.

Guilt may be rationalized through confession, but shame can only be handled by regaining a sense of personal control, developing a stronger sense of self and purpose, and reversing the negative view of death as punishment.

SLEEP DISTURBANCE

Difficulties in sleeping continue through this phase of bereavement. Paradoxically, this phase is a time during which the bereaved desperately need sleep. Everyone advises the bereaved to get rest and sleep, but because of the body's continued state of alarm, both rest and sleep generally evade the griever. As mentioned earlier, a mild tranquilizer or antianxiety agent at this time could be beneficial to allow the body much needed rest. There is no indication that a small amount of medication inhibits the grief process. On the contrary, the bereaved is better off gaining the rest needed than overextending physical limitations. Because sleep disturbance has been reported so frequently in the literature (Clayton et al., 1971; Parkes, 1972; Parkes & Weiss, 1983), the caregiver should consider relieving this symptom when possible.

FEAR OF DEATH

Death anxiety is higher during bereavement than at other times. The bereaved may believe that they are now closer to "the veil" after the death of a significant person (Hine, 1978). In the Tampa study, one widow told me that at the time of her husband's death, she felt that she too had come close to seeing what it was to die, that she experienced an eerie proximity to death herself. Others have said that they realized for the first time in their lives that they were vulnerable to death.

This vulnerability to death was especially true of middle-aged children whose parents died. These people reported that they now felt next in line for death. One grown son put it this way:

> You are in a new position, particularly when you are getting older. One thing I have thought about lots since Mother died is how many years do I have. I'm 52 and I feel that if I live to be 70, which I think I will, I'm dealing with 18 years. So I sometimes think a little bit about what do I want to do with those 18 years. I didn't think about this before.

Bereavement also is a time of personal death anxiety in which fear for one's own safety is experienced. This fear seems incredible to most bereaved people because, like sleep, it is so paradoxical. On the one hand, they could not care less if something happened to them; but on the other hand, they are fearful lest something does. One woman told me about taking a plane trip several months after her son was killed. She had never been afraid to fly before, but she said that this time she was highly anxious about the trip. She needed a tranquilizer even to board the plane. All during the flight, her shade was down because she was so afraid to look out. It took several days to recover from the stress of that trip, but she has never been afraid to fly since then. "I just couldn't understand my behavior," she said. "I have never been afraid before or after."

PSYCHOLOGICAL ASPECTS OF PHASE 2

Oversensitivity • Searching • Disbelief and denial
• Sensing of the presence • Dreaming

OVERSENSITIVITY

People are more sensitive in early bereavement and often react to what others say more quickly and negatively than they would at other times. This sensitivity can be a problem in two respects. First, it can cause others to withdraw their support when they do not understand this reaction. Second, it can cause the bereaved persons deep anguish because they themselves do not fully understand their actions and are beginning to question their own sanity. A young widow told me,

I don't understand why I was so rude to my neighbor when she came over to offer her sympathy. All she said was, "I'm sorry" but it got me mad. In the first place, she didn't even bother to come for a whole week, and in the second place, I don't want her feeling sorry for me. But usually I'm more easygoing and that wouldn't have ticked me off so.

Another widow was so angry with everyone that when people called, she would invariably become irritated about one thing or another. As a result, by the time I first saw her at 4 weeks after the death, she said few people had called recently. "I guess I'll have to learn to be more patient with them," she said. But other bereaved persons found it difficult to understand the change from being a fairly nice person to being so quick to take offense.

SEARCHING

The bereaved tend to search for the deceased in familiar places (Bowlby, 1960a; Jacobs & Ostfeld, 1980; Parkes, 1972). There is a desire to curl up in his favorite chair or sit at her desk and just stare into space. Many people find a special comfort in going to the cemetery. They feel closer to the deceased there than at any other place. Others unconsciously search a crowd for a sign of the deceased, often catching their breath when they see the back of a person's head that resembles him or her.

One young widow found it comforting to put on an old plaid shirt that had belonged to her husband. She said it made her feel like his arms were around her. Others have said that they saved a favorite piece of clothing just to take out of a box or drawer to hold from time to time.

Each of these behaviors is an embellishment of the bereaved's desire to search for and find the lost one (Bowlby, 1960a). By searching for the loved one, grievers hope to catch a glimpse or even feel the presence of the deceased.

DISBELIEF AND DENIAL

Disbelief and denial abound during this phase of bereavement: disbelief that such a loss could occur in the first place, and continued denial of the emotions that surround a profound loss. When denial is profound, grief is difficult to resolve. Levitan (1985) found that severe cases of asthma were exacerbated by massive denial on the part of the patients. People find it impossible sometimes to accept the fact that death is irreversible. Grievers find it difficult to imagine that a person can "not" be. Although the bereaved may have rationally accepted life and death, when death occurs, the finite mind cannot grasp such absolutes. Stories are confabulated and even believed in order to distract grievers from the truth until they are confronted with the truth over and over.

For example, Mrs. Houston's husband died after 55 years of marriage. They had known each other for more than 60 years. When he became ill, she knew that he could not recover. Yet they had been together so long that she felt they would be together always—that he could not die. When he did, she could not believe it. Relatives were amazed that she was so shocked and seemingly unprepared. Mrs. Houston died within 6 months of her husband, still in profound grief—still not believing that he had left her.

SENSING OF THE PRESENCE

During the "awareness of loss" phase, the presence of the deceased may still be felt. This phenomenon has been described as the cognitive counterpart of yearning (Worden, 1982). Many grievers have described an experience that I have termed the "flicker phenomenon." This is a perception in the peripheral vision of the eye seen as a flickering shadow. Immediately, thoughts of the deceased come to mind, but when the bereaved quickly turns to look, nothing is there.

Others have reported actually seeing the deceased person standing in a doorway or sitting in a favorite chair. One widow said that often when she was washing the dishes she would catch a glimpse of her husband turning the corner in the small hallway that separated the kitchen from the rest of the house. In another case, a widow saw her deceased husband walk into the bedroom, tell her that he was okay, smile, and walk out of the room. A widower spoke of when he felt his wife's presence:

> I will be washing windows, for example, a job we always did together, one on one side and one on the other, and I will suddenly see her on the other side of the window. Or, I will be sitting here and suddenly look up and she is sitting across from me.

These experiences were not frightening; they seemed to have brought a sense of comfort to the bereaved.

DREAMING

Dreams may be an extension of the desire to sense the presence of the lost person. Because there is intense longing to regain the absent one, the bereaved thinks of the deceased almost constantly. It is therefore not unusual that unconscious thoughts are also in that same focus (Raphael, 1984).

In the Tampa study, one widower told me of dreaming several times of his wife in very ordinary situations around the home. These dreams soothed him and helped him feel a little more secure without her. "It was like having her come in occasionally to visit," he said.

Worden (1982) states that dreams can be helpful to the therapist in giving some diagnostic clue as to where the bereaved is in the process of bereavement. He relates a dream of an adult daughter who had been suffering several years with guilt over her mother's death. In a significant dream, the daughter was able to release her mother along with her own feelings of guilt (p. 26).

Many of the dreams that people in the Tampa study related were dreams of premonition. Several told me that these precognitive dreams had been a lifelong experience. A widow explained these phenomena,

> I have a lot of dreams that are sometimes scary. If I have a dream about something, and it strikes me as being something different and I tell it to my husband or I told it to my children, it really happens. Like this is one I dreamed: My husband had been married before, and of course, I didn't know him until 9 years after they were divorced—but his wife was living—he had two children like I did when I married him. And I got up one morning and I told my husband, "You know, maybe I shouldn't say this, but I dreamed of Jane last night." And I told him how she died. And 2 days later I was on the phone talking with my stepdaughter, and emergency broke in and said that they wanted to use the phone and I got off. And she called me right afterwards and told me that her mother had died.

This widow also dreamed of her husband before he died.

> I said to my daughter, "Well, I really shouldn't tell you this, but I dreamed of your Daddy last night. We were both standing real still, side by side, but were naked." And he died 2 days later. The same thing happens every time I dream of someone. I wish I'd written them all down.

It was during this phase of bereavement that dreams seemed to be the most prolific. For most, they brought a sense of comfort and security, as though the deceased were assuring them that they were all right in the next dimension. These "visitations," as they were often referred to, were experienced by the bereaved person as an opportunity for the lost person to say "goodbye."

MOVING ON TO THE NEXT PHASE

There is a limit to the amount of emotional arousal one can experience until sheer exhaustion forces one into retreat. This exhaustion is what actually initiates the third phase of bereavement—that of a need to withdraw from others and conserve precious energy. However, this shift does not happen overnight. The bereaved may experience periods of tiredness and fatigue interspersed with high emotional output and activity over a long period of time. But once withdrawal is initiated, it gradually becomes the rule rather than the exception, and the bereaved person begins a progressive "winding down," which moves the bereaved into the next phase.

CHAPTER 6

The Third Phase:
Conservation-Withdrawal

I can't understand the way I feel. Up to now, I had been feeling restless. I couldn't sleep. I paced and ranted. Now, I have an opposite reaction. I sleep a lot. I feel fatigued and worn out. I don't even want to see the friends who have kept me going. I sit and stare, too exhausted to move. I am really frightened by my behavior. Just when I thought I should be feeling better, I am feeling worse.

Bereaved parent, age 45

THIS PHASE OF grief is experienced by many as the "worst period of the entire grief process." It is a time of withdrawing from others, of feeling the need to be alone. It can be one of the most frightening periods in the grief process because it seems so like clinical depression. Most people are not familiar with the symptoms of depression; therefore, they associate this need to withdraw with a more pathological picture. As a result, many bereaved people push themselves beyond their physical limits in order to prove that they are not depressed. The bereaved may even fear they are losing their minds. This fear was expressed repeatedly by bereaved people in the Tampa study as they were approaching the year's anniversary of the death. They would say, "I thought I was going to feel better by now. Instead I feel worse. I'm afraid I'm going crazy." It was hard for them to understand.

Briscoe and Smith (1975) supported the notion that bereavement is not typical of unipolar affective disease when they compared bereaved depressives with divorced or hospitalized patients. The bereaved individuals presented a different pattern from the other two groups. The divorced or hospitalized depressives shared the usual symptoms typical of severe depression, such as slowed ideation, suicidal thoughts, loss of ability to concentrate, and irritability, but the bereaved group showed distinctly and significantly less intensity of these symptoms. It would seem that the withdrawal behavior of the bereaved ostensibly resembles depression, but it does not possess the authentic underlying qualities for primary affective disease, unipolar depressed.

GENERAL DESCRIPTION OF PHASE 3

Withdrawal • Despair
• Diminished social support • Helplessness

WITHDRAWAL

George L. Engel (1962) has proposed two primary biological modes of response to danger, which have already been described in Chapter 2. The first is the fight-flight response, which is akin to anxiety and triggered when danger is initially encountered. The second, which concerns us here, is the conservation-withdrawal mode, which warns that the individual is close to exhaustion. He adds, "Its most ordinary expression is probably to be found in the daily pattern of fatigue and need for rest" (p. 96).

What is being experienced as depression is the body's need to conserve energy, both physically and emotionally. After the near exhaustion of the preceding phase, the bereaved needs to pull back and conserve what little strength is left until the body has rested and recouped some of its former energy. This phase is a time of hibernation until necessary resources can be replenished. Most often, these resources take the form of renewed physical strength, which eventually produces a faint feeling of hope. But this renewal comes slowly.

Much has been learned about the effects of separation and loss from the studies of nonhuman primates. Following their initial period of agitated distress, infant monkeys separated from their mothers experience a quieter period of persistent distress. This quiet period was proposed as an adaptive response calculated to allow the animal to regain comfort and to conserve energy (Kaufman & Rosenblum, 1967).

Spitz (1946) and Bowlby (1960b) both discuss this withdrawal response in their detailed descriptions of the problems of institutionalized infants.

Spitz used the term "hospitalism" (1945) to describe infants who lost their mothers permanently after age 6 months. These babies were characterized (1) by massive failure to develop, both mentally and physically, and (2) by frequent illness and often death. The seriousness of the distress culminated in a giving-up attitude after all efforts had failed to retrieve the lost mother.

DESPAIR

The term *despair* fits this phase of bereavement better than does *depression*. For one thing, depression connotes pathology, a nonadaptive form of responding. This period of bereavement, to the contrary, is a most adaptive phase. As has been shown, this phase is a necessary time for the body and mind to decelerate in order to focus on the task of relinquishing the lost person. Up to now, all the crying, yearning, and searching of the previous phase have failed to produce the results for which they were intended—namely, to regain the beloved person. Intellectually, it is known that the lost person is dead, but emotionally, the fact has not been confirmed. There is still the longing, the need to have him or her back. Finally, a sense of utter despair pervades, as exhaustion takes over the mind and body of the bereaved. This phase is a time of turning inward, of reviewing the loss, of reviewing the life together and realizing that the life that has been lived up to this point will never return, that the lost person is gone forever. This is the true meaning of despair.

DIMINISHED SOCIAL SUPPORT

During this time, social supports have diminished for at least two reasons: (1) Friends allot less time and energy to continue the stream of nurturance that was provided soon after the death; (2) family and friends expect the bereaved to be over grief in 6 months to a year, rather than the 3 or 4 years that is generally required. Our culture has not been educated to acknowledge the length of time necessary to overcome a major loss. This lag in information adds to the burden on the bereaved because they themselves feel that they should have been "back to normal" long before this.

HELPLESSNESS

The feeling of loss of control contributes to the helplessness still being experienced. Helplessness has been defined as a "psychological state that frequently results when events are uncontrollable" (Seligman, 1975, p. 9). An event is uncontrollable when there is nothing more *to be* done and when nothing that *is* done matters anyhow. The sheer frustration of uncontrollability leaves an individual despairing that nothing will ever matter again. Engel (1967) refers to this as the "Giving Up–Given Up" complex, experienced as feelings of powerlessness in which the bereaved place blame on external circumstances rather than accepting personal responsibility for them (p. 553).

Often helplessness can result in secondary gains for the bereaved. This gain is especially true in cases in which the bereaved either have depended heavily on the one who died or have identified so closely that much of their personality has been buried with the lost family member. In these cases, the bereaved find greater satisfaction in having others do for them than in learning independence and thereby gaining control over their lives. For these persons, nurturance for the bereaved should continue, but it should gradually be reduced, to encourage greater self-sufficiency. Yet support is often withdrawn because those who are trying to help become exasperated or simply exhausted. One thing leads to another, and it appears to the helpers that the bereaved can never be satisfied.

A minister talked with me about a parishioner he had been counselling. She began asking favors from the beginning, which he was delighted to do. Other friends were being asked to do things too, but they became discouraged sooner than did the minister. Eventually, he was the only one who could be called upon to help. He had just about reached the end of his rope, telling me, "She has worn out everyone who has tried to help. There is no stopping. Nothing seems to be enough." This unfortunate woman had gotten stuck in the third phase, and feelings of helplessness persisted in all her activities until she relied completely on others to do for her.

When the minister realized that she needed a push to move on, he was able to refuse all but the most urgent requests, compliment her when she did anything for herself, and thereby assist in putting her on track again. Learned helplessness can sometimes be as painful for those who need help as it is for those who are called on to help.

PHYSICAL SYMPTOMS OF PHASE 3

Weakness • Fatigue • Need for more sleep
• Weakened immune system

WEAKNESS

Typical of this period are feelings of weakness. People have told me of their inability to do even the simplest of chores. One widow said, "I get out the vacuum cleaner thinking I should do something about this hopeless mess. Then I sit down and stare for 2 hours without getting the strength to even lift the handle. I can't understand it." Another complained about having to lie down all the time. Others could not get the needed energy to do errands, leaving it to other members of the household. This weakness bothered these otherwise active people and added to their feelings of inadequacy.

FATIGUE

It is not difficult to understand why the bereaved feel weak and exhausted much of the time. In the Tampa study, most of the bereaved expressed feelings of debilitating fatigue during this period. It was evident that even the smallest extra push to do anything left them exhausted and irritable. One widower, aged 57, said, "I barely seem to get my work done during the day. I have a job where I see a lot of customers, and they expect me to be up all the time. When I come home at night I don't even want to watch television. I just collapse into my chair and sometimes just sit doing nothing." For those who had to work outside the home, the need to present a front to their peers became such a drain on their physical stamina that they were left with greater feelings of despair than those who were in a more protected environment. The evenings, for these individuals, were spent stretched out on the couch watching television, neither processing what they saw nor caring much.

NEED FOR MORE SLEEP

In contrast to the insomnia of the previous two stages, this stage is marked by the need for more sleep. Actually, excessive sleep is one of the best indicators that one has reached this phase of bereavement. The grieving person, however, is sometimes frightened by the large amount of time spent in sleep, thinking it is being used as a means of escape rather than as a restorative process. The truth is quite the opposite. The message is clear that the body needs more rest immediately.

In one case, the accidental death of a promising young attorney left his wife shocked and inconsolable. She experienced the first phase of bereavement for nearly a year, and the second phase was equally prolonged. When she entered the third stage, she was near complete exhaustion. She began sleeping longer periods, often napping in the afternoon and then going to bed at 6 or 7 in the evening. This need for sleep frightened her because she had never slept this much before. Too, she had always stayed up until her children were in bed. Now, she felt like she was not taking proper care of them. Even though this guilt added tremendously to her grief, she felt that she had no control over her quasi narcolepsy. Worried about her health, she underwent a complete physical exam by her internist and was given a clean bill of health. Once she learned that sleep was an adaptive response that was facilitating recovery, she was able to give in to it and not feel guilty or afraid.

WEAKENED IMMUNE SYSTEM

When the first two phases of bereavement have been protracted and intense, both physical and emotional exhaustion tends to reduce the body's natural adaptive responses. Selye's General Adaptation Syndrome (1956) has been used as a model to explain the effects of inordinate stress on the body. He has delineated three stages that, when connected, form the entire syndrome: (1) alarm stage, (2) stage of resistance, and (3) stage of exhaustion.

The alarm stage is a general call to arms of defensive forces. This stage is followed by a stage of resistance, which describes the period of chronic stress in which the body attempts to repair or compensate for the stressors. Finally, during the stage of exhaustion, the body has used the reserve and resources normally available for adaptation and succumbs to disease or death (Selye, 1956). Selye says that individuals go through the first two stages repeatedly in life, and the body repairs itself. In this way, one learns adaptive responses. Even the third stage need not be irreversible as long as it affects only parts of the body and not the entire system.

It has been shown that stress produces changes in blood pressure and heart rate as well as in the chemical makeup of the blood (Parkes, 1976). Further, emotional distress has been connected to infections and autoimmune diseases (LeShan, 1963; Solomon, 1969). Prolonged grief actually suppresses the immune system of the body, which consequently exposes the bereaved to a variety of external pathogens (Fredrick, 1976–1977; Schleifer, Keller, Camerino, Thornton, & Stein, 1983). Under the impact of prolonged stress, corticosteroid production is distinctly altered. This excess secretion then acts to suppress the body's immune mechanisms, causing the bereaved to be at considerable risk of illness or even death.

Fredrick (1976–1977) proposed a physiological-endocrine model that explains the chain of events set into motion by grief:

1. Increased release of ACTH from the pituitary.
2. Stimulation of the adrenal cortex for either the release or activation of corticosteroids.

3. Corticosteroid depression of the immune mechanism of the body.
4. Sustained high activity of corticosteroids, which further suppresses immune protective processes.
5. Disease: infection or malignancy.

Engel (1961) pointed out that grief fulfills all the requirements of a disease process. Investigative studies have shown that this finding might be true. Rees and Lutkins's (1967) study on the mortality of bereavement reported five times as many bereaved died of cancer as did control cases. Another well-known study (Schmale & Iker, 1966) involved 51 women who were awaiting a Pap smear. It was predicted that those women who had experienced a bereavement within 6 months of the test would be more likely to show cancer cells than would those who had not. Results showed that the cancer rate was indeed 212 times greater for the bereaved group than it was for the nonbereaved women.

Fredrick (1976–1977; 1982–1983) pointed out that the immunity of an individual represents a complex interaction of factors. Until further research is completed, it is difficult to draw hard and fast conclusions concerning grief and the direct effect on disease. However, the extent of grief as a major stressor cannot be ignored. The research to date points to the need for the bereaved individual to be helped to greater psychological safety and security as soon as possible. This stability would act to reduce corticosteroid levels to normal secretion, thus strengthening the immune system before the system becomes entirely depleted.

PSYCHOLOGICAL ASPECTS OF PHASE 3

Hibernation or holding pattern • Obsessional review
• Grief work • Turning point

HIBERNATION OR HOLDING PATTERN

As stated earlier, Phase 3 is the longest, most despairing time of the grief process. The entire world of the bereaved person is in chaos. The bereaved feel that a part of the self is gone and all that is left is meaningless and irrelevant. As mentioned in Chapter 4, grieving is like learning to live without an arm or leg—awkward, frustrating, and painful—and, in fact, a part is gone. A significant loss undermines the bereaved's confidence and sense of security in the world. One bereaved parent explained to me that she felt she was becoming stagnant, unable to see or even think about the future. The forward motion of her life was halted for the time being.

While going through this phase, the bereaved feel that they are in a holding pattern (Engel, 1962). They feel as if no progress is being made, and—even worse—that they may be regressing. Typically, at this point (usually out of fear that they are facing a clinical depression), the bereaved want to accelerate their activities. They feel that they should be doing something useful or purposeful, something that would move them faster out of their grief. The informed caregiver can offer beneficial advice and can support the bereaved in their desire to simplify activities and have more rest. Overextending at this time can have dangerous side effects (Selye, 1956).

A Tampa widow described how well-meaning friends urged excessive activity, which she considered too much too soon for her own well-being.

It was Thanksgiving and Christmas, and they were having parties. And they pushed me into these things with all these people, and I don't know if it was good or bad, but at the time, it was just a real pressure. I just wanted to tell everybody, "Leave me alone. Let me be by myself. Leave me alone." But everybody was saying it was good for me. But it wasn't good for me. I was very, very . . . I couldn't be myself and yet I had sense enough that I didn't want to be rude. But I felt like being rude. I wanted to just tell all of the people to leave me alone and just let me . . . let me either go off by myself somewhere or just leave me alone. But they didn't.

You need rest. Your body has gone through a very physical thing, too, besides mental. And you feel like you've lived a hundred years. I lost 20 pounds, which was good, but still losing it in just 3 weeks. I would have been happy to have been left alone. Just a little help. And I wouldn't have felt like they were neglecting me either. I would have been happy if they would have just done it.

OBSESSIONAL REVIEW

The mind has been called a "magnificent filtering system" (Kavanaugh, 1972). The loss of a significant person cannot be realized suddenly; the bereaved gradually grasps the loss by mentally reviewing it repeatedly. This mental repetition is called obsessional review. No matter how much the lost person is wished or yearned for, no matter how many dreams have seen the loved one well and alive, reality coldly and harshly confirms the fact that the beloved is gone, dead. This testing of reality, then, finally allows the bereaved to realize the finality of the loss.

Because the meaning of life has been badly shattered by the death, it is important for the griever to begin somewhere, somehow, to build a meaningful, purposeful world. New assumptions must replace old ones. It is through obsessional review that the griever begins to work through the quagmire of confusion that has plagued the griever since the death.

Going over the events of the death, as well as the memories of a lifetime, occupied most of the waking hours of the bereaved in the Tampa study. The hours spent at work provided a respite during the day for some, but when they returned home in the evening, the same circular review began again. Obsessional review seemed to be intensified for those people who had lost a child. The impossibility of surviving a child remained foremost in their thoughts and seemed to go against the natural order of the universe. It had shattered their worldview.

GRIEF WORK

Obsessive ruminations are a necessary part of working through the grief. There seems to be no shortcut. Just as the emotional venting was necessary to the second phase of grief, so are the obsessional thoughts and preoccupations central to the third phase. In doing the work of grief (Freud, 1917)—the ruminating and unfocused concentration—there finally comes an acknowledgment that old conditions are no longer attainable. The deceased is gone, and life will never be as it once was.

Evolving from that position, one realizes that new approaches and new relationships must be found if life is to have any forward motion. Harriet Schiff (1977) said it well in her book, *The Bereaved Parent:*

> Ultimately, though, facing the reality is what we need to go on with life when a child is dead. Facing it could well begin with something as simple as language. Robby did not "pass on." Nor did he "fly to heaven" or "go to his just reward." He died. Those two words are cold, brutal, and true. During the time before I decided to live and not [just] exist, I used such euphemisms in even my innermost thoughts. It was only when I could think "Robby is dead" that I could also think, "but I am alive." (p. 7)

Grief work depends on accepting the loss and the consequent change in one's life. Once the bereaved person can tolerate the idea of having to find substitutes and replacements, a certain degree of acceptance has been accomplished. In order to move to the next phase, the bereaved must come to acknowledge that the old conditions of living, including old gratifications and goals, are no longer attainable and that new ideas, approaches, and relationships must be found.

TURNING POINT

It is through thoughts such as the ones expressed in Schiff's book that the turning point in the grief process is recognized. Perceived as only a glimmer in consciousness during the latter part of the third phase, it becomes the motivating force that moves the bereaved person from the third to the fourth phase and continues more prominently as healing takes place.

Three Choices
The turning point in grief is marked with a decision either to move forward—and in doing so relinquish the past as it had been lived with the deceased—or to remain in the status quo, not making changes. Many older spouses resolve grief in this way, feeling that major life adjustments would take more strength and energy than they possess or wish to expend. A third choice is seldom discussed as an alternative, but it is selected far more often than is realized: the decision to die. Sometimes this decision is not a conscious one but is more an unconscious desire, and death results from illness or accidents. With the rising rate of suicides among bereaved spouses, there is growing indication that some bereaved persons have chosen not to continue their lives without their beloved mates.

Up until this point in the bereavement process, the bereaved have had little conscious control over the movement from one phase to another. Biological mechanisms have been the primary motivating forces. Impact (shock) led to anxiety (arousal), which eventually caused exhaustion (withdrawal). The importance of the withdrawal phase is found in the need to conserve what energies are left until supplies or resources can again be generated. A period of hibernation is essential if one is to regain the strength lost in the prolonged expenditures of energies during the preceding phases.

If resources are supplied, then one gains the impetus to move on to the next phase. *Resources* refer either to external elements such as the amount of nurturance one receives or to internal elements like the inner resolve one possesses, the determination to overcome grief, the ability to change, or just the amount of sheer physical and psychological endurance with which one is endowed.

If resources are not available, however, the bereaved person is like a vitamin-deficient organism, with little strength to move forward, heal, and grow. It is at this point of deep exhaustion, when frustrations and deprivations have diminished life forces, that individuals are most susceptible to various illnesses and diseases. One can usually expect various physical disturbances during the grief process. However, a number of investigations of grief reactions have indicated a substantial mortality rate among bereaved individuals (Kraus & Lilienfeld, 1959; Rees & Lutkins, 1967; Stroebe & Stroebe, 1983; Young, Benjamin, & Wallis, 1963). In the Tampa study, the rate of infections, diseases, and accidents rose significantly in those suffering a loss as compared to those who had not. These incidents primarily occurred from the ninth month through the first year and a half. Illnesses around the anniversary of the death were prevalent.

CASE STUDY: THE DECISION TO MAINTAIN THE STATUS QUO

In most cases, the turning point in bereavement depends on the determination to survive and change. As mentioned earlier, some grievers will opt to maintain their lives with as little change as possible. An example of this is a 55-year-old widow, Mrs. Walsh, who was married to a successful television executive for 32 years. Mr. Walsh died suddenly of a heart attack in his office. The shock and grief Mrs. Walsh experienced were profound, but she tried to maintain a brave front. She grieved privately, for as she said, "No one wants to see a sad face." She never cried in front of her family, but she told me that often she would cry all night in her room when no one could hear her. Everyone commented on how wonderfully she was getting along and as she said,

> You just have to live through it, that's what I've heard. We always thought widows were great, that they got along so well, but you don't know until you get into that situation. There is no choice. You can't, just as I said, you might like to . . . I'd like to a lot of times sit in here and not open the door. But you can't do that, and of course, my children won't let me. I've had so little time alone that I don't have a chance to cry. I'm sure that's good.

Mrs. Walsh had grown up in Tampa, so she was surrounded with a loving family and friends. She made few changes in her lifestyle. She built a small home next door to the large family house so that her daughter and her family could occupy the larger one.

Underlying all this, she said, was a large degree of aloneness, not loneliness. She went to several parties but felt like she was the "odd man" during the evening activities when husbands were included, so she decided only to go out to lunch with her friends. She said that she would rather stay home in the evenings alone.

There was a sense of desperation in her voice as she told me that she felt her life was over. She said that it would be lived from here on as an old woman. She feels old now. It was her husband who had made her feel young, she said. It was not that she would object to remarrying, but it would have to be someone who had the same friends, the same lifestyle, who traveled in the same circle as she did. Even so, she added, she could never start over with another husband at this late stage.

Mrs. Walsh made the decision to go on as before, maintaining her contacts with friends and family as always, still feeling married, only with a missing husband. Grief for a lost lifestyle finally replaced the grief for her husband.

CASE STUDY: THE DECISION TO CHANGE

There are other situations, however, where radical changes take place after a significant loss, and such was the case with Mrs. Rogers. She had been married to a man who was prone to depressive episodes as well as alcoholic binges. He had been hospitalized for pneumonia, but in his weakened state, he developed complications that led to his death. Mrs. Roger's grief was compounded by the ambivalence she had experienced toward her husband. Guilt was profound, as was anger, but it did not surface for several months. She continued work, but she came home each night to her empty house and an even emptier life.

One day, she was invited by a friend to join her for a drink after they finished work. She said that it was good to be out where there was life and activity. Later, when the same friend asked her to join a singles' club, she refused at first. That night at home, she gave it some serious thought and realized that she was grieving over an ideal, rather than her real husband. He had actually been a burden most of their married life. From that moment, she made up her mind that she was going to change her life and begin to do some of the things she had always wanted to do.

Mrs. Rogers joined the club and met both men and women who were in the same situation. She began dating, much to the displeasure of her neighbors, who thought that she should be in grief for at least a year.

She said that she found it necessary to change the old friends she knew. Women, it seems, became more possessive of their husbands, and she felt like a fifth wheel when she was with them. Primarily though, she had little in common with them any more.

When I last saw Mrs. Rogers, she appeared exuberant and enthusiastic about her new life. She said that she felt 16 years old again and was enjoying herself thoroughly. Along with her new social life, she was taking some courses at the university, exploring avenues she had never thought possible.

Alternative Decisions

Most of the bereaved in the Tampa study made decisions somewhere between the decision to remain in the same place with their lives and the decision to make drastic changes in restructuring a new identity. Only one that I know of chose death, but many had varying degrees of illness, some of which were serious and certainly could have caused death. The important point is that each person chooses a unique way of dealing with grief, and that each person's way is the right way. There is no good or bad way to resolve a significant loss.

MOTIVATION TO MOVE ON

During this phase of bereavement, feelings of hopelessness and worthlessness still pervade the thoughts of the bereaved, but there is indication that by this time, they are beginning to turn their attention from the initial needs for coping to the eventual needs for looking and planning ahead (Blanchard, Blanchard, & Becker, 1976). When the decision has been made as to the direction of grief resolution, the next phase has been reached. Healing has begun.

CHAPTER 7

The Fourth Phase:
Healing—The Turning Point

One morning, I woke up to a brand new realization. For the first time—maybe for the first time in my whole life, I was aware that I could do whatever I wanted to do, be whatever I wanted to be. This was such an overwhelming thought that I began exploring what it was I wanted to do. Then it hit me. I had always been what others wanted me to be, done what others wanted me to do. And I never even knew it until now.

Widow, age 57

GENERAL DESCRIPTION OF PHASE 4

THE CONCEPT OF "healing" may connote illness or disease to many. For that reason, some researchers and writers in the area of bereavement are reluctant to use terms that imply a medical model. This reluctance is understandable in that society does not see the bereaved as sick nor do the bereaved view themselves that way (Osterweis et al., 1984). Yet *healing* is an appropriate term when describing grief. Bereavement has been spoken of as a "wound" or a "blow," or likened to an amputation. A broken bone or stump "heals," though the afflicted individual was not considered ill or diseased. It may take months of physical therapy and medical attention to recover. It may produce consequent symptoms of distress, which must also be treated before the person is considered fit and able again. All the while, healing is taking place.

Grief, like a fracture or an amputation, is the severing of a bond so strong as to be considered an extension of one's physical self. The breaking of that bond can be analogous to the most severe of fractures. Grieving persons may seek medical attention and may receive prescribed medication for a particular symptom or complaint. But a large part of healing in bereavement has to do with changing the bereaved person's internalized concept from "learning to live without my beloved" to "learning to live more independently with myself." The caregiver can act as a guide, pointing out alternatives and choices, weighing the consequences with the advantages. As Silverman (1987) appropriately points out, bereavement is a time of change —oftentimes a new stage in the life cycle, which makes it not only an ending but also a beginning.

Three steps in the healing process have been delineated by Parkes and Weiss (1983): The bereaved must (1) accept the loss intellectually, (2) accept the loss emotionally, and (3) change their worldview to match the new reality. Herein lies the key to the fourth phase of bereavement.

CHARACTERISTICS OF PHASE 4

Turning point • Assumption of control
• Identity restructuring • Relinquishing of roles

TURNING POINT

The turning point, which was barely contemplated during the final part of the preceding phase, pushes its way into consciousness during this phase. The Tampa study revealed few clearly defined marks of change in the lives of the bereaved—no sudden jumps to signify the transition. Statements such as "I don't think I was aware of any one thing; there was just a change in my attitude" or "I realized that something was different; I didn't feel as tired or depressed as before" were the rule. However, some participants did report that something made a difference in turning their grief around; nonetheless, at the time of its occurrence, they were not aware that it had contributed to a change.

In one situation, a 52-year-old widower, Ted, whose wife had died a year before, was planning to marry a woman whom he had met about 6 months after his wife's death. She had been a strong support, helping him get through many rough times during his bereavement. Although she had separated from her husband 5 years before, she had never divorced. As their love grew, they began to talk of marriage. Ted told me that he could not pinpoint an actual event that accompanied his improvement, but he had felt a "turning point" experience 2 weeks before our interview. He simply felt better, but he did not tie it to anything. Upon questioning, however, I learned that his fiancee's divorce had become final on the previous weekend, so now they were free to move on with their marriage plans. He had not made the connection with his new, more optimistic mood.

The turning point can sometimes be effected by other changes in the environment. For example, while on vacation the bereaved can get away for a while and gain a better perspective on the situation. Other changes can trigger a turning point, such as beginning a new job, returning to college, starting volunteer work—anything that moves the bereaved out of a rut and into a different routine or around new people.

Often an event can precipitate the turning point by making the bereaved angry enough to act in new ways. In one case, a widow had remained in her house for almost a year following her husband's death. She only went out occasionally to go to the store, but even then she refused to drive her car. Neighbors had transported her since the death. Meanwhile, she became caught up in phone conversations and letters with the Social Security office over some red tape concerning a hospital bill. It was taking forever to untangle. One day, after a particularly frustrating phone conversation with a Social Security representative, she got so angry that she dressed herself, got in her car, and drove all the way across town to the Social Security office, where she settled her case once and for all. She had become so angry that she had not even thought of herself; she had not even realized what she had done until she was on her way home. In this case, she had managed to turn her anger away from herself momentarily in order to focus it outward. As a result, her anger and determination motivated her to take action. After that, she began going out more often and became less fearful.

ASSUMPTION OF CONTROL

Taking control of one's life differs in kind and degree from person to person. One widow, whose husband had always handled business matters, had to take over a large estate, and she gained a sense of competence in being able to do it. A bereaved mother took a job as a receptionist in a law firm and regained her confidence in dealing with people once again. A widower, whose wife died suddenly after surgery, learned to cook, at first grudgingly; but later, he began to prepare gourmet meals for friends. As he realized a sense of competence over what had been his "wife's territory," he said that he wished he had done this before she died so that they could have shared it together.

Assuming control can be frightening, especially if it means drastic changes. One Tampa widow was unable to move on with her grief because she could not bring herself to move from the isolated lakeside home her husband had built. One day would blend into another. She hated to leave her home, but she was becoming more lonely and isolated the longer she stayed there. Finding a reason for her life was difficult. As she stated,

> It just seems like you're trying to figure out a way to put in your time alone and it's really hard to do. He died a year ago January and you say, well, now you've got to do it. You've got to make up your mind to fill up your time some way, but it is hard. I've gotten a little more used to being alone, but—like I say—it's awful lonesome.
>
> You wonder what you are sticking around for. I just can't see where I'm worth that much to be around. I mean I have no tendency to destroy myself, but I sometimes wonder what He put you here for.

Making decisions about future life changes can be burdensome at any time, but in grief this task is doubly intensified. The bereaved fear that what they decide for the future will create even greater problems than the present ones. This fear often freezes the bereaved into no action at all, creating a greater problem of stagnation. In the preceding case, this widow had been sitting in her house alone, wishing that things could be different—afraid to make a change. She felt an implicit loyalty to the house because her husband had built it and loved it. Abandoning it seemed like she was abandoning him too. Yet being alone meant that she had no one with whom she could talk over alternatives and choices.

For some, even trying to assume control is not always successful. And further failure may end in a sense of continued helplessness. One widower, in reaction to the terrible feeling of loss of control when his wife died after a long bout with cancer, began ordering his fellow workers around, even going so far as to tell his manager how to work out a particular negotiation about which he knew very little. He eventually lost his job, which furthered his sense of helplessness and loss. It was not until he took stock of his emotional situation that he realized how anger was blocking his way to healing.

Gaining a sense of control comes slowly, often in bits and pieces. Caregivers need to maintain a balance between offering support and providing strategies for change in order to boost the bereaved without overwhelming them.

The Tampa study indicated a distinct sex difference in the need for control. Men seemed better able to gain control of their emotions, which generally were channeled in the direction of aggressive actions. Women's greatest needs, on the other hand, were directed more toward gaining better control over the world about them than toward control of their emotions. Women needed to gain a renewed sense of competency and order in the environment, which allowed them greater feelings of security once again. The world can be a frightening, threatening place during bereavement, leading the bereaved to retreat to safe but nonadaptive modes of behavior.

IDENTITY RESTRUCTURING

Suffering a major loss leads to a crisis transition akin to that experienced in adolescence. Teenagers often vacillate between independence and dependence. Maturity means accepting the responsibility of a new and different existence in which they learn to depend more on themselves than on their parents. The bereaved, during the early stages of grief, have lost a sense of confidence in themselves and the world, which interferes with the ability to take charge of their lives once again. The return of confidence is gradual and erratic. The bereaved often tend to sequester themselves in the safe haven of the protective home or to avoid people at work. Yet, this hiding cannot become a way of life if one is to move forward in the grief process, because the assumptions that were appropriate in the past are no longer operable. An identity based on life with the deceased must now be replaced with a new identity, structured without the beloved person (Parkes & Weiss, 1983).

In the early phases of grief, when the realization dawns for the first time that death is final and that the loved person is gone forever, the bereaved often feel panic—a fear so intense that it seems overpowering. Bereaved persons have said that when they feel this panic, they wish that they, too, would die—that too big a part of themselves has already died with the deceased. When personal identity is so connected to the person who has died, it takes enormous courage to carve out a new one. Gerald Corey (1977) writes about this:

> The trouble with so many of us is that we have sought directions, answers, values, and beliefs in the important people in our worlds rather than trusting ourselves to search within and find our own answers to the conflicts in our lives; we sell out by becoming what others expect of us. Our being becomes rooted in their being and we become strangers to ourselves. (p. 44)

Many bereaved people are strangers to themselves and are groping blindly. A physician's wife in the Tampa study told me that all her life she had been just that. Her community work and her social life all revolved around her husband's status and profession. When he died, she lost her identity and felt like an empty shell. She then had the arduous task of searching within herself for her own individual worldview.

Parkes and Weiss (1983) discuss the concept of identity this way:

> What we mean by an "identity" here is simply a reasonably consistent set of assumptions about one's own self. It is on the basis of such sets of constructs that we make choices and plans. They should, therefore, correspond reasonably well to our actual wishes, potentials, and situations. (p. 160)

RELINQUISHING OF ROLES

Identity restructuring does not occur overnight. Roles must be relinquished if growth is to develop. One immediately thinks of the role of wife or husband because they have been so carefully delineated in our culture. But I have heard many adult children speak of the pain of relinquishing the daughter or son role when a parent dies. They expressed sorrow at never having anyone to love them again in the special way that a parent does. These grievers were becoming orphans in an adult world and could never be a child again to that parent.

But the loss of a child may require the most restructuring of identity. The parent's role has changed because that particular child is no longer there. A parent's identification with his or her child is a given. The parents and child are biologically connected. Living without that child means the restructuring of the persons they were into the new persons they are becoming. One parent told me that in relinquishing one small aspect of his role as a father—that of being father to a son who played in Little League—he gave up the role of armchair coach, adviser, and team rooter—in that one situation alone.

It is when the bereaved relinquish roles that the work of changing an identity begins to take place. This process is essentially one of transformation—a death and rebirth process (Bridges, 1983). Caregivers need to recognize that bereavement takes a long time. The process is far from complete simply because the bereaved have stopped crying or are sleeping better. In this phase the caregiver actively participates in helping the bereaved develop goals and make decisions (Parkes & Weiss, 1983).

PHYSICAL SYMPTOMS OF PHASE 4

Physical healing • Increase in energy
• Sleep restoration • Immune system restoration

PHYSICAL HEALING

Biologically, during the stage of healing, the body is repairing itself. There is a gradual diminution of the effects of prolonged stress, causing a release from abnormal states of hyperarousal. From this period of emerging health and restoration springs a more positive attitude, which works to create new energy sources for the healing process. Several bereaved have described it as a time of rebirth, signaling that physical and psychological repair is in progress.

INCREASE IN ENERGY

A healing organism will naturally develop more energy as it develops greater health. However, if the bereaved have developed habits of inactivity, these habits will need to be gradually changed. A moderate exercise program should be initiated, in order not to succumb to what Selye terms as the "retirement disease" (1956). This is a condition of enforced rest that continues until the individual is debilitated by the lack of activity. The mental health professional can encourage the bereaved, who are now ready for more diversion but who may be still in the stress-behavioral mode. Although the bereaved will probably still tire easily, it is important to good mental and physical health that the body is exercised and strengthened.

SLEEP RESTORATION

Stress prevents restful sleep. The hormones produced during acute stress are meant to prepare the individual for alarm or peak accomplishment (Selye, 1956). As stress diminishes, sleep patterns return to normal. It is during the healing phase of bereavement that the griever usually finds that sleep has returned to normal and the bereaved can expect to have fairly unbroken periods of sleep during the night. But if sleep patterns have been disrupted over a long period, if stress has been of a chronic nature such as it is in bereavement, sleep habits may be broken and will need to be reinstated.

The mental health professional can help the bereaved learn methods such as progressive relaxation techniques, autogenic training, and biofeedback (Pelletier, 1977). Because these procedures are self-regulatory, the bereaved can derive a sense of control by learning to master any one of them.

IMMUNE SYSTEM RESTORATION

The generalized state of stress reduction restores the body's natural ability to ward off disease through the immune system. Renewed feelings of safety and security, while growing tentatively, are nevertheless acting to strengthen the body during this phase. The bereaved find that they are no longer having as many health problems as they had during previous phases of bereavement. Corticosteroid levels are returning to baseline values (Fredrick, 1982–1983). Because the body's natural state is to heal itself, it seems logical that relief from stress would produce greater competence in the immune system. Surviving a major bereavement is akin to reversing the aging process. Rather than seeing a sequential diminishment of health resources, these resources gradually increase over time.

PSYCHOLOGICAL ASPECTS OF PHASE 4

Forgiving • Forgetting • Search for meaning
• Closing of the circle • Hope

FORGIVING

The stage of healing is also a time of forgiving and forgetting. Forgiveness works two ways. First, it implies self-forgiveness by working through emotions such as guilt, anger, and shame that were initially felt when the bereaved blamed themselves, in some way, for the death. The bereaved also need to forgive themselves for not having been the ones to die—for surviving. At the same time, the ones who left must be forgiven for leaving, for causing such suffering and agony in the first place. Forgiving the deceased is usually the harder task because there are so many lonely and frustrating times to live through. The act of forgiveness in this complete sense is time-consuming, arriving slowly, bit by bit. Once realized, however, forgiveness can be a blessed emancipation.

FORGETTING

Forgetting involves "letting go." This is perhaps the most difficult task of bereavement. As Colin Parkes (1972) so aptly puts it, "love is a tie and the strength of a tie is its resistance to severance" (p. 120). When we have been deeply committed to a person, the ties are strong and letting go is difficult. But it is in the act of saying goodbye to the past, to the yearning and longing to be with the lost one, that grief work can be resolved.

One Tampa widow who had been married for 44 years was trying to manage her grief without crying all the time. At the same time, she was trying to establish a new life for herself. She found that the best way for her to manage was to remove her husband's things from view. She knew that she did not want to deny his death, but she found it better if she was not constantly reminded of it. She told me that a friend of hers had asked why she did not have his picture up. She had answered, "Because I'm trying to forget him." She went on to tell me,

> I don't know whether that's being inhuman or not, but I'm really trying to forget him. I don't dwell on bad things. I don't have any pictures around. I don't have any of his things around at all. I really don't. And it's not that I want to go with somebody else, you know what I mean. It's just that it's my way of coping and surviving.

This widow was determined to somehow get through her grief. She had grieved intensely the first year, but she had become tired of this way of life. Her resolution to stop crying became a shift point in the bereavement process, but she also needed to put away reminders that brought on her tears. In saying that she was trying to forget him, she was implying that she was trying to let go of her wish to have him back, to stop herself from yearning for him the way she had during the first year after his death. She was not trying to forget the 44 years of marriage, because these years were very precious to her. Her decision to forget him was made because she was tired of her own responses to grief, not tired of him. The act of putting away his things meant that she was now looking toward the future rather than lingering in the past.

Forgetting does not mean either that the bereaved will not experience poignant memories from time to time, or that anniversary reactions will be erased. If the bereaved were to erase all memories, it would also erase the meaning of the life of the deceased. Letting go refers to the act of turning to new encounters, trusting in the future. This act establishes expectations that move toward the rebuilding of a life with new rewards and reinforcements.

A woman in the Tampa study whose father had died felt that she needed some way to ritualize her decision to let go of her grief. She had kept an old hat that he use to love to wear and had it hanging by the back door much the same as he did when he was alive. Every time she passed that hat, she had what she called "bittersweet" feelings. She loved seeing something that was so beloved by him, but she felt pain that he could no longer be there to enjoy it.

One day, after a good cry at the kitchen table, she decided that she must begin to let go of the pain of her grief. On the spur of the moment, she took his hat plus a copy of a favorite poem of his to the beach not too far from her home. Standing on the shore in that bright Florida sun, she tossed his hat onto a wave, which carried it slowly out to sea. While the hat slipped away, she read the poem to herself, silently saying goodbye to her father. When the hat had disappeared from view, she turned and went back home, feeling a weight had been lifted from her heart. Little self-made rituals can be affirming and therapeutic. They have a power of their own as they carry out the expectations of change with them.

SEARCH FOR MEANING

It would be a waste of time to suggest to anyone in the earlier phases of grief that they could ever find meaning in the death. Few people who have ever suffered a significant loss have been able to find this comfort initially. Before creating some meaning from the death, the bereaved must take time to process what the deceased has meant—both to the bereaved and to others. Most often, in the Tampa study, the bereaved found meaning by doing something as a memorial to the deceased. One widow volunteered in the cancer ward where her husband died and was able to bring comfort to the families who were waiting there. A bereaved parent taught a course at her church to describe the needs of newly bereaved people. Through this effort, she started an ongoing support system for anyone who had had a significant loss. Others involved themselves in support groups of one kind or another and became an integral part of those groups, in a sense, finding a family of understanding people.

One outstanding characteristic of bereaved people is that they generally become more compassionate to others who are suffering a loss of any kind.

One widower who prided himself on being pragmatic said that he never thought about going to funerals before his wife died. She had always done that for him, acting as a sort of surrogate mourner. When she died, he realized how important the supporters were for him and said that he never misses an opportunity to help a newly bereaved person. Attending the funeral appears to be a major way in which others can support the bereaved. Their presence there speaks for them and their personal concern. One newly bereaved mother, whose 16-year-old son had been killed in an accident, made it a point to read the obituary column and pinpoint any adolescents who had been killed. She would then call on the family and let them know that she was there to offer what comfort she could. She told me that everyone had been grateful when she visited them, but she never would have dreamed of intruding before.

Because the search for meaning from the death goes on relentlessly until some conclusion has been reached, caregivers should offer opportunities to the bereaved to actively carry out this search. Discussing spiritual values often helps, although caregivers should be careful not to introject their own values or philosophies. The bereaved should do the talking.

Closing of the Circle

Closing the circle is analogous to closing the wound, which is the true meaning of healing. Scar tissue will remain, probably permanently, but the open wound is closing. Many primitive societies offer rituals following a death: Families close the circle by joining hands, sharing a ritual meal, or burning sacrificial foliage that creates dense smoke symbolic of the departing spirit. In each case, the idea is to separate the living from the dead, to provide the survivors with impetus to continue their lives with renewed commitment (van Gennep, 1960). Usually, these rituals occur over a period of time after the death.

Unfortunately, our society provides few rituals that give the bereaved this opportunity. The funeral is over too soon to provide the mourner with a sense of finality. Closing the circle is usually done in less symbolic ways, such as beginning to associate with newfound friends who were not a part of the life that was shared by the deceased. This process actually facilitates healing.

One family in the Tampa study had lost a 14-year-old son, but they had kept up with his friends for more than 2 years. They entertained them frequently, went to football games to watch "the team" play. As a matter of fact, their social life centered around this group of teenagers. Finally, at a

Christmas family dinner, the remaining children, aged 17 and 19, confronted the parents with their own discomfort concerning the constant association with these boys. Their parents were not only keeping these boys from moving on with their lives but also curtailing the acceptance of their own need to resolve their grief. The parents were shocked and hurt with their children's directness, but after discussing it with their minister, they began to see what they were doing. As difficult as it was, they began to close the circle and to find a new group of friends who could share in their present world. They still kept up with the teenagers, but on a much more diminished level.

The realization of the need to find new ways of sharing life comes slowly. Several widows in the Tampa study found that they had little to talk about with their married friends and began to seek others with whom they had not been involved before. They just seemed to have less in common with the old crowd now.

The phase of healing is a long, drawn-out period with false starts and regressions. Trying out new lifestyles can be perilous and disappointing. Seeking replacements or substitutions to fill the void left by the death of a family member is in and of itself discouraging, especially when one is reluctant to let go, to even admit that something is needed to fill the empty place.

Hope

The very fact that the bereaved is beginning thoughts of a future of any kind signals a faint formation of hope. Friends and caregivers who are alert to these signals will be ready to gently help the bereaved seek alternatives. Self-help bereavement groups are especially helpful at this time because they themselves recognize from their own experience the signs of healing and can suggest and even push the bereaved into taking some action.

Yet a time comes when the bereaved person can look back past the events of the death and see happy memories, joyful times. The griever views a more realistic picture of the deceased rather than the idealized one that developed after the death. Idealization can be functional shortly after the death, when one needs a balance for ambivalent feelings. But if idealization is carried over the entire bereavement, it can produce an unrealistic picture of the one who has died, blocking out memories of a more complete person. The bereaved must recognize their frailties as well as their strengths. When the bereaved can think in these terms, they are ready to move on to the final phase of grief, that of renewal, that is, a new level of functioning.

CHAPTER 8

The Fifth Phase: Renewal

There are sad days, but it is easier to remember the good times and other happy special events that we shared. I do not like to dwell on sad, unhappy events; these I must put away. I will always remember them, but on the more positive side rather than negative side.

Bereaved parent

AFTER THE BEREAVED have (1) tested and come to grips with the social losses of bereavement, (2) developed higher self-esteem, and (3) set about to secure substitutes for the lost person, they move on to the final phase of bereavement—that of renewal, of a new level of functioning. When this level is reached, the bereaved are markedly improved and well on the way to a new life they have worked to attain. This is not to say that they are the same persons as before the death. Far from it. The agony and suffering of loss create scars that remain forever. However, the pain, for the most part, is gone. The bereaved will continue to deal with anniversary reactions, perhaps abject loneliness.

Grief is akin to a death and resurrection experience. As part of the old self dies with the old life, there is almost simultaneous preparation for a rebirth into a new life. And when that rebirth comes, so does a deeper compassion for others as well as a new strength that pervades the entire lifestyle.

GENERAL DESCRIPTION OF PHASE 5

New self-awareness • Acceptance of responsibility
• Process of learning to live without

NEW SELF-AWARENESS

The strength of grief derives from a new self-awareness, which in turn provides the avenues for a sense of freedom. When one recognizes the alternatives in life and the freedom to choose them, amazing possibilities are opened. One young widow in the Tampa study said,

> During this time of recovery, I learned many things about myself—mainly that I could cope. I found myself able to do things and handle affairs which I never dreamed possible—and do it in a businesslike manner. I also became aware of the outside world around me instead of being in a sheltered world of homemaker.
>
> I find it easier to accept disappointments and to take life at an easier pace on a day-to-day basis. I don't take anything for granted anymore.

Most of the Tampa bereaved found that out of a new sense of competence came an inner strength that was not there before. To survive a tragedy that for some was the worst thing that could have happened to them brought a realization of their own stability and courage that they had never thought possible prior to the death.

ACCEPTANCE OF RESPONSIBILITY

Existentialists insist that persons are responsible for their existence and their own destiny. They believe that humans can escape neither from freedom nor from aloneness—that ultimately we are all alone (Frankl, 1959; Jourard, 1968; May, 1953). Unless the bereaved have learned autonomy and independence before the death, this realization of personal responsibility causes fear and uncertainty. A sense of isolation comes when the bereaved recognize that they cannot depend on anyone else for their own confirmation—that they alone must give meaning to their lives, find their own answers as they go.

Many bereaved people feel that they can take care of themselves, are financially independent, and certainly are physically self-reliant. They provide themselves with clothing and shelter, take care of their bodies, and supply their social needs. Yet the one area that causes the most trouble is the lack of emotional independence. Many people tend to gain emotional security from someone else rather than supplying it from within. This attitude is learned early through identifying with parents, later with spouses, then with children. Moods and good feelings depend on the reinforcements, positive or negative, offered by these other people. Abandonment issues are the bottom line with these feelings: If we do not behave as others wish, they will leave us. When a loss occurs, these emotional responses are brought into play at an unconscious level. Grief epitomizes the ultimate isolation that has been so deeply feared. Learning to take care of personal emotional needs can become one of the most freeing experiences of a lifetime; it is a guarantee that the unconscious abandonment issues will not be overwhelming when a loss occurs.

The bereaved person must learn eventually to focus on the positive aspects of this new freedom. But in the beginning of grief, this attitude adjustment is hard to comprehend, and—like everything else in the process of bereavement—it takes a long time to realize. However, experiencing conditions of loneliness, meaninglessness, emptiness, guilt, and isolation—without becoming buried by them—leads the bereaved to become stronger and freer (Corey, 1977).

CASE STUDY: DEALING WITH LONELINESS RESPONSIBLY

One wonderful woman at the university was working toward her bachelor's degree at age 70. Her husband, who was retired, drove her to school each day and waited for her in the lobby of the building where she was taking courses. I got to know them well and admired her striving and his patience. They were inseparable. When he died suddenly of a heart attack, she was bereft. Her children, who lived in other parts of the country, all came home, but the family seemed to experience one misunderstanding after another, even during the rituals.

Because she was 70, they felt she was incapable of taking charge of her needs. They made all the decisions. One decision was a heartbreaking disaster for this widow. While she was out of the house having her hair done for the funeral, they donated all his clothing and personal effects to a local charity. When she returned, she was shocked to find every drawer and closet empty; even treasured photographs had been thrown away. They had believed that she would recover from her grief sooner if she were not reminded of her husband by his things. But it had just the opposite effect. She felt emptier than ever, for she had nothing of him left. Later, she found a torn photograph of him in the bottom of the desk drawer, which she cherished. It was all she had left.

The daughters stayed on for 2 weeks, but at the end of that time, they said, "Mama, it is time for you to stop crying and get back to school. Tears won't help anything now." But she soon learned that grief is not so quickly dealt with. She and her husband had grown together as two trees entwine—even the roots had become as one. She tried to do as her children wished, for she could not bear to risk losing them, too. She returned to her classes at the university while they left for their homes in other cities, content with the knowledge that she was not "stuck at home alone with her grief." Yet she was alone. Her husband had been with her even when she went to school, and now she had to make the trip without him. Evenings were the worst; she hated the awful emptiness of being alone.

Some of the students in her class sensed her loneliness and began seeking her out for coffee or lunch. She was surprised at first that young people would want to be with an "old woman," as she said. However, she had kept herself interesting, and even in her grief, she shared something with her classmates. She began to shift her need for relatedness on to these students rather than clinging to her own children as she had done in the beginning. To her surprise, she found many new friends with whom she could begin to share her life. Things would never be the same for her, but she began to deal with her aloneness in a way her children could never help her do.

It is not always easy for the bereaved to accept responsibility for their lives, especially if they previously had relied on others too heavily. The deprivations of loss, however, teach that if the bereaved are to survive, they will have to shoulder some of the new responsibilities themselves. Often there is no one else to do it. One widow, who had been having some trouble sorting out her husband's affairs, gained a sense of mastery when she was able to handle things on her own. She told me,

> We had some government bonds that had to go back to Washington. And all that got straightened out. Then I think it hit me. I said, "All right now, Mary, you're on your own." I think I woke up to that fact, for the first time, but I also think that it was a feeling that I had accomplished these things and that I was able to do these things without somebody else. You know, without leaning on a brother-in-law or something like that.

Some widows in the Tampa study had assumed responsibility for their lives before their husband's death so they did not have this task during bereavement. In one case, the husband had had a series of heart attacks, which culminated in his doctor's telling him that he was not to work again. Because he had owned his business, it was up to his wife to learn how to handle it. During the interview, she said,

Well, he had had five heart attacks. After the third massive heart attack, we were still in business, and he began training me. He taught me the rudiments of the business, which was the laundry and dry cleaning business of the old type, the big old laundries, the old dry cleaners. And I had to learn how to buy the materials. I had to do all that, just like he had done all the years before. He was preparing me for his death so that I would not have this period of grief. The business had to operate. It was our livelihood. And he knew I had to do it.

Because of her preparation, she was able to carry on the work of her husband, but even more important, she was prepared for his death by their open and frank discussions. They were ready for alternatives should the need to choose arise.

Process of Learning to Live Without

Losing a family member means learning to live without the resources once taken for granted: a husband or wife who filled lives with meaning and purpose, a child who was an object of nurturance, a parent who was a life-long role model. In order to begin a new life, the bereaved need to find substitutions and replacements to fill the voids caused by the death. But searching for replacements can be disastrous if done before the bereaved are able to recognize that they can never find an exact replacement. Early decisions following a major loss can lead to inappropriate substitutions. For example, some people try to find a husband or wife just like the one who died. Parents have tried to replace a child by quickly having another and then trying to mold this child into the pattern of the one they lost (Cain & Cain, 1964). In such cases, bereaved individuals will be disappointed and miserable because of their own choices and because of what they do to the people they have chosen. To avoid this danger, bereavement must be worked through until a new level of functioning is realized. Once this renewal is achieved, then the bereaved may more wisely seek replacements, taking into consideration the change that has occurred within themselves.

CASE STUDY: TRAVEL OFFERS RENEWED INTEREST

Appropriate replacements can be anything that interests the individual or provides a sense of purpose. One Tampa widow, Mrs. Paul, found that traveling brought her a renewed feeling of participation and joy.

I joined a Sixty Plus Club that's really sponsored by the Presbyterian church. They decided they would lease a bus and go to Nashville about the middle of May. And I decided that I'm going too. And I have this friend that's a few years younger than I am and she says, "Oh, I'll look after you. Come on." So she got a leave of absence from her work; she works with the blind. We went, and I just had a ball. I had the best time. Everybody was my age. Most of them were widows, and we just had a real good time. And you would never believe it if I was to tell you . . . the bus trip to Nashville cost about a hundred dollars and we paid for our food, and that's just about all. All our meals, I mean all our sleeping and all our entries. We went to see the Grand Old Opry. We went just like a tourist, we took in everything.

But this same widow had to face social pressures from several people she had known before because they saw her as moving too quickly into the social mainstream. Even though she had not joined the Sixty Plus Club until well into her third year of grief, some people felt she was not showing the proper loyalty to her husband. As she described her feelings,

I think my traveling has . . . so many people have made slight remarks since I've lost him and said, "Well, you haven't missed him, have you." That's not true. It's because I fill my life full of substitutes, which are not replacements certainly, but they help.

Mrs. Paul is a very positive and determined person, but even so, she suffered greatly from the loss of her husband of 52 years. After the death, she was overcome with the memory of the day he died. Although she has laid a throw rug over the place where he fell in the living room and where rescue efforts took place, she relived the event over and over in her mind. She had his chair recovered, partly because she felt so sad looking at it without him in it and partly because the chair needed it. She senses his presence and knows he is with her and always will be.

Mrs. Paul was helped by the fact that they had talked about the time when only one would be left, and she says she is better off than most because of it. They, along with their daughters, planned their burial and funeral arrangements so that when death occurred, she simply put the plans into gear. This forethought, she said, made a big difference in grief resolution because she knew she was doing what he would have wished.

Still, it is easy to see how social pressure often deters the progress of grief resolution by imposing outdated mores and personal values on the bereaved. Many of the bereaved in the Tampa study were afraid to act for fear that they would make a mistake. However, when they overcame their fear of change, life became an adventure in which excitement replaced anxiety. Learning to accept responsibility for personal decisions is a big step toward realizing the new equilibrium necessary for renewal.

PHYSICAL SYMPTOMS OF PHASE 5

Revitalization • Functional stability
• Caring for physical needs

REVITALIZATION

The phase of renewal is one of gaining a new sense of vitality. After the death of his mother, D. H. Lawrence wrote,

> Then, in that year, for me everything collapsed, save the mystery of death, and the haunting of death in life. I was twenty five, and from the death of my mother, the world began to dissolve around me, beautiful, iridescent, but passing away substanceless. Till I almost dissolved away myself and was very ill; when I was twenty six.
>
> Then slowly the world came back: or I myself returned: but to another world.
>
> Introduction to *The Collected Poems of D. H. Lawrence* (1928)

Having come through the long process of grief, the bereaved often feel like nothing short of a miracle helped them survive. Yet with renewed vitality, a faint optimism tentatively allows the bereaved to assume greater confidence in physical activities.

FUNCTIONAL STABILITY

The bereaved survivor has the potential of developing into a stronger, more capable person. Just as a broken bone sometimes heals to become stronger than it was before, so the grieving individual can realize a similar outcome in bereavement. Biologically, the system has had time to heal and renew itself. Although special times and dates, such as anniversaries, continue to be stressful, the overwhelming shock of death's impact has subsided, and the body has healed itself from that assault. The despair that was felt in the third phase has lifted, and its departure coincides with a return of functional stability (Schulz, 1978).

CARING FOR PHYSICAL NEEDS

Having experienced the sleeplessness, loss of appetite, and fatigue of grief, the bereaved find that renewal brings a returned vitality that motivates them to take better care of their personal health. The bereaved must assume responsibility for educating themselves about exercise and proper nutrition in order to build in a preventive, protective mechanism that will defend against trauma in future losses. Feeling in control of their lives once again brings renewed confidence. Most bereaved individuals must learn new health skills in order to survive. These skills, in turn, allow them to venture into activities previously thought unnecessary or inappropriate.

PSYCHOLOGICAL ASPECTS OF PHASE 5

Living for oneself • Anniversary reactions • Loneliness
• Reaching out • Time for the process of bereavement

LIVING FOR ONESELF

After they had become more independent, many bereaved in the Tampa study expressed a concern that they had a hard time getting used to the new persons they had become. Most were referring to the fact that they were living for themselves now and not for others. They were talking about their new ability to center on themselves and find a sense of purpose in fulfilling themselves rather than trying to satisfy others. Having lived much of their lives through others—their spouses, their children, their parents—they had now begun to discover who they were and to focus on being that person.

In the course of learning to be this new person, they needed to become selfish, to take care of themselves first and allow others the opportunity to take care of themselves as well. Yet, when others showed their disapproval, the bereaved sometimes faltered, becoming anxious and insecure. Many found that in the process of changing, they were in conflict within themselves. They found that often they did not know or even like the new persons. They had leaned heavily on their support systems during the earlier phases of grief. Now it was difficult to become strong and confident all at once. As one bereaved mother told me,

> Sometimes I lose perspective of where I've been or where I'm going. Sometimes it's hard for me to like myself—other times I border on conceit. Sometimes I wonder who I really am—other times I know exactly. Most times, I'm aware of how I "feel" but can't always channel it constructively.

Learning to center oneself takes concentration on inner ideals. This focus can be done through the process of meditation, prayer, analysis, psychotherapy, reading, or study. So often, the bereaved have a tendency to overlook this need by distracting themselves—keeping constantly busy, spending much time with friends or acquaintances, or whatever it takes to maintain life as it had been. Granted, some in the Tampa study wished their lives to remain the same; they lived as though they thought the deceased would return and were marking time until it happened.

Isabella Taves (1974) writes in her book, *Love Must Not Be Wasted*,

> The early days of grief—although they may not seem so—are easier. Tears, anger, anguish come spontaneously; people around you are understanding. There is also the cushion of shock, the courage that comes with unreality. The second part, the long road back, is more difficult. It consists of rehabilitating yourself, rebuilding your life with an eye to the future, destroying your old self so that you may live again . . . but once again, if you accept the challenge of creating a new and more liberated life, your own growth will be your reward. (p. 174)

Anniversary Reactions

The bereaved will always experience moments of poignant memories. Bereaved parents have spoken of breaking down every time they passed the cereal section in the grocery store. Special anniversaries or other dates are probably the hardest. When these reactions come after the bereaved thought their grief was over, it can be disheartening. One widow told me. "I was in a panic because I thought it was starting all over again. If I thought I had to live through all that again, I would go off the deep end." Caregivers should alert the bereaved to the fact that anniversary reactions should actually be expected so that they will not come as a shock or a setback. Anniversary reactions can be experienced throughout a lifetime, popping up when least expected. I'm not saying that they necessarily will appear but that the bereaved should not be devastated by the reactions when or if they do.

Loneliness

In one study (Lund, Caserta, & Dimond, 1986), loneliness was found to have caused the greatest difficulty of all following the death of a spouse. In the early phases of grief, loneliness stems from not having that one particular person nearby, in wishing and yearning for the return of the presence of the deceased. But as the bereaved work through the reality of the loss, recognizing the impossibility of retrieval, they begin to wish for other sources of supply. When they open themselves to new people, places, ideas, and experiences, they expand horizons of hope and new possibilities. Reaching out is a sure cure for loneliness.

REACHING OUT

One of the most difficult tasks for the individual emerging from a major loss is that of reaching out to others. During the phase of renewal, when a new level of functioning is undertaken, it is imperative that the bereaved tap into new sources of energy and support. For some of the people in the Tampa study, support systems changed or fell away during the long period of bereavement. The death of a parent least affected the lives of their adult children, who had friends removed from the lives of their older parents. But when a child died, many friends who were parents of their child's friends gradually drifted away, their common interest gone. When a spouse died, the couple's companionate friends closed the circle, making the widow or widower feel like a fifth wheel.

One widower who had stayed pretty much to himself for nearly a year after his wife died and who had resisted taking a trip even though his therapist had recommended it, particularly at Christmas, finally complied. When he went to the travel agency to purchase his ticket, the woman who waited on him was a person that he and his late wife had known. In the meantime, her husband had also died. It was not long before they were seeing each other regularly and finally married. He wondered later why it took him so long to reach out.

TIME FOR THE PROCESS OF BEREAVEMENT

Predicting how long it will take for an individual to complete the process of bereavement is difficult. Intervening variables create differing patterns. Some individuals can complete the entire process in a month; others may require years. So much depends on the relationship of the bereaved to the person who has died, what resources the bereaved person possesses, internal and external mediators, and the degree of shock produced at the time of death. A phasic model of bereavement allows caregivers to determine where each grieving individual is in the overall bereavement process in order to provide the appropriate intervention for each phase.

In the first three stages of grief, the bereaved person needs an abundance of nurturance and nonjudgmental listening. During the stage of healing, caregivers need to (1) encourage the bereaved person to try new directions, (2) help the bereaved initiate new actions, or (3) provide comfort when things do not work out as planned. Failure can be a devastating experience if support is contingent on success. The bereaved must explore many avenues before encountering the right one. Compromises require discussion with a fully supportive person. Finally, during the phase of renewal, some success already has been realized, but the bereaved individual still needs to have backup support systems.

Actually, this concept of a support system offers a message for us all. Hans Selye told us (1974) that to combat stress we need to develop "altruistic egotism"—earning your neighbors' love. He said that this commodity should be hoarded, saved up, to be used in times of stress. Selye's advice is good. We must learn to reach out to others in order to build strong insurance against hard times when losses occur. When participants in the Tampa study were asked what had been the most important thing in helping them through grief, they overwhelmingly answered, "friends, family, neighbors. Anyone who would take the time to listen." Millions of dollars are spent on life and health insurance each year, yet individuals often forfeit the one kind of insurance that will help in surviving a major loss: person insurance—hoarding their neighbors' love. The returns on that insurance can make all the difference in surviving a loss.

PART THREE

THE MULTIDIMENSIONALITY OF GRIEF

CHAPTER 9

Personality Variables

All my life I've had problems getting close to people. Everyone made me feel like I was on the outside—except for Tom (my husband). He always made me feel wanted. But now he's gone and I think . . . how will I ever manage without him?

Widow, age 59

PERSONALITY FACTORS do contribute to the manner as well as the extent to which an individual responds to stress. Several writers have hypothesized that personality variables probably do affect the manner in which an individual survives grief (Clayton, 1980; Parkes, 1972; Raphael, 1984; Sanders, 1979; Vachon, Sheldon, et al., 1982). Yet few systematic studies have been directed toward this hypothesis.

Parkes describes a "grief prone" person as one "who tends to react strongly to separation" (1972, p. 133). He concluded that the intensity of grief varies according to personality factors deriving from the bereaved, which results from genetic givens as well as previous life experiences. Clayton (1982) noted that poor physical and mental health is an important determinant of bereavement outcome, but Clayton did not describe a personality that would explicate this effect. Raphael (1984) was more specific in describing certain personality characteristics that would confound or inhibit the grief. She wrote,

> Although no specific risk factors have been demonstrated, it may be suggested that people with personal characteristics that lead them to form dependent, clinging, ambivalent relationships with their spouses are at greater

risk of having a poor outcome. Those who, perhaps because of their own personality styles, make relationships with others who are unable to accept the expression of feeling and review the lost relationship may be at greater risk. . . . It may also be that those who have difficulty with the acceptance of the expression of negative affects or of powerful feelings generally may be more likely to inhibit their grief and mourning. (p. 225)

In a single case study, Alarcon (1984) reported on the grief reaction of a 28-year-old female following the death of her nephew, who had been acting as family provider. She was hospitalized with a 2-year history of drug abuse and was suffering severe hallucinatory experiences. She also showed typical features of histrionic personality disorder as well as symptoms of antisocial behavior. Because the histrionic individual uses depression as a way to manipulate others, gratify dependency needs, and get needed help, this behavior intensified during her bereavement, blocking the way to resolution. Alarcon stated that her personality became the pivotal complicating factor in her bereavement.

Bowlby (1980) discusses various personalities prone to what he described as disordered mourning. Even before their bereavement, these individuals were anxious and ambivalent and were often compulsive caregivers. They tend to be either overdependent and temperamental on the one hand or extremely emotionally independent and self-sufficient on the other. Either way, they represent a particular personality type that is severely hampered by an inability to grieve adequately.

Whereas certain personality patterns have been shown to be detrimental to grief resolution, other positive personality variables have been shown to facilitate grief resolution (Vachon, Rogers, et al., 1982). In a well-designed systematic study using the General Health Questionnaire (GHQ; Goldberg, 1972) and the 16 Personality Factor Questionnaire (16PFQ; Cattell, Eber, & Tatsouka, 1970), Vachon and her group focused on discerning those individuals who not only indicated low distress after a bereavement but also showed high distress for a period of 2 years. By pairing the GHQ scores with those of the 16PFQ, the researchers were able to show personality styles of those individuals who coped well and those who did not.

Of the 72 women who completed both instruments, 23 (32%) demonstrated "low distress." These women were described as emotionally stable and mature, conscientious, conservative, and socially precise. The 14 women in the "high distress" group (19% of the sample) were found to be apprehensive, worrying, and highly anxious, indicative of low emotional stability. The authors noted that social support was also low for this group. The authors caution that there might be a confounding interaction between these two variables. Were these individuals isolated (1) because they were ordinarily unable to maintain relationships or (2) because the grief situation had warranted or caused their isolation?

Yet it must be pointed out that those women with low distress showed little stress in other areas of their lives. Vachon and her group wrote,

> The enduring "high distress" observed in 26 women was not attributed to factors intrinsic to bereavement (e.g., loss of closest confidant, conflicted or unresolved mourning) but to factors consequent to any major loss (e.g., disruption of social network, health consequences). The enduring "low distress" for 30 women can perhaps best be understood not as the absence of mourning but as the presence of personality characteristics which promote adaption into the new role. (p. 787)

It is thought that personality variables would be among the most important determinants of adjustment following loss. Perhaps the paucity of data on this subject speaks to the basic difficulty in tapping into studies of this nature. Using what they have developed to place the study in a heuristic framework to guide their research, Stroebe and Stroebe (1987) devised what they call the Deficit Model of Partner Loss (p. 209). This adaptation of interactionist cognitive stress models to bereavement is based on the premise that critical life events are stressful because they require major readjustments. As the writers state, "The intensity of the stress created by life events depends on the extent to which the perceived demands of all the situation either tax or exceed an individual's coping resources, given that failure to cope leads to important negative consequences" (p. 225). According to this model, risk factors in bereavement are not only seen as a function of the relationship to the deceased but may also include other factors that may be relevant. This model views social support as an important coping resource. It is seen as an intrapersonal resource that buffers the individual against the impact of loss.

Stroebe and Stroebe (1987), in a well-thought-out study known as the Tubengin study, used two personality variables—emotional stability and locus of control—to measure personality and health in bereaved individuals. The researchers reasoned that (1) persons who were emotionally stable would be better able to cope with the stress of bereavement and (2) locus of control would be a good indicator because people who believe that they have little control would react to loss in a depressed manner. A control group was given the same measures. The Eysenck Personality Inventory (Eggert, 1983) and the Interpersonal Control Scale (Levenson, 1973) were used to measure these variables. Results indicated that those individuals high on neuroticism and low on internal control beliefs were found to be more depressed than were those with low neuroticism and high internal control beliefs. In sudden death situations, loss of control was even more significant, which would be predictable based on a learned-helplessness model. This study was important in pointing out the need for emotional safety in bereaved individuals.

A further benefit of the Tubengin study was to measure the extent to which grief work actually furthers the process of grief. The authors felt that emotionally stable persons would be better able to cope with the stress associated with bereavement. On the other hand, they reasoned that people who have little faith in their own self-control would feel depression during the loss. Results of their study revealed that individuals high on neuroticism showed more depression and that this effect was stronger for the widowed rather than the married control group. Along the same lines, the widowed who showed less emotional stability appeared to have greater difficulties in dealing with their loss.

Older persons react to life stresses in characteristic ways of coping, and these ways are mediated by personality traits. Personality traits that inhibited or accentuated the emotional aspects of coping with a loss could place older adults at greater risk for complicated, unhealthy outcomes. Recent research has shown that an emotionally repressive coping style can have a deleterious effect on physical health.

One study examined the influence of personality style on bereavement outcome to determine if a negative outlook could be viewed as a risk factor in complicated grief reactions. The study argued that personality may indeed contribute to factors that curtail a full grief response. For example, the study noted that individuals scoring high on repressive defensiveness tend to maintain a controlled restraint, never sharing their true feelings or needs with others. These individuals fall into the same category as those observed as having "compulsive optimism" in my Tampa study; this group employed strong defense mechanisms to avoid the vulnerable position of sharing too much. Such defensiveness could serve a protective function in modulating the intensity of people's grief reactions, especially when they are reminded of past losses. Although the sample size in my study was relatively small and nonrandom, whatever data can be gathered concerning the impact of personality on bereavement outcome will add meaningful empirical data to this subject, which needs more testing. These results suggest that widow(er)s high in characteristic distress may be at particular risk for complicated grief reactions. While on the surface, repressiveness, defensiveness, and denial may work as shields for protecting the individual from emotional intensity, it is well to remember, as mentioned by the writer, that the denial of emotions may not be healthy if it disrupts positive healing.

The findings of these studies suggest that no one strategy meets the needs of all bereaved people and point to the need for interveners to take accurate and complete histories when dealing with bereaved people. The caregiver can use the basis of past coping behavior to see how the griever will deal with the present stressful situation. If the griever is engaging in nonfunctional defenses, the caregiver can work to modify those responses toward more adaptive ones.

ANGER

Anger is a natural by-product of grief. Frustration, helplessness, and deprivation all create feelings of anger and hostility, which are often directed toward others. In many situations, the bereaved person feels anger at being left to handle everything alone.

For some individuals, conflict becomes a way of life. Events are seen as amphitheaters in which conflicts may be acted out over and over. These people see the world as a threatening place in which at any given moment they must stave off a verbal attack. These people are basically contentious people who have a hard time living peacefully with the world. When faced with a serious loss, these people need someone to blame, some reason to feel ripped off. This behavior can sometimes be associated with pathological dependence on the one who has died (Raphael, 1984). The relationship is often more like that of mother and child than like two adults—a relationship of powerful symbiotic themes. The sense of desertion is great and the bereaved feel that their very survival is threatened by what has happened. They want to punish those who leave them so deprived: the deserting spouse who died and left them, or those survivors who will not fill the spouse's place and meet the bereaveds' immense dependency needs. Early childhood losses can contribute to this reasoning. Then, as now, the bereaved feel that death has cheated them from the security that belongs to them. It doesn't matter how the death occurred; someone is to blame and must be punished.

CASE STUDY: AGNES AND TOM

Agnes and Tom had an idyllic marriage, or so everyone thought. Tom was the perfect husband, taking care of Agnes's every wish. Their friends marveled at what close attention Tom paid to her. Actually, Agnes told me, she suspected that some wives were jealous of the care she received. When Tom died suddenly of a heart attack, Agnes was bereft. She seemed to have no idea how to handle the affairs of the estate or take care of the household tasks, aside from the usual housekeeping chores. Having had no children, the two had seemed to live for each other. Agnes turned her despair into resentment, saying that Tom should have prepared her for managing the money, for managing the house, and for managing a myriad of other tasks for which she was ill prepared. When the funeral was over and friends departed, Agnes didn't know where to begin. But rather than doing something, she did nothing. It wasn't until the bills and her affairs seemed to go haywire that a neighbor asked if he could help her straighten out the tangled mess. But she blamed the mess on her thoughtless husband and initially turned down the neighbor's offer. Neighbors eventually left her alone (she couldn't understand why), and finally, in desperation, she contacted someone at the bank to help her. She told me later that she didn't trust anyone but her husband to do these businesslike tasks. His suspiciousness of others left her without the friends that she badly needed. She was put in touch with a support group but left, saying that the participants often discussed financial problems and solutions. Yet her anger and resentment, as far as I know, never left her. She always felt that her situation was unique and that no one else was ever left in the very difficult position in which she found herself.

According to Raphael (1984), these lingering bouts with anger seem to go on for a long time. This anger falls into the category of chronic grief. The overriding power of these emotions have the potential of destroying the life of the bereaved. Few supporters will wish to linger on in a relationship so fraught with unpleasantness and negativity.

Yet anger is not necessarily present in all bereaved individuals. I have seen many cases in which no anger is evident at all, either initially or after several years following the death. Anger is an individual reaction that depends on the many variables involved. Caregivers should be aware of the possibility of hostilities and realize that anger is a natural response to loss that can be manifested in a number of various ways. The angry bereaved person is most helped by having a supportive listener who will not leave when angry outbursts occur.

DEPENDENCY NEEDS

If the bereaved relied on the deceased for personal safety, whether physical or emotional, then following the death, the bereaved experience fear, excess anxiety, and worry as well as feelings of hopelessness and helplessness (Lopata, 1973; Parkes & Weiss, 1983; Raphael, 1984).

Dependency needs are so closely correlated with safety needs that once the bereaved have no one on whom to depend, they are thrown open to excessive anxiety and worry simply because they do not have the strong, reliable source that once was available. Stroebe and Stroebe (1987) further support this notion, comparing grief to the insecurity of overdependent children separated from their mothers. Those who experience early losses are often more prone to grief than those who have had a more secure early beginning (Parkes, 1972; Parkes & Weiss, 1983; Sanders, 1979). Parkes describes the "clinging," dependent relationships as those leading to excessive yearning and chronic grief, consequently placing the grievers in a high-risk category.

CASE STUDY: DIRE YEARNING

In the Tampa study, it was noted that those people who had experienced losses in early childhood were at greater risk for poor bereavement outcome than those who had been given a firmer security. In one case, a 47-year-old widow had grown up in several foster homes, never quite sure of where she would be living next. On her own at 18, she found work in a local café, which was also near an Army base. During the time before she met her husband, she went out with many men stationed there but always felt that she had been "dumped" at the end of each affair. Her self-concept and ego strength were low, and she looked to each man in her life to give her a sense of purpose and security. However, her relationships were always doomed to despair and disappointment.

But when she met her husband, she found him to be different from the other men. He treated her with the caring and respect befitting his first relationship. From that moment on, her life improved tremendously while she leaned on him for her sense of self and security. The world was safe as long as he was near. She was unable to have children; instead, she became her husband's child. After a lifetime of being no one's child, this situation was like heaven. Of course, the problem was that she never matured enough to deal with the monumental loss of her husband's death when it happened. She struggled to maintain a safe equilibrium following her husband's sudden heart attack and subsequent death.

After his death, she sequestered herself in her house, going out only to do the most necessary tasks. When I first saw her, she was still in shock, although it had been nearly 3 months since the death. On the 6-month follow-up, she was even more frightened. A general paranoid ideation had gained a stronghold, causing her to be suspicious of even her well-meaning neighbors. By the end of the first year, she required hospitalization. Yearning for her husband was acute, and the anguish of being without him for the rest of her life was impossible to contemplate. It took several years of psychotherapy before she was able to stand alone and begin to trust another person.

This case study is an extreme example of dependency behavior, but it indicates to what extent this phenomenon can debilitate the bereaved individual. In a society traditionally trained to place wives in physical dependency and husbands in emotional dependency, dependency behavior is a factor that cannot be overlooked by caregivers as they look for signs of complicated grief.

Parkes and Weiss (1983) also support this finding in their study of bereaved spouses in Boston. When the partner had died, the dependent widow or widower organized her or his life on the assumption of being helpless without the deceased. The bereaved needed to cling to the relationship with the deceased in order to maintain this role of helplessness and inability to cope. This behavior can become a way of life unless intervention is attempted.

Ambivalent Relationship with the Deceased

Related to dependency is ambivalence. It is not difficult to imagine why ambivalence in a relationship would cause difficulty once the relationship was ended by death. If the relationship had been one of passive/aggressive acting out, then the bereaved might be indefinitely trapped in an intrapunitive form of grief. Freud (1917) argued that an important precondition for depression in grief was an ambivalent relationship with the deceased before the death.

Any relationship includes a certain level of ambivalence, whether it is a marriage, a child-parent relationship, or emotional involvement with any other close family member or friend. No relationship is perfect. The difficulty in bereavement lies in the fact that the hostility and guilt are usually repressed and not dealt with because it is not socially accepted to show these negative feelings toward the deceased. These relationships contained greater violence and anger.

At the time, the bereaved usually deny that there had been problems in the relationship. Raphael (1984) suggested that when denial is profound, it probably indicates that exaggerated idealization is being used to cover up the ambivalence. The caregiver can gently proceed to open up the possibility of greater honesty with the bereaved, thereby releasing them of the burden of these negative pent-up emotions.

In the Tampa study, more ambivalence was noted among bereaved spouses than with either parents of children or adult children grieving their parents. One interpretation is that for bereaved parents, the longitudinal follow-up of 18 months to 2 years may not have allowed time to see them through much more than the first two phases of grief. Because parental bereavement needs to be measured in terms of many years, it could be that the identification factor initially far outweighed the ambivalence involved. On the other hand, the loss of a parent is usually resolved in a much shorter time, and ambivalence is easier to acknowledge socially.

The relationship with one's spouse is more of a partnership. There is greater opportunity for a power struggle. Yet it is in this struggle that so many difficulties and battles arise, anger stirs, and trust is jeopardized. Ironically, among those people who seemed most content with their marriage without showing undue idealization, a larger percentage said that they would want to remarry. This finding is in line with what Parkes and Weiss (1983) noted in their Harvard study, in that they found among those people who reported a lower level of conflict with their spouses, there was less anxiety, depression, guilt, and yearning for the dead spouse. These writers concluded,

> It seems to us that the most obvious inference is that a report of a conflict-laden marriage can be taken as an indication of a relationship marked by ambivalence. Marital conflict had produced anger, and perhaps desire for escape, but coexisting with the feelings were continued attachment to the other and even, perhaps, affection. Anger interfered with grieving, and only with the passage of time did persisting need for the lost spouse emerge in the form of sadness, anxiety, and yearning. (P. 111)

Ambivalence, when carried over from real-life situations, often results in conflict for the griever after death. Because all relationships contain some element of ambivalence, all grievers must deal with mixed emotions, attitudes, or behaviors. It is easy to understand how ambivalence, when present in a relationship before death, would cause problems after a death. Certainly, the couple would have much unfinished business to complete as well as anger and self-reproach. Fenichel (1945) believes that the greater the love-hate relationship and the greater the self-reproach, the greater the grief. Freud (1917) felt that if the griever experienced ambivalent feelings, grief resulted in a pathological form that he called "obsessive reproaches," a constant form of self-denigration caused by the conflict of ambivalence.

Rando (1993) outlines five main problems that often complicate grief when ambivalence is present:

1. People possess a natural reluctance to acknowledge negative emotions such as anger and difficulty when facing less than positive feelings about the deceased.

2. Most individuals have difficulty handling dichotomous feelings that deal with emotional situations. The ensuing conflict causes confusion, immobilization, or attempts to suppress one or both sets of feelings.
3. Hostility can become a strong bond; however, people often fail to recognize the connection produced by the ambivalence.
4. Hostility within the ambivalence causes the bereaved to experience guilt after trying to avoid remembering the relationship. Some survivor guilt can cause undue discomfort and encourage the griever to avoid thoughts of the deceased.
5. The bereaved may have difficulty adjusting to the world with the negative experience still so close to proximity. The negative experience may produce chronic anger, mistrust, or alienation, keeping the griever from dealing appropriately with his or her grief.

The griever must be educated as to the complexity of competing emotions in ambivalence. At the same time, the caregiver can open the door to the bereaved to help them understand and work through negative feelings and memories that are acting as roadblocks for reinvestment in others.

GUILT

Rarely does one encounter a significant loss without a certain amount of guilt. Guilt appears to be a by-product of grief itself and can result from many types of interpersonal problems between the bereaved and the deceased. It may be only a small nagging remembrance of something that should have been done and wasn't, or it can be a full-blown, persevering guilt associated with a lifetime of rejection or other hurts. Either way, guilt can be one of the most self-disparaging and self-defeating responses one can deal with in bereavement.

Guilt has been defined as resulting from a sense of inadequacy or perceived offenses. Of course, a certain amount of guilt helps to maintain a clear conscience when it is feared that one has overstepped social bonds. This notion is generally only a perceived one but it leads to much anguish and mental pain. Rando (1993) lists six primary occurrences associated with guilt:

1. Falling short when acting out a character of one's own self-perceived image.
2. Violation of a conscious or unconscious personal standard.
3. Ambivalence.

4. Imperfection in relationships.
5. Surviving when others have died.
6. Feeling that one contributed in some way to the death.

Guilt can serve the functional purpose of protecting the bereaved as a defense against helplessness. Helplessness can arise when grievers perceive their own actions as incorrect behavior and, through personal guilt, feel less disenfranchisement and more like part of society simply by maintaining their own stature. Along with this helplessness, guilt can act as a self-punishment sentence, again helping guilty grievers find a way out of bad feelings toward themselves.

Guilt comes from a wide variety of sources. Unfortunately, when grievers carry guilt for a long period of time, it can slow down the bereavement process and keep them stuck in the awareness-of-loss phase (Phase 2). Instead of using their energies to heal, they stay churned up with guilt, wasting valuable strength on useless thoughts (see the section on guilt in Chapter 5).

Guilt leads to feelings of unworthiness, shame, and self-blame. If these feelings continue, the result is a lifetime of misery. The best way to deal with this ugly emotion is to share those feelings with a trusted friend or counselor. If healing is to take place, it is best to bring feelings out into the light where they can be truly seen and acknowledged. Unattended guilt can become a real source of complicated grief that lasts a lifetime.

TYPES OF BEREAVEMENT

It has been difficult to evaluate the assumptions regarding types of bereavement because the assessment material used in bereavement studies has not attempted to tap basic personality characteristics. Heretofore, types of grief have been represented in terms of response to grief, such as "chronic grief," "delayed grief," or "pathological grief," rather than as a basic function of the premorbid personality of the bereaved. Although few prebereavement personality measures of a grieving individual are available, researchers nevertheless feel that maladaptive functioning is always exacerbated by the stress of grief. In other words, the person who manifested disturbed reactions as a trait syndrome displayed the same disturbed reactions in an exaggerated form to bereavement as a trait syndrome. Similarly, those people who use denial as a protective defense mechanism display those characteristics to a greater degree when coping with a loss or inordinate stress.

The challenge of the mental health professional lies in the need to chart the course of therapy to fit each separate case. In determining therapy, it is imperative to look at whatever information may be available on the premorbid personality traits of the bereaved individual. For example, what characteristics has this person found useful in resolving stress, and which ones are no longer functional? Which enduring behaviors are standing in the way of this person's grief resolution?

In order to investigate the issue of premorbid personalities in bereaved persons, a longitudinal study was initiated (Sanders, 1979). Researchers using the MMPI (Hathaway & McKinley, 1951) to examine personality constructs and the Grief Experience Inventory (GEI; Sanders et al., 1977) to look at bereavement patterns and intensities discovered distinct types of grief.

By interviewing bereaved people soon after the deaths of significant family members and by retesting these same individuals 18 months to 2 years later, when grief intensities had somewhat subsided, personality baselines could be established. These baselines, in turn, could determine the effect of bereavement on various types of coping patterns.

Four types of bereavement emerged from this study: (1) a disturbed group; (2) a depressed, high-grief group; (3) a denial group; and (4) a normal, grief-contained group. It must be pointed out that individuals in the normal grief-contained group experienced severe losses, too. They felt their grief and they expressed sadness, many weeping openly at times during the interviews. However, these persons recognized that losses must occur in a lifetime and were attempting to make an honest response without repression. The essence of their personality was not lost in a crisis situation.

DISTURBED GROUP

The disturbed group might be analogous to what is called "pathological grievers." Their MMPI profiles looked like that of a schizoid personality with depressive reactions. Personality problems—particularly feelings of inadequacy, inferiority, and insecurity—appeared to be of a chronic nature. One common denominator in this group was clearly an ongoing difficulty with living. One widow who had nursed her husband through a long cancer illness needed psychological day-care treatment for more than a year. She said, "I feel extreme disbelief and horror that it [his death] could happen, even though I should have been prepared because of his long illness." She felt abandoned by everyone around her. She lost her self-confidence, her religious faith, and her financial security. She became hyperanxious and fearful of the future. At follow-up, she was even more grief stricken than she had been initially.

People in the disturbed group have few defenses that could offer relief or freedom from distress. They rarely learn to profit from their life experiences. When this personality suffers a severe loss, the result is one of long-lasting desolation.

Depressed Group

The depressed group complained of tension and low mood as well as inordinate oversensitivity. Almost invariably, these people showed a history of multiple family losses. Too, these individuals were plagued with unusual situations not conducive to healing. After her husband's death, one widow's two daughters and their families moved into her tiny house, leaving her with the grandchildren to care for during the day. Her daughters were trying to keep her company, but the widow lacked the stamina to deal with the confusion and extra work. She had grown up in foster homes and had always been shy and nonassertive. When I saw her, she was unable to tell her daughters that they would have to find other places to live. As a result of that living situation and her grief, she grew even more anxious, eventually becoming agoraphobic.

Because anxiety exists as a trait phenomenon, when inordinate stress occurs, the depressed individuals were subject to intense fear and emotionality. Horowitz and his group (1980) use the term *frighteningly sad* to describe these reactions. For these individuals, early losses or strained interpersonal relationships have left the individual with a tenuous grasp on security. In order to survive, they develop a relationship based on dependency, which compensates for their earlier sense of weakness and aloneness. Even though they appear to compensate well by controlling their world, when a loss occurs, the dormant negative self-images are activated, with resultant feelings of panic, rage, and deflated self-image. As the authors write,

> With loss of the other, the person remains dependent and the need becomes frightening. The most frequent self-image in these states is that of a weak, abandoned waif in desperate hope of rescue, with intense fear that such a rescue will not occur. (p. 1160)

They then show reactions similar to Seligman's learned helplessness model of depression (1975), in which the individual lacks the ability to control life events. This reaction eventually leads to a traitlike sense of help-lessness that can generalize to any number of negative situations.

At follow-up, this group still showed pervasive sadness, but the intensity had diminished since the initial interview. Still remaining, however, were feelings of isolation and of being alone in their grief, which resulted from their extreme sensitiveness.

Denial Group

Of particular interest to many health professionals is the third typology: denial. Individuals in this group employ strong defense mechanisms to deal with crises, often using physical symptoms as a means of solving conflicts or avoiding responsibilities. But the characteristic seems to be so ingrained that the person is not even aware that such a defense is being used. They were reluctant to admit to common foibles and, instead, kept a "stiff upper lip."

Many managed to survive grief by a flight into activity, intensifying their personal work, community activity, or church involvement. This is not to say that they were not sad, but they sped up their normal activity in spite of their loss. The expression "determined optimists" suits them well.

Their thoughts and energies, however, were constantly occupied by physical problems, particularly backaches, headaches, chest pains, or abdominal discomfort. One bereaved widow casually mentioned that she was suffering from a torn muscle, osteoarthritis, osteoporosis, and degenerative ambulation. Yet she underplayed these problems, as she underplayed her own grief. This indifference regarding physical symptoms was typical of this group.

Some health care professionals have been concerned that grieving individuals who do not ventilate their emotions will be at risk for poor outcome. Such was not the case with this denial group. Their coping mechanism appeared to be facilitative. They did not deny death itself, but rather they denied their overt emotions surrounding the bereavement. Denial is apparently an adaptive defense that serves them well in crises.

Normal, Grief-Contained Group

As indicated earlier, the normal, grief-contained group made the best adjustment of all to bereavement. They showed emotional control with little expression of confusion or unreality. High ego strength was evident, and they were able to find meaning in their lives.

IMPLICATIONS FOR THERAPY

The significance of this study (Sanders, 1979) lies in its implication for intervention. Recognizing that personality differences do exist and that these differences create coping styles that are enduring, mental health workers are in a position to better predict bereavement outcome. By making careful assessments of an individual's history of prior losses and by evaluating specific adaptations to these events, caregivers will be able to offer intervention that can be facilitative. This approach may also render a baseline from which to normalize various grief situations.

DISTURBED TYPE

Because these individuals are operating on the ego of poor mental health before the death, the current loss greatly depletes what few sources they possess, leaving them feeling vulnerable and hopeless. The caregiver will need to supply greater support than usual and for a longer period of time. These grievers need tremendous nurturance and empathy. Caregivers must have a high tolerance for dependent behavior to avoid a growing resentment toward the demands imposed by disturbed grievers. That it takes these people longer to move through the grief process has been indicated (Sanders, 1979). Therapists and families should become sensitive to the needs of individuals represented by this typology and provide even more service and support than would ordinarily be expected.

DEPRESSED TYPE

When a depressive suffers a severe loss, the course will be slow and painful. That early losses contribute to chronic anxiety and depression is supported by bereavement literature (Bowlby, 1961; A. Freud, 1965; Furman, 1974; Klein, 1940; Parkes, 1972). The therapist is dealing not only with the most recent loss but with multiple previous losses as well. Loss after loss has created an expectancy for disaster, reinforcing the devastating feelings of being out of control. To these individuals, it appears that no matter what they do, how hard they try, they are destined to face setbacks, leaving them with thoughts of failure and worthlessness.

This description is much the same picture that Schmale and Iker (1971) presented in the predisposed character traits of predicted cancer patients. These researchers reported that patients' reactions to hopelessness within 6 months before the diagnosis of their cancer provided evidence of psychological traits that could be associated with a high predisposition of hopelessness. Depressed persons, then, seek more than a healing. They want the return of all their previous losses as well. These grievers show strong indications of being in the victim's role, unable to counteract the mass of negative situations at hand. Although this need may be primarily unconscious, recognizing it will help therapists who, in turn, must recognize their own limitations in supplying patients' expectations.

Because of the multiple loss aspect, the process of grief is lengthened for the depressed typology as it was for the disturbed. Anger and guilt may be submerged, requiring careful and painstaking probing. The edge of paranoia may become apparent, resulting from the extreme loneliness experienced by the bereaved. These emotions must be dealt with in a nonthreatening manner. These grievers need time and space to explore their feelings, but always in an atmosphere that is highly supportive and reassuring.

DENIAL TYPE

This type shows a psychological state nearly opposite to depression: optimism. There are similarities here to conversion neurosis in that the source of anxiety is represented by a physical symptom rather than an emotional one. Although the anxieties of grief are relieved, the physical symptom bears the weight of the conflict of grief. For some, an ache or pain is easier to discuss than one's feelings or emotions and is much safer, certainly more socially acceptable.

Others in this group simply employ the strong defense mechanism of "determined optimism." They find it important to display a positive attitude when dealing with the public. This attitude helps them get through the day without breaking down or revealing their emotions. They may cry into their pillows all night, but to everyone else, they appear strong. The illusion that they are managing well seems to allow some hope. These people are often able to turn threats into challenges (Goleman, 1979). And for them, a challenge facilitates positive functioning. The critical determinant, of course, is whether they are denying the fact of death or simply trying to maintain an inner strength by denying emotional involvement.

Control is the prime ingredient in these individuals. Because they feel such a lack of control over themselves, they need to control everything in their world. This need leaves little time for them to focus on taking care of themselves. Counseling should work to encourage these people to release their hold on things and begin to allow themselves the opportunity to grieve. When this reversal takes place, physical symptoms will diminish.

NORMAL TYPE

Persons of this type will probably not be seen in therapy except to work out life changes resulting from role loss and consequent adaptation. Because of good ego strength and optimal reality testing, they are usually able to work through the immediate crisis of grief. Using their ability to share feelings with others and recognize that grief will not last forever, they manage to get through their bereavement by focusing on a better future.

SUMMARY

The types of grievers listed in this chapter offer a sound basis on which to dispute the stereotypic notion that it is bereavement per se that causes complications rather than the psychodynamics of the personality itself. Certainly other moderator variables share the influence as well. Although investigations into preexisting personality factors in bereavement outcome have been meager, a consensus among writers in this field suggests that moderator variables represent a fruitful avenue for investigation. Indeed, through such studies as those by Vachon et al. (1980), Sanders (1989), and Horowitz, Daniel, et al. (1984), it can be seen that core personality factors can either facilitate positive coping skills or, on the other hand, act to prolong or intensify painful grief. There is a need for more studies along these lines.

On the basis of the identification of these premorbid characteristics in controlled studies, intervention by caregivers and families can be more finely focused. But even further, it is seen that wider latitude may now be allowed the grieving individual. It becomes clear that no one intervention strategy meets the needs of all grieving persons but rather that a variety of approaches may be carefully tailored to individual characteristics.

CHAPTER 10

Social-Situational Variables

Maybe it would have been better if it hadn't happened so suddenly. We just weren't prepared, that's all. We hadn't been able to save any money ahead and there wasn't even any insurance money to pay for the funeral—I had to get the whole family to pitch in. But it wasn't just the money, you see. The main thing was, I didn't have him anymore.

Widow, age 39

THERE IS CONSIDERABLE agreement among writers that certain social-situational moderator variables can have a debilitating effect on bereavement outcome. These variables contribute heavily to the concept of complicated bereavement, and in many cases, if experienced strongly enough, they may be the sole reason for the complication. Among those variables often mentioned are social variables, such as age, gender, socioeconomic status, and religiosity, as well as situational variables surrounding the death, sudden versus anticipated death, alcohol abuse, dysfunctional grief, lack of social support, and concurrent crises.

SOCIAL CHARACTERISTICS OF THE BEREAVED

AGE

Studies of age differences having an effect on poor physical or emotional outcome has been fairly limited to conjugal bereavement. It would be expected that increasing negative health consequences accompany increasing age at the time of bereavement. This conclusion, however, is not necessarily the case (Kraus & Lilienfeld, 1959). Ball (1977), in comparing the age differences among three groups of widows—young, middle-aged, and old—found that the youngest group was more symptomatic than either of the other two groups. Severity of symptoms was further isolated for those younger widows who had experienced the sudden death of their husbands. It is quite possible that a sudden death compounded by a younger age interacted to produce a more intense bereavement reaction in the younger widows.

Maddison and Viola (1968), in a well-developed retrospective study carried out in Boston and in Sydney, Australia, investigated grief reactions of widows less than 60 years of age with matched controls in both locales. Differences in health deterioration of bereaved compared to controls was significant. Emotional symptoms were found most clearly to differentiate widows from controls: One widow in eight sought help from her physician for depression. Because there was no comparison of the younger widowed group, the results of this study could be explained in one of two ways: Either aging is the main effect, and bereavement is an interaction effect; or bereavement is the main effect, and aging is an interaction effect. This unclear interpretation points to the need to include a comparison group as well as controls.

Early studies of bereavement posited a disengagement theory, in which researchers claimed that a mutual withdrawal by both society and the elderly themselves acted as a defense against emotional upheaval (Chappell, 1975; Cumming & Henry, 1961; Stern, Williams, & Prados, 1951). In another study (R.G. Brown, 1960), which examined responses of individuals 60 years and older, broad variations in rates of disengagement were noted. Social contacts had actually increased rather than decreased for many individuals, indicating that disengagement is typically neither gradual, inevitable, nor irreversible. The study seemed to indicate that, although the loss of a spouse is a major cause of disengagement, the disruptive event of death itself, rather than the number of years lived, produced the effect. In general, Brown concluded that most elderly persons neither prefer disengagement nor are satisfied with it. As Lopata (1971) has stated, "Far from voluntary disengaging from activity when the husband dies, they (widows) are lonely and pining for greater involvement" (p. 55).

In a study comparing younger to older widows (Sanders, 1980–1981), bereavement intensities were examined in a group of 45 widows (21 were more than 65; 24 were 63 or younger) covering an 18-month time period. The GEI (Sanders et al., 1977) was used to assess grief reactions, and the

MMPI was employed to look at personality variables. Initially, younger spouses showed greater intensities of grief; yet when this group was seen again 18 months later, scores were lower on all scales except for guilt and anger. Socially, this group was seen as having adequate support, and they looked ahead to a better future with some new feelings of hope. Older spouses, however, initially showed a diminished grief response, but on final interview, they showed elevations on 12 scales of the GEI, especially for physical symptoms and for denial. The MMPI profiles showed increases on all scales except hypomania. Loneliness and anxiety were the greatest problems for this group and feelings of helplessness were often expressed, yet none of the older participants indicated a desire for remarriage. The results of this study suggest that being older does not appear to contribute directly to grief symptoms per se but rather to the constellation of debilitating variables that universally plague the elderly.

Parkes and Weiss's study (1983) of Boston bereaved indicated that between younger and older widows, the younger participants suffered with more psychological problems whereas the older participants dealt with more physical ones. This discrepancy could be explained by noting that older persons in our society are reluctant to complain of grief reactions, which are often thought of as psychological or emotional. Instead, they channel their symptoms into physical difficulties, which are considered more socially acceptable, leaving them free to seek medical assistance and to openly discuss physical difficulties with cohorts.

In addition to the difficult problem of loneliness is the lack of skill among older bereaved spouses to deal with problems of everyday living. Older men lacked the ability to cook, shop, and clean the house, whereas widows felt a deficiency in doing home repairs or managing legal or financial affairs. These tasks were a source of frustration for these older spouses; however, when they learned to perform a certain task, they immediately felt better about themselves (Lund, Caserta, & Dimond, 1993). The researchers found that although older men and women differed in their lack of specific skills of daily living, they were quite similar in their emotional, psychological, social, and health adjustments.

Although Lund and his group (1993) observed that support received from others was extremely important, they also suggested that personal resources unique to each individual made the biggest difference in bereavement outcome. By personal resources, Lund was referring to grievers' ability to take control of their lives during the major adjustment that followed losing a spouse. Such resources include motivation, pride, flexibility, and of course, some help from others. But all this requires time because most of the problems of single living emerge slowly, without much forewarning.

From the preceding discussion, age does appear to create an interaction factor but not a deciding one. When social isolation is parceled out, age might not make a significant difference in bereavement outcome. For risk to be excessive, factors other than age would need to have greater impact on the bereaved.

Gender

There is a lack of agreement as to the effects of gender differences on bereavement outcome. The gender difference in the expression of bereavement becomes more pronounced as adults mature and have experience with loss. This is not to say that masculine grief becomes more open and expressive or that feminine grief becomes less open or seeks support less often. Rather, particularly in marriage, wives take care of the emotional aspects of the marriage and allow their husbands to take a more stoic position. This arrangement is not necessarily a satisfactory one, as the opening epigraph in this chapter indicated. Rather, this arrangement points to the fact that custom becomes the overriding rule and habit takes precedence. A number of researchers have concluded that widows suffer more health consequences following the death of a mate than do widowers (Carey, 1979; Lopata, 1973). On the other hand, considerably more writers find that widowers sustain greater problems (Helsing, Szklo, & Comstock, 1981; Parkes, 1971b; Parkes & Brown, 1972; Rees & Lutkins, 1967; Stroebe & Stroebe, 1983; Young, Benjamin, & Wallis, 1963). And still other writers have noted no significant differences (Clayton, 1974; Clayton, Halikes, & Maurice, 1972; Heyman & Gianturco, 1973). These data were compared on such outcome measures as mortality, physical symptoms, depression, and other emotional sequelae as well as positive circumstantial events such as remarriage.

In studying adult bereavement, I have found several patterns that are consistent with the reactions described by Martin and Doka (1996). They have noted that masculine grief can be described by the following patterns:

Feelings are limited or toned down.
Thinking precedes and often dominates feeling.
The focus is on problem solving rather than expression of feelings.
The outward expression of feelings often involves anger and/or guilt.
Internal adjustments to the loss are usually expressed through activity.
Intense feelings may be expressed privately; there is a general reluctance
    to discuss these feelings with others.
Intense grief is usually expressed immediately after the loss, often during
    the postdeath rituals.

As Martin and Doka (1996) point out, caregivers tend to overlook much of the masculine reaction to grief and focus instead on feminine grief, ignoring the potential differences that exist.

Feminine grief has been shown to have these characteristics:

Can express anguish in tears and laments.
Is socialized to be nurturing and empathetic.
Is not afraid to discuss grief.
Seeks support.
Has difficulty expressing anger.
Is prone to guilty feelings.
Is caregiver to friends and family.
Is keeper of the family circle.

Examining the health aspects of these data, Parkes and Brown (1972) found that widowers complained of fewer symptoms than did women in both the bereaved and the control groups. They found the difference to be so large that in several cases, the control women indicated that they had nearly as many symptoms as the bereaved men. Some explanation was offered by the writers, who felt that the reporting characteristics of men may be different from that of women. Too, men are less prone to develop neurotic symptoms during a bereavement and consequently suffer less psychological illness than do women. Interestingly, whereas widows had higher depression scores than did widowers 1 year after bereavement, on followup (2 to 4 years later), the widows were no more depressed than were married women of the same age; yet widowers remained significantly more depressed than married men. Parkes and Brown felt that this depressed state may have reflected what Cumming and Henry (1961) described as disengagement, in that widowers often showed signs of withdrawing from others and feeling more remote and apart from friends.

In an excellent review article, Stroebe and Stroebe (1983) outlined the many methodological obstacles that often confuse the researcher, causing biased results and unclear interpretations. For example, remarriage taken as a criterion of good outcome may present some problems. Widowers tend to remarry sooner than do widows, leaving a larger proportion of widows in long-term follow-up studies. Stroebe and Stroebe point out the problems in determining what kind of person is selected for remarriage. If one assumes that the healthiest remarry, then how does one account for dependent widowers who remarry in haste? If the widowers did not have a potential remarriage partner (like many widows who, even if they wished to remarry, usually must wait to be asked), would they succumb to poorer health by virtue of their physical and emotional needs remaining unmet? Perhaps, as Stroebe and Stroebe (1983) point out, the unhealthy might remarry more quickly. Yet Helsing and his group (1981) found mortality rates lower among remarried widowers than those who have not remarried. Clearly, the multiple interactive effects related to this issue must be clearly planned for and parceled out.

The refusal rate among widowers is higher than for widows. In the Harvard study (Glick, Weiss, & Parkes, 1974), it was reported that 44% of widowers who were contacted opted not to participate in the study compared to a 49% acceptance rate for widows. This refusal rate combined with the fact that men die earlier creates a smaller widower-to-widow ratio in studies, which presents a sampling problem.

Men typically report fewer symptoms and less affective distress than do women, making widows appear to be more severely distressed than widowers are (Weissman & Klermann, 1977). This gender effect can lead to incorrect interpretations regarding severity of bereavement symptomatology.

There has been noted a gender differential effect in the grief of parents who have lost a child. In the death of a young child, gender differences may be attributed to the bonding of mothers to their infants (Fish, 1986). It was found that younger fathers grieved less than did the mothers. When the child died at an older age, the disparity grew smaller, but mothers continued to report higher levels of grief than did fathers. The isolation effect may also be a factor, in that following the death of a child, mothers feel more isolated than do fathers, primarily because work envelops fathers and keeps them occupied through a greater part of the day. In the evening, widowers are normally alone whereas fathers usually have other children with whom to interact, plus a wife who, even though deeply grieved, will normally still maintain housekeeping duties. Therefore, deprivation and sense of loneliness in a man who loses a child is not as great as in a man who loses his wife.

Lack of social support has been used as an explanation as to why widowers do less well than do widows. Men depend on their wives for emotional support and nurturance as well as an entrée to social interaction, and when these services are no longer available, widowers have little practice or inclination to develop these new skills but instead bury themselves in work. Women, on the other hand, cope by searching for social support, which in turn facilitates the bereavement process (Stroebe & Stroebe, 1987).

Gender differences across the life span do appear to exist in bereavement. These differences gradually shift as the bereaved moves from childhood to terminal old age. The cultivation that comes from the layering on of experiences in which loss was the centerpiece teaches each person the importance of valuing moments, relationships, family. People begin life by being attached to one person, then two, then gradually a whole array of familiar and important people, things, animals. Each attachment creates a web of connections with friends and family members that grows steadily as a person creates larger and more inclusive circles. Yet each connection must eventually be broken, separation must be suffered and dealt with.

Grief, it seems, is no different at one level of life or another. Pain still grips everyone. With the accumulation of losses, people don't get better at dealing with the pain, despite their gender, but they suffer nevertheless in ways that are traditionally and culturally gender biased.

SOCIOECONOMIC STATUS

Economic difficulties often plague the bereaved, complicating their already painful existence. Because the majority of widows are aged, their economic circumstances are usually below average. The financial plight of widowhood has led Harvey and Bahr (1974) to write, "typical in studies of the effects of widowhood . . . the negative impact sometimes attributed to widowhood derives not from widowhood status but rather from socioeconomic status" (p. 106). They concluded that lowered morale and a decrease in affiliation are more directly correlated with change in income than with change in marital status. This observation was supported by a study by Atchley (1975) of an older working-class group of widows in which inadequate income led to reduced social participation and consequently greater loneliness and anxiety. A Canadian study (Sheldon, Cochrane, Vachon, Lyall, Rogers, & Freeman, 1981) found that low socioeconomic status contributed to poor adjustment and had a definite effect on how widows answered a health questionnaire.

Marris (1968), in studying London widows, went to some length to describe the deprivation encountered by these women as they endeavored to maintain households, care for dependent children, and engage themselves in outside jobs, many working for the first time in their lives. Similar findings by Glick et al. (1974) led these writers to conclude that poor adjustment following bereavement is a consequence of insecure economic positions. In a study that used controls to examine socioeconomic aspects of bereavement, Sanders (1979) found that income does not contribute to poor outcome directly, but instead is a preexisting factor that contributes negatively to any stressful situation.

This hypothesis is supported by Morgan (1976). In statistically parceling out the effects of income differences, using analysis of covariance (ANCOVA), he found that lowered morale is not attributable to bereavement in and of itself, but that it is caused primarily by the deprivation brought about by lack of income. Thus, the outcome of widowhood per se can probably never be fully separated from the financial situation involved because the lack of adequate funds usually adds a further burden to the survivors following a significant death.

RELIGIOSITY

Members of a society are held together by the symbolic ties and the sharing of a common set of definitions—knowledge, beliefs, and expectations. In the case of death, the social nature of human interaction is often given a religious or spiritual interpretation, and those religious interpretations can frequently be an important sustaining factor to the bereaved individual. At these times of extreme pain or sorrow, the individual becomes acutely aware of this social nature, and it is for these experiences that some religious or spiritual explanation is needed. The bereaved turns to something or someone outside of the self in which to seek explanations and find answers. The catastrophic nature of death can then be placed in a larger perspective and dealt with as part of universal law rather than as individual persecution. Firth (1957), for example, suggests that the use of religious interpretations and ritual at a time such as death may prevent the bereaved from giving way to fear and horror, which in turn would cause disintegration.

Immortality is an important element in the beliefs of many bereaved persons, particularly of religious involvement. Yet Gorer (1965) found that only about half his sample admitted to believing in an afterlife, and it was voiced by only half as many men as women. Marris (1968) found only 9 out of 72 widows expressed a belief in an afterlife. If anything, the shock of a husband's death seemed to make them less confident in the possibility of immortality. On the whole, these women did not seem to find much comfort in religion and religious beliefs.

Parkes (1972), on the other hand, noted that those widows whose religious beliefs helped them to place the bereavement in a meaningful perspective coped better than did those who had no such faith. He found, however, that faith in God and regular church attendance were not necessarily related to good outcome following bereavement. Sanders (1979–1980) noted that frequent church attenders (once a week or more) were more likely to respond with higher optimism and social desirability, but with more repression of bereavement responses, than were less frequent church attenders. The most striking results were noted, however, when subsamples of frequent church attenders with known family interaction were compared to attenders with infrequent family interaction or few family members nearby. The first group responded with fewer somatic experiences and physical symptoms, less depression, anger, and feelings of isolation, and higher levels of social desirability and optimism. These results not only point out the emotional effects of isolation during trauma but the high intensity of psychological problems encountered as well. That these differences were not found when church attendance alone was studied presents strong support for the important element of family interaction during periods of stress.

Bereavement and religion taken apart can both become confounded by the multidimensional nature of these variables. Whether religious conviction is a result of a substitutive process or a consecrated faith in a supreme being will have differing effects on the outcome of the bereavement. More studies are needed before parallels may be drawn concerning the effect of religion on the outcome of bereavement.

SITUATIONAL CHARACTERISTICS OF THE DEATH

SUDDEN VERSUS ANTICIPATED DEATH

There is a general agreement that sudden, unexpected death produces a shock that has a debilitating effect on the bereaved, which both prolongs grief and produces excessive physical and emotional trauma (Brown & Stoudemire, 1983; Lundin, 1984a; Parkes & Weiss, 1983; Rando, 1984; Raphael, 1984; Sanders, 1979; Vachon, 1976). In the Harvard study (Glick et al., 1974), sudden death was seen as such a shock that the capacity to cope was diminished and full functioning was not realized by some, even 4 years following the death.

Engel (1971) studied 170 cases of sudden death, reporting that 81 died following a significant loss—many within hours of the death of a loved person. Although these cases are anecdotal, the study points to the compelling incidence of inordinate stress in bereavement.

Parkes (1975), in looking at bereavement outcome among 68 bereaved spouses, found that the mode of death was one of the primary predictive factors involved. Variables affecting a poor bereavement outcome were short duration of a terminal illness, cancer not being the cause of death, and no opportunity to discuss impending death with the spouse. From his analyses of the data, Parkes describes what he terms "Unexpected Loss Syndrome," characterized by social withdrawal together with continued bewilderment and protest. This syndrome is seen as impairing functioning so severely that uncomplicated recovery cannot be expected (p. 94).

Lundin (1984) used controls who had experienced an expected death to examine the consequences of sudden, unexpected death. The 45 sudden-death respondents showed greater somatic and psychiatric illness over the 65 respondents who grieved an anticipated death. Although the health of the controls had been poorer before bereavement, they suffered no increase in health consequences after the loss. Eight years later, when both groups were asked to complete the Expanded Texas Inventory of Grief (Fasching-bauer, Devaul, & Zisook, 1977; Zisook, Devaul, & Click, 1982), the study found no difference between the groups that related to good versus poor outcome.

On the other hand, some writers have found no correlation between anticipation of death and postdeath grief experience (Clayton, Desmarais, & Winokur, 1968; Maddison & Viola, 1968; Schwab, Chalmers, Conroy, Farris, & Markush, 1975; Wolff et al., 1964). These findings may suggest that there could be instances in which death was impending but, for one reason or another, the family did not grieve in anticipation, either from a denial of impending death or from a misunderstanding of the warnings (Parkes, 1972; Rando, 1986b; Vachon et al., 1976).

Still other studies have indicated a definite qualitative difference between sudden death and one that has been anticipated. Sanders (1982–1983) and Rando (1983) found that both sudden and long-term chronic-illness deaths produced poorer bereavement adjustments than those deaths that took intermediate lengths of time.

In the Tampa study (1982–1983), Sanders found that survivors of a sudden death situation showed longer-lasting physical repercussions as well as more anger and guilt than did those who survived a short-term chronic-illness death. Survivors of a long-term chronic-illness death showed greater feelings of isolation and alienation, which prolonged their grief and gave rise to loss of emotional control. The group making the best adjustment to bereavement were in situations in which the individual died of a short-term chronic illness. Although these respondents had initially indicated levels of grief similar to the other two groups, when seen at follow-up 2 years later, they showed considerable diminishment of grief. The sudden-death group indicated an internalized emotional response described as an "anger-in," or intrapunitive response, causing them to sustain prolonged physical stress. The long-term chronic-illness group expressed an "anger-out" response, which, while creating a picture of defection, frustration, and loneliness, did not cause them to sustain the prolonged physiological component.

These findings, then, indicate value in some preparation for loss, as long as it is not extended over a protracted time period, which then may result in withdrawal of social support.

SITUATIONAL CHARACTERISTICS
OF THE BEREAVEMENT

LACK OF SOCIAL SUPPORT

Feeling isolated and alone is a basic characteristic of every loss experienced. At one point or another, almost everyone disengages from supportive friends for a short period in order to complete the grief work necessary to gain renewed strength. This disengagement does not usually continue as a way of life. Problems arise, however, when a support system is actually lacking or if the bereaved individual permanently withdraws from others. The same feelings of isolation exist if social support is actually there but is perceived not to be; in such cases, anger with the death succeeds in separating the bereaved from others. Maddison and Walker (1967) showed that widows who were most open to risk perceived themselves as having more unmet needs in interpersonal relationships than did those with good outcome. The widows felt that they were not given an opportunity to express their grief, particularly emotions such as anger and guilt. They also felt that they were sidestepped when they wanted to talk about the lost spouse. These findings were supported by other writers (Lopata, 1979; Raphael, 1977; Vachon, Sheldon, et al., 1982). Sanders (1980–1981) found that bereaved spouses of either sex who had had a closed relationship in which the deceased had provided the total social outlet suffered deeper despair than did those bereaved spouses who had been more socially independent.

In the Tubingen study (Stroebe et al., 1985), measures were included to examine both perceived social support and actual social network. Respondents were divided into high and low perceived social support groups. A Social Support by Marital Status by Gender analysis of variance (ANOVA) resulted in a main effect in each of the factors for depression and physical symptoms, without a buffering effect in each of the Social Support by Marital Status interactions. This finding seems to indicate that it is not so much the quantity of individuals that one has available but the quality of good, dependable friends who can be called on. One trusted confidant could possibly supply all the needed interaction. Being alone and in pain strikes at the deepest level of an individual's personal safety. Fear and anxiety are natural concomitants of this stress, which, when continued, tends to create a feeling of distrust, further undermining personal health.

Parental bereavement produced the greatest feelings of isolation and stigma in the Tampa study (Sanders, 1980–1981). Parents were aware that what they had experienced was one of the worst things that could ever happen to a person and that few other individuals wanted to connect with anyone who had experienced this kind of tragedy. One mother compared it to being a leper without a colony. Several spoke of walking down the street and seeing friends a distance away actually cross the street to avoid having to speak to them. Yet some of these parents would hesitate to mention these incidents for fear of sounding unduly paranoid. In reacting to their own projections as well as to the real reactions of friends and relatives, they created a world of sequestration that was akin to quarantine.

DISENFRANCHISED GRIEF

> I came to church alone . . . found a seat in the rear of the chapel and tried to be as invisible as possible. The funeral began on time after the family had been seated. I was heartbroken and couldn't hold back my tears—sobs really. I was an intruder at the funeral of the man I loved. It was horrible . . . not to count in a person's life when you had meant so much to each other. I wasn't allowed to show my grief or even acknowledge that I knew him—certainly not that way.
>
> Bereaved mistress

The funeral is only one of the many areas in life in which disenfranchised grief holds particularly poignant memories. Ken Doka (1989) defines the term *disenfranchised grief* as that felt by "persons who experience a loss that is not or cannot be openly acknowledged, publicly mourned or socially supported" (p. 4). In effect, Doka says, such a person bypasses the grieving rules of society that spell out a set of norms specifying who, when, where, how, how long, and for whom people should grieve. Grieving rules, for example, specify whether one should take a day off to attend a funeral or perhaps take a week off to gain equilibrium after the shock of death. Such time off from work can vary, depending on the leniency of the boss or person in charge, but this rule applies to recognized losses. Disenfranchised grief has no rules, and the disenfranchised griever must hold back tears, refrain from any show of grief, and for the sake of appearance, go about business as if nothing sorrowful has happened. Three reasons are offered for disenfranchised grief: (1) the relationship is not recognized; (2) the loss is not recognized; (3) the griever is not recognized.

1. *The relationship is not recognized.* The nonrecognized relationship is illustrated by the grieving lover in the opening epigraph. She recognized that she would have little support within the community. Therefore she kept quiet about her pain. And because secrecy is certainly not conducive to grief resolution, hers was a long and arduous grief.

There can also be dire consequences when the recognized lover is abandoned for another partner. When feelings of hopelessness and helplessness band together to create a lonely and desperate situation, the abandoned partner sometimes feels as if the only answer is to destroy himself or herself. Anger left unattended without benefit of a confidant can often lead to self-destruction. A woman who had been the right arm of her boss was replaced by a younger assistant after years of working closely with her boss and having a long sexual relationship as well. He had been promising a life together after his divorce. When she was confronted with the new assistant, who now took her place not only in the office but in the bed as well, she drowned herself in her bathtub. Her loss was accompanied by rage and shame. Feeling helpless in a hopeless situation, this woman took her own life. Disenfranchised by her own secrecy, she was left with no resources to use at that time.

2. *The loss is not recognized.* When a pregnancy ends—regardless of whether it ends in miscarriage, stillbirth, or abortion—the loss is cruelly disregarded by the community as being the loss of a child. No matter how the pregnancy ends, if the parents are left without acknowledgment of a child, they experience an emptiness and void over lost dreams. Even in cases in which the child was unwanted, there is usually some guilt. In cases of prebirth loss, mothers are often angry with their body's betrayal. However, the loss does not affect the community, so little support is offered to the parents. Many friends and relatives even ignore the death. They have a hard time imagining grief over a baby that was never seen or held. Many people feel as if, for grief to be valid, there should have been years to establish a relationship.

But prebirth and infant losses are real. The relationship between parents and child often begins before conception. If the parents wanted that child, they have a right to their grief. They have an equal right to be supported through their grief, whatever it takes.

For many women, an abortion is coupled with the breakup of a relationship, which causes even deeper loss and sadness. The woman must go through the procedure alone and without support. Even though legal abortion has been practiced for some years in many states, a great deal of shame, stigma, and secrecy still surrounds this procedure.

The death of a pet can cause deep emotional sorrow and pain. Many people feel that a pet death is inconsequential. However, new research into pet bereavement is showing that the loss of a dearly loved pet can have psychological and physical repercussions. The growth of pet cemeteries, headstones, and mausoleums attests to the fact that the stigma of pet grief is now changing.

3. *The griever is not recognized.* There are situations in which characteris-

tics of the bereaved seem to negate their being qualified to grieve. The very old and the very young are often perceived by others as having little understanding of the death of a significant person.

Along the same lines, mentally disabled persons are often disenfranchised in bereavement. Families often ignore the emotional responses of a mentally disabled family member and their right to grieve.

Doka (1989) speaks to the problem of disenfranchised grief as a paradox. He says, "The very nature of disenfranchised grief creates additional problems for grief, while removing or minimizing sources of support" (p. 8).

Disenfranchised grief is a growing issue. Millions of Americans are involved in losses in which grief is effectively disenfranchised. Higher percentages of divorced people are in the cohorts now aging. The AIDS crisis means that more homosexuals will experience losses in significant relationships. "The very nature of disenfranchised grief and the unavailability of informal support make it likely that those who experience such losses will need to seek formal supports" (Doka, 1989).

ALCOHOL ABUSE

The influence of alcohol in bereavement outcome has been alluded to but not well documented. However, the alcoholic may represent a significant suicide risk (Chenoweth, Tonge, & Armstrong, 1980; Murphy & Robins, 1967). One study has shown an increase in hospital admission of bereaved alcoholics (Blankfield, 1982–1983), but these occurrences were not well documented because the first admission can occur months or years after the event. There is some thought that the use of alcohol and other drugs can postpone or inhibit the grief response (Parkes, 1972). Alcohol withdrawal during grief can cause varying responses, ranging from complete concealment of grief reactions to a pathological response.

In her survey of clinical case histories in an alcohol treatment center, Blankfield (1982–1983) found known grief reactions in 24% of 50 consecutive admissions. Variants of pathological grief were present in one quarter of those individuals, relating to a premorbid alcoholic personality. However, alcohol intake did not necessarily inhibit the resolution of bereavement symptoms. There appeared to be more problems for bereaved alcoholics when the deceased had acted to inhibit their alcohol intake. Blankfield suggests that alcohol can be an aggravating influence in bereavement as well as an increased suicide risk but adds that because data is inconclusive, more studies are needed before risk factors can be outlined conclusively.

CONCURRENT CRISES

Because grief itself is a major stressor, when one is assailed by other debilitating stressors, the outcome may produce an overburdened situation that further depletes the griever. Parkes (1965) and Raphael (1984) speak to the serious sequelae that follow multiple death situations, particularly when several members of a family are lost in the same disaster. In one situation, a mother lost her husband and two small children when their home burned to the ground. Only she and her infant son were saved when her husband pushed them to safety and then went back for the other children. In another case, a husband was driving the car when the accident that killed his wife and small daughter occurred—he did not receive a scratch.

Concurrent stressors may also have to do with other losses that the bereaved may be experiencing, such as loss of employment, divorce, loss of physical health, financial setbacks, and so on. Sometimes, several incidents may happen concurrently. When there are too many stressors or when they become too debilitating, a condition known as *psychic numbing* occurs. This term is used by Lifton (1979) to describe survivors in Hiroshima who were so besieged by their own multiple losses and by the constant horror of death itself that they behaved almost like robots and, as such, adopted probably the most extreme defensive position that could be managed. Lifton uses a phrase from a Hiroshima survivor, "paralysis of the mind," which aptly describes the temporary shutting down of psychic processes in order for the bereaved to tolerate the inordinate stress. When this paralysis happens, grief is either inhibited or exacerbated and needs extra time and effort on the part of the caregiver.

The adaptive resources of the bereaved may already be at a minimum when a major bereavement occurs, leaving the bereaved more vulnerable and helpless. Studies have shown that individuals involved in these multiple crises are at greater risk than others who may not be so assailed (Parkes, 1975; Raphael & Maddison, 1976).

PHYSIOLOGICAL VARIABLES

VULNERABILITY TO ILLNESS

The death of a loved person is one of the most intense stressors known. Holmes and Rahe (1967), who devised the Social Readjustment Rating Scale, have listed the death of a spouse as the most intense stress experienced in a lifetime. If the bereaved already has a chronic illness or shows vulnerability to an illness, then he or she is at greater risk of developing serious physical consequences that could even result in death (Maddison & Viola, 1968; Parkes, 1972; Vachon, Sheldon, et al., 1982).

The death of a child can cause chronic and severe grief that continues for a period of years, sometimes evolving into serious psychological problems (Rosen, 1988). It is at periods of such intense stress that the body reacts with an increased cardiovascular rate accompanied by high blood pressure. In addition, a growing body of research points to the high correlation between stress and the immune system function (Kiecolt-Glaser & Glaser, 1992). Such data leads to the assumption that grief, representing a substantial psychological stressor, carries a negative effect on the immune system (Irwin & Pike, 1993; Kim & Jacobs, 1993; Mason, 1991).

In a review of research literature regarding the relationship between grief and immunology, Irwin and Pike (1993) state that "cell-mediated immunity . . . may be altered in men and women undergoing severe, acute psychological stress such as bereavement" (p. 166). Chronic grief such as that following the death of a child might pose a serious threat to the immunological functions of the bereaved individual. For people with cancer or AIDS or who are HIV positive, the threat is even greater because the immune system has already suffered a serious compromise.

Jacobs and Ostfeld (1977) found five health conditions that may operate to produce higher morbidity or mortality as a consequence of loss:

1. Change in the health practices of the survivor.
2. Neglect of early disease warnings.
3. Poor management of chronic diseases such as diabetes and hypertension.
4. Alcohol abuse.
5. Absence of care that used to be provided by the deceased.

These writers also feel that stresses such as social isolation and retirement play an important role in explaining the mortality of older widowers that has been reported by several researchers (Helsing, Comstock, & Szklo, 1982; Maddison & Viola, 1968; Stroebe & Stroebe, 1983).

Jacobs and Ostfeld (1980) think that the vulnerability to illness is directly related to alterations in immune functions brought about by the conservation-withdrawal phase of bereavement. It is largely at this time, when the body shifts from sympathetic nervous system exhaustion to parasympathetic nervous system dominance, that illnesses have been reported. These writers conclude that most of the causes of mortality among the bereaved already exist in the form of chronic disease, which is exacerbated by the stress of grief. As they state,

Bereavement increases the risk of premature illness or death in widowed persons who are already vulnerable by virtue of a diathesis or pre-existing disease. This is consistent with the observation of a "compensatory dip" in mortality among the bereaved in the third, fourth, and fifth years after their conjugal loss. (p. 358)

Zisook and Devaul (1985) support this interpretation and add that failure to resolve the conservation-withdrawal phase of bereavement can also lead to chronic hypochondriasis. They found this problem in 20% of their sample who, because of their preoccupation with health, were unable to reinvest interest or energy in social relationships. There is a reported tendency for the bereaved to adopt a sick role as a result of their loss (Maddison & Viola, 1968). This sick role then allows the griever to receive nurturance through socially sanctioned channels rather than by appearing emotionally dependent. In keeping with these findings, Schmale (1958) noted that states of helplessness or hopelessness, characteristic of the third phase of bereavement, increased vulnerability to illnesses. He attributes much of this susceptibility to early unresolved object loss, which leaves the person vulnerable to continued assault. Illness then, he feels, may be either an adaptive attempt to resolve bereavement or a nonadaptive consequence of unresolved bereavement.

If an individual's health—mental or physical—is tenuous before bereavement, the stress of grief will aggravate a current condition. Studies have indicated an exacerbation of congestive heart failure and essential hypertension when an individual is faced with the threat of grief and loss (Chambers & Reiser, 1953; Weiner, Gerber, Battin, & Arkin, 1975). As Parkes (1985) points out, "The effects of emotion on coronary arteries are, of course, well known, and it is not unreasonable to suppose that people with severe heart disease may be vulnerable to the psychological accompaniments of severe grief" (p. 13). On several occasions, Parkes (1964, 1975) has reported a link between poor bereavement outcome and premorbid mental illness. Bunch's (1972) study of suicide in bereaved persons noted that 60% of those who succeeded had undergone psychiatric treatment prior to the bereavement. It is easier to trace premorbid physical symptoms and diagnoses than it is to determine severity of psychiatric problems. Individuals are more prone to volunteer information regarding their physical problems than they are their emotional ones, especially if they have remained in outpatient treatment only. Several writers have supported the fact that those persons who utilized health services before the death were most susceptible to poor bereavement outcomes (Mor, McHorney, & Sherwood, 1986). Yet Heyman and Gianturco (1973), in a study that examined health factors both before and after bereavement in elderly spouses, found few differences in health functioning of these participants, although there was a small increase in depression for widows following the death. Even then, the widows maintained active contact with friends.

Ample evidence indicates that nervous and emotional stimuli such as fear, rage, or pain can act as stressors. In addition, grief is one of the most potent psychosocial stressors known. When continued for a prolonged period, grief can cause emotional disturbances, headaches, insomnia, high blood pressure, gastric and duodenal ulcers, and cardiovascular and kidney disease (Selye, 1956). Several researchers have examined the correlation between stress and bereavement. Casuta and Lund (1992) looked at the stress experienced by a group of recently bereaved widows and widowers and compared it to those people's coping skills. The researchers then compared their data with the anticipated levels of a nonbereaved control group. The bereaved group reported moderately high stress levels over a 2-year period. Not surprisingly, the control group reported less stress and grief. The study found that significant levels of both stress and grief were extremely intense and continued throughout four years.

Neuroendrocrine abnormalities produced by stress seem to be an underlying issue with certain bereaved persons. The locus coeruleus (part of the central nervous system) produces norepinephrine, and the adrenal medullary system produces both norepinephrine and epinephrine. These catecholamines regulate blood pressure, heart rate, and cardiac output and mobilize blood glucose. Both systems are strongly affected by stress (Kim & Jacobs, 1993). Mason (1975) noted that when animals were exposed to unfamiliar surroundings, they reacted not to the stressor per se but to the psychological relevance of the stressor. If the animal was not upset or exposed to strange circumstances, the adrenal system was not activated. Rose (1980) carried this finding further and saw significant differences shown by human subjects when confronted with potentially threatening stimuli. People simply did not respond in the same ways when confronted with frightening or challenging stimuli. Because bereavement is a highly novel and distressing experience, neuroendocrine responses can be stimulated by individual differences such as the survivor's gender and relationship to the deceased, and the circumstances of the death. Unique coping styles vary with each person; the many new situations in life without the deceased may lead to anxiety, depression, or both, and the neuroendocrine responses become highly mobilized. The fluctuation from acute distress to chronic distress changes with varying circumstances, such as reduced financial difficulties, a new locale, adapting to a new social role, and so on; all these circumstances require adaptation to a different and novel situation. Life becomes a roller coaster, and the bereaved finds it difficult to reach a homeostatic level.

Freeman wrote in 1948,

> One of the basic weaknesses of behavioristic theory is an apparent inability to relate the motivated behavior of a total organism satisfactorily to the behavior of its more limited organ systems. An extension of Cannon's principle of homeostasis seems to fill the gap. This states that the organism is designed to react to change in a way calculated to restore disturbed equilibrium. (p. 5)

Psychological responses to distressing life events correlate positively with immune disfunction in persons suffering severe life stressors such as loss (Irwin & Pike, 1993). Psychological depression or anxiety itself may be connected with immune changes. These negative responses can leave the bereaved open to various health problems.

If an individual's mental or physical health is tenuous before the loss, the stress of grief will exacerbate that condition during bereavement. Early studies showed an exaggeration of congestive heart failure and essential hypertension in individuals who faced the threat of grief and loss (Chambers & Reiser, 1953; Weiner, Thaler, Reiser, & Mirsky, 1957). Tracing premorbid physical symptoms and diagnoses is easier than tracing the severity of previous psychiatric problems.

Certain risk factors have been identified as seriously debilitating to people who have suffered a severe loss (Sanders, 1993). Those risk factors include the following:

- Sudden unexpected deaths, including suicide, murder, catastrophic circumstances, and stigmatized deaths.
- Ambivalence and dependency.
- Parental bereavement.
- Health before bereavement.
- Concurrent crises.
- Perceived lack of social support.
- Age and gender.
- Reduced material resources.

Most people do not become seriously ill or die after a significant loss, but caregivers, without knowing what long-term health risks their patients had before the death, have to be alert to certain dangers that might be encountered. Sudden or untimely death creates such systemic shock that, for some people, the impact does indeed cause immediate consequences.

Grief affects everyone unequally. Some people are severely affected and die, whereas others seemingly take it in stride, acknowledging a loss but somehow managing to go on with their lives. Researchers and caregivers must work to lessen the ill effects of complicated bereavement.

CHAPTER 11

Early Childhood Impact

BILL WAS EIGHT when his mother died. She had been ill for two years and her death was anticipated because curative treatment for her metastatic cancer was no longer an option. Bill had never experienced a death in his family—even the death of a pet—and he did not know what to expect.

While he was at summer camp he came to understand that his mother's death was imminent. His uncle arrived to take him home two weeks before the session was over saying only, "It's time to see your mother." After his arrival at home, Bill's mother called him to her bedside to say good-bye. She died within two days.

Bill recalls feeling "extremely sad" but unable to express his emotions. Although he did hear his father's crying late at night in the privacy of his bedroom, it seemed to Bill that no one else seemed sad. People were nice to him and the reception after the funeral brought together family and friends, but in Bill's estimation, it seemed that no one expressed sadness or missed his mother as he did. It appeared, instead, to be a party atmosphere in which people dropped by the house, food and drinks were served, and folks carried on polite conversation not unlike that which would have happened on a normal Sunday afternoon. In fact, it seemed to Bill as though everything was normal except that his mother was dead.

This lack of validation and recognition of Bill's significant loss led him to a state of disenfranchised grief that is experienced when loss is not (or cannot) be openly acknowledged, publicly mourned, or socially supported (Doka, 1989). Children often disenfranchise their grief because they are either not capable of grieving or believe their behavior will be unacceptable. Bill's mother died in the late 1940s when little was known about grief and

154

its effects. It was an era in which people tended to display a minimal public reaction to death, preferring instead to mourn privately. At that time, it was thought best to protect children from a negative reaction to death and although the family and friends of Bill's mother were deeply affected by her death, they reacted to him as if they were not. Bill's need for support was unmet. Doka suggests that the "simultaneous availability of support and lack of receipt is worse than complete unavailability because it tends to increase secondary loss and intensify such normal grief feelings as despair, depression, anger, abandonment, shame, victimization, anxiety, guilt, search for meaning, and social withdrawal." Bill felt all these reactions at various times during the 30 years subsequent to his mother's death. His adult relationships were seriously affected by his unresolved feelings of abandonment. He was often depressed, and his level of guilt in dealing with many aspects of his life was high. He felt that his life was, with rare exception, simply "sad." Bill lived with this unresolved grief until he was 50. It was not until he entered treatment for alcoholism that a counselor encouraged and supported him in grieving his mother's death.

Each human being forms his or her own personal perception of death from distinct experiences. Book (1996) reminds us that experience is the source of all knowing and the basis of behavior. Deaths that we experience as children . . . become ingrained within us as we seek to create meaning for ourselves. Meaning is constructed by individuals "between the self and the object and also between one person and another" (p. 323–342). In Bill's experience, meaning for his life was stunted at an early age because well-meaning adults sheltered him from a realistic awareness of mortality. Contemporary thought suggests that children are capable of experiencing an understanding of death and dying as a natural process and that the lifelong relationship that an individual has to dying and death is based in no small measure on the experiences of childhood.

What, then, are the feelings that children have in relation to their understanding of death? In a study conducted by Orbach, Weiner, Har-Even, and Eshel (1994/95), the emotional impact on children's understanding of death was examined. Fifty-four children, tested in groups ranging in age between 6 and 11, participated in an investigation of the relationship between the understanding of death and the degree of interpersonal closeness to the deceased. Their findings indicate that among these groups, the child's comprehension of death and dying is "multifaceted, dynamic, and changes with circumstances with his or her state of development, social attachments, and anxieties." The data suggest that children's views of death depend on the context and that their knowledge is organized not in a static but in a dynamic way. As the emotional context changes, so does the fluidity of the schemata. The question arises as to whether this attribution is to the emotionally loaded concept of death or to the egocentric reality processing or immature cognitive functioning of children. This study replicates other findings regarding comprehension of death at various ages. The older the child and the more experiences that child has had related to death, the greater the ability to carry out abstract reasoning and comprehension of mortality.

A child's separation from a parent or significant other is a tremendously difficult experience. The literature has failed in providing caregivers with new research into the complexity of the child's response to loss as well as the impact that a loss may have later, particularly when that child deals with subsequent death experiences. Early researchers focused on adults' retrospective analyses of their personal childhood bereavement and related that information to the form it took in adult emotional adjustment. In some of these research studies, psychiatric patients were interviewed with an emphasis on early death experiences that pointed to severe adult personality disorders. More productive research would place less reliance on psychiatric patients and concentrate instead on identifying those factors in the present and past environments of the bereaved child that enhance (or detract from) adjustment (Papadatou & Papadatos, 1991). The focus clearly needs to be on the bereaved child rather than on retrospective reports.

In a 1987 report, Stroebe and Stroebe emphasized that loss of key attachment figures during childhood is indicative of poor outcome in antecedent bereavement experiences. Unfortunately, in the case of many children's death experiences, the loss has been unsuccessfully dealt with. As the child gains more experiences in later life, including the death and dying of others, difficulty in dealing with these early issues could surface in the face of a current loss. The extent to which prior losses from earlier experiences were not integrated successfully may interfere with a healthy adaptation to a current death experience. Prior loss, particularly that which has not been resolved from childhood, can leave the individual at high risk for complicated mourning (Rando, 1993). Early, unresolved loss can deplete one's coping mechanisms, compromising mental health and interfering with appropriate personality development (Raphael, 1984). An individual may experience further complications if there are concurrent stresses associated at the time of subsequent deaths, such as coincidental associations, same circumstances, multiple loss, secondary loss, or unfinished business of earlier losses (Rando, 1993). If complications in mourning exist because of any of these conditions, it will be critical for the caregiver to uncover and address these issues in treatment. Naturally the extent to which the complications are multiple will directly impact the nature and duration of treatment. The *perceptions* that a person has attributed to a loss cannot be ignored because they provide the meanings people give to their experiences. Perceptions are the result of many variables. Age, although quite significant for this purpose, is but one variable. The caregiver, therefore, is charged with the responsibility to examine all other variables when dealing with complicated conditions in treatment, and these complications will surely evolve from the impact of unresolved childhood bereavement.

The specific form of a child's attitude toward death will correlate to the nature of the involvement with that subject and to the developmental, personal, and cultural resources that shape the child's interpretation and responses to the individual experience. Young infants, for example, show very clear evidence of separation anxiety even though they have little experience or conceptual clarity for death. Older children may blame themselves for the death of a parent although they had no role in the death. They may feel anger and a sense of helplessness, especially when death is preceded by changes brought on by illness: If daddy can change this way and act less like a father, can the child help but fear loss of identity too? Certain aspects of the death experience for the child may be avoided or "forgotten," or fantasy may be used to deal with the loss. Some children may manifest disturbances in their affective and cognitive functioning. Children's attitudes toward death are complex. They are the result of many sources and cannot be defined in a neat package of conceptions attributable to chronological or cognitive factors alone (Corr, Nabe, & Corr, 1994). Early experiences and their impact in later life will therefore be as unique as the individuals themselves.

Prior losses from childhood may indeed imprint an impact on the individual's future loss responses. Avoidance of the feelings associated with the prior loss may prevent dealing with a current loss if the avoidance pattern becomes firmly entrenched. A depletion of the ego could also occur from past experiences with the resultant amount of ego insufficient for coping with current loss. Expectations of prior loss may influence feelings and anticipation of future loss, which may affect coping strategies or defense mechanisms. If these experiences were negative or have not been accommodated, the present loss can be adversely affected through specific learning (Rando, 1993, p. 459).

If adaptive resources are minimal at the time of an earlier loss, an increase in one's vulnerability may surface with the present experience. Feelings of helplessness brought on by the current loss may be overwhelming, thereby challenging both the caregiver and mourner with complicated mourning. Loss from an early dependent relationship may invoke feelings that resurface in later life. If, for example, the mother of a young child dies, the same feelings of anger, abandonment, and helplessness could arise at the subsequent death of an older sibling or spouse, leading the mourner back to a vulnerable, defenseless place.

Children who were neglected or abused by a deceased parent or guardian may be conflicted in their mourning, and this conflict may present itself in future death experiences. In these circumstances, the mourner may have a tendency to grieve about what the abuser has taken away, such as innocence or the loss of a happy childhood. Caregivers who work with mourners from victimizing relationships should always be prepared to deal with anger, either latent or manifest, as well as feelings of ambivalence, which are often exacerbated by self-blame. Inappropriate idealization of the abuser is also common in these situations. Both the victimization and the issues resulting from complicated mourning must be addressed. Careful attention must be paid to processing all emotions, thoughts, and memories relating to the abuser, with the ultimate goal of assisting the mourner in reshaping his or her self-image and relearning ways to establish trusting and healthy relationships (Rando, 1993).

Although anger expressed over a death experience is not unusual, it is an important characteristic for caregivers to note when working with children because it may well present itself as a complex emotion resulting from the early death experience. Raphael (1984) reports that in the loss of an extremely dependent relationship, distorted mourning of the angry type can be the resultant reaction. Extreme anger of this nature is intensely bitter and is often displaced on others. Consumed with anger at the loss, the mourner lashes out at those whom he feels may be responsible, a direction that may include the self. Intense anger, as it relates to children, may be a reaction from deaths associated with extreme dependency and in which the sense of desertion or abandonment is great. If this type of anger is not treated or assimilated properly, the death of a subsequent loved one may bring back feelings of insecurity caused by earlier losses. This recurrence is especially true when the earlier loss was of a dependent relationship, such as a parent or guardian. The death of a loved one appears to bring back feelings of insecurity caused by earlier losses, particularly those experienced in childhood. Feeling helpless again, the mourner in this situation may feel rage resulting from the earlier loss. A degree of dependency seems to fuel the infantile state, leaving the mourner with feelings of intense anger and of unmet needs and expectations. Anger toward the new death experience may be difficult to recognize because it can take on many forms, including anxiety, negativity, aggressive behavior, withdrawal, and other debilitating patterns. Clinically, complicated mourning can result from prior loss, especially if the loss occurred in early childhood and was not integrated appropriately.

Conversely, the impact from early experiences can have a positive effect on subsequent losses if the early experience was handled in an open manner and the child assimilated the experience appropriately. Learning from early death experiences may provide a person with more resources to fall back on and, if those resources are processed effectively, can provide insight and experience that will serve the bereaved well as he or she moves through the various losses in life. When the challenge of a new death surfaces, this person will have prior meaning structure in place and knowledge that the distress will eventually subside. In this regard, the early impact has had effectual value for the individual. Useful coping skills that were developed at an earlier time provide a repertoire for dealing with the immediate crisis. Sadly, however, this situation rarely occurs because adult caregivers are so often caught up in their own grief that children's needs are either ignored or are handled insufficiently. In many cases, the intrusion of death thwarts the natural movement for a child's hopes and anticipation about his or her own future. The basic human sentiments—to possess love, recognition, and physical security and to maintain membership in a stable group—are suddenly disrupted. How these sentiments are obstructed after a death experience is important in examining the early childhood impact.

What, then, can be done to assist caregivers in helping children grieve appropriately, and what have we learned about the effects of early impact on children?

The unknown carries with it an element of fear, especially where children are concerned. When a child experiences a death, it is most likely a new experience and the natural reaction to this new experience is fear. Excell (1980) suggests that caregivers determine the following objectives in dealing with the affected child: (1) promotion of an honest, nonjudgmental environment in which questions may be asked and feelings may be discussed openly; (2) exploration into the experiences, if any, that the child has already had with death; (3) provision of correct information for any misinterpretations concerning death; (4) identification of a model for the many feelings a child may have in the process of mourning; and (5) provision of alternatives for the child to say good-bye. The most essential element in resolution of grief is the ability to engage in communication. Supportive communication helps a child's thoughts and emotions become clearer and makes it easier for them to share their particular beliefs about the death and its meaning for them. Caregivers may want to ask the child to draw a picture of what he or she thinks death looks like, a process that can be subdivided into three distinct conditions: how the death occurred, the personification of death (as an angel, monster, etc.), and actions that the child witnessed after death (scenes from the funeral or burial, etc.). Depending on the child's focus, much information can be gained from such drawings, which can lead to a deeper understanding of the child's feelings.

Lammers (1995) reports that there has been a revolution in the practices and perceptions surrounding death and dying in the last 20 years, but little has been done to effectively transmit these changes to children. She suggests that our modern society provides little material that would introduce children to the reality of death. Lammers berates children's cartoons, lamenting that in the presentation there is a consistently distorted view of mortality and, in some cartoons, a sense of fostering the conclusion that death is somehow reversible. However, books and fairy tales do offer material that helps make death a subject that can be constructively discussed between caregiver and child. Lammers cites *Charlotte's Web, The Yearling, Little Women,* and *The Dead Bird* as some of the best children's literature available on the subject.

Charlotte's Web, in which E. B. White presents a classic tale of animal fantasy, was one of the first children's books (published in 1952) that faced death squarely, helping the reader (and listener) to view death as a part of life. This story revels in the best of life amid the occurrences of nature in which pleasure and pain and life and death merge into a comfortable, loving existence. After Charlotte dies, when her children begin to hatch, Wilbur trembles with joy and his heart is filled with happiness. The fact that Charlotte's newborns repeat the very word she herself first used to greet Wilbur underscores the cyclical continuity of life. The story ends with White's heartwarming reminder that we can hold on to our feelings for our loved ones forever as we honor and value what each creature brings to life: "Wilbur never forgot Charlotte. Although he loved her children and grandchildren dearly, none of the new spiders ever quite took her place in his heart. She was in a class by herself. It is not often that someone comes along who is a true friend and a good writer. Charlotte was both" (White, 1952, p. 184).

Through fairy tales, children can be exposed to a host of new experiences and can learn modes of behavior that fit into their own needs. For example, children can learn through fairy tales that one can confront new or frightening circumstances and not only survive, but grow in new ways. Rather than exposing children to Saturday morning cartoons, parents can instead read fairy tales and books that introduce children to the types of situations that will enhance their experiences as they encounter life as it really is.

Bibliotherapy can also be an effective tool for helping children who are troubled by death. When grieving children read (or are read to) about others who have experienced similar situations, they may not feel as alone or different and, with the help of a skilled caregiver, may find positive solutions to their problems. It is important, however, that the child be able to see similarities between themselves and the characters in the book. Identification and projection are critical to the success of bibliotherapy, and skillful caregivers will be attuned to the goals of this therapy. A number of books are available on the subject of death that are suitable for reading to children from ages 3 to 8. *The Fall of Freddie the Leaf* is a fine example of a children's book that can help a young person learn about the delicate balance between life and death.

Caregivers can take a direct approach to helping children who are in the early stages of mourning through meaningful listening, interpretation, and encouragement of shared feelings. Discussions of death should be guided by the child's curiosity and include considerations of life as well as death. Discussions must be honest and allow the child to make appropriate deductions, according to Papadatou and Papadatos (1991). Factual information for any misperceptions must be relayed to the child in his or her language as much as possible. Excell (1980) states that factual information for children younger than age 6 must be repeated because it is more difficult for this age group to grasp the finality of death. If the child's cognition is more developed, however, a child's perception of death will be that death is final and inevitable.

One of the earliest means of communication with young children is teaching them to say good-bye. Most parents will wait proudly and patiently for their toddler to wave "bye-bye" to friends and grandparents, infusing in the child a sense of importance to this most elemental means of closure. It is only appropriate then, that we provide the child with an opportunity to say good-bye to a loved one either before or after the funeral.

One very effective way of helping children accept the reality of death is to permit a viewing of the deceased. Preparing the child appropriately for this sacred experience is extremely important. Explaining that the deceased is unable to talk and at the same time encouraging the child to talk to the deceased may present a constructive way for a child to deal with any unfinished business. With a caring adult nearby, it is also beneficial to respect a child's need to be alone with a loved one, an engagement that may well begin his process of mourning (Excell, 1980). A child may wish to place a drawing, a photo, or some other article in the casket with the deceased, and this desire should be honored as well. Older children may wish to take part in the funeral or memorial service by reading a poem or letter. Honoring these desires can help a child move through the mourning process in a meaningful and constructive way.

When any mourner does not receive a perceived need for support, difficulties nearly always surface. When children perceive that their support needs are unmet, the problem can be exaggerated in both the short and long term. Identification of the type of support the child needs is one step that caregivers must undertake, particularly since the social support of children is limited. For this reason, structured support groups are available for children who have experienced the death of a significant person. These groups provide a safe environment in which exploration of emotions can be validated and normalized and in which children can learn from and share with their peers their reactions to loss. The structure will vary from group to group but many are organized into weekly sessions in which the discussion topics and themes are identified (Fleming & Balmer, 1980). Unanswered questions, misconceptions, and misunderstandings as well as painful emotions, thoughts, and memories are explored in these special settings.

The healing that time supposedly brings to the grieving process may not necessarily come with the passing of time alone. Time is seen "more as a function of dissipation of grief emotion with its debilitating and paralyzing effects and a shifting of focus to the tasks of coping" (Attig, 1991, p. 389). The notion of helplessness that children encounter through death can be shifted only through inclusion in the process. When a child sees an adult express sadness, it invokes a healthy response message that is valuable not only in the present but also in the future as other losses are experienced (Excell, 1980). When children are permitted to ask questions and explore their range of emotions, they participate in a process of communication, the most essential element in grief resolution (Gilbert, 1996). When children share, they heal. When children listen, they learn.

Excell (1980) emphasizes three major considerations when working with children in the process of mourning. First, inclusion is much healthier than exclusion, for if children are left out, they only have their imagination on which to rely. A clear understanding of what has happened and a presentation of the facts in a simple way is essential. Second, adults need to provide healthy role models for children to realize that their open and honest expressions of grief will be accepted and welcomed. Finally, personal boundaries of the child must be respected. Individual reaction to loss may take one form or another; forcing a child into one particular coping alternative may be as unhealthy for the child as excluding the child from any participation. If age permits, discussion of the alternative directions is a caregiver's responsibility, as is guiding the child with awareness and possibility. The final decision belongs to the child and is owned by the child. Children who are helped with their current distress can become the future adults who will be better equipped to view the cycle of life and death in a natural and healthy way.

CHAPTER 12

Death and the
Family Constellation

It is strange. I never felt particularly close to my family before Dad's death. Oh, we got together on special occasions and everyone got on all right, I guess. It's just that when we were all together at the funeral, there was a closeness that had never been there before—and it's still there 2 years later. It was like Dad's love that he had for each of us now drew us all together under one umbrella.

Bereaved adult daughter

BEREAVEMENT RESEARCH has focused primarily on the responses of individuals following the death of a beloved family member rather than on the family as a group. Widows and widowers have been targeted most often, but lately there has been a growing concern for parents of children who have died. Research in this area is on an upsurge, yet even here grief has been approached in terms of the mother's or father's reaction. But make no mistake, grief is typically a family affair. Although it is important to think in terms of individual reactions, if caregivers begin to lose sight of major effects within the family constellation, important strategies for family intervention will be missed. Bereavement profoundly affects the cohesion of the family unit. When links in the familial chain are broken by separation or death, disturbing social and psychological disruptions are often created (Raphael, 1984).

Anthropologists agree that the universal family is bound by two common characteristics: (1) They are held together by kinship ties, and (2) they share a common residence (Landis, 1977). In most cultures of the world, the joint family is the most typical behavior. Several families join in one large household. The extended family can offer varied supports for each other while spreading the emotional investments across a larger network. When death is experienced, the network bands together. Grief is shared. However, in American culture the kinship ties are narrower. The nuclear or companionship families far outweigh the extended kin network. As a result, love is spread among fewer family members. Emotional investment, therefore, becomes more focused and intense. Dependency needs, rather than being spread across a broad network, are relegated to a small familial circle. And this smaller size, of course, creates the greatest difficulty in bereavement outcome for family members. When someone dies in a nuclear family, the loss is greater because there are fewer members to share the attachment bonds. A large investment is shattered.

Another serious problem for the nuclear family is the continued mobility of the American society. It is estimated that 35 to 40 million Americans change residence every year. Only 35% of the heads of families are living in the place of their birth. One family in five is living 1,000 miles from the place of their birth. Although most of the 35 to 40 million Americans who change residency every year may only be moving within the same city, more than 5 million of the families do move across state lines (Landis, 1977). Studies of relocation have shown that the cohesiveness of the family is greatly threatened by the death of one of its own, leaving them feeling stripped and vulnerable. Although families travel to reunite during the rituals of death, they quickly disperse, leaving the immediate family to manage alone. As Secundy (1977) points out, "one or two days are allowed to attend funerals of immediate family only. One is expected to return to work promptly and efficiently as opposed to days gone by when one's employer allowed 'as much time as you need' " (p. 649).

Yet there is no question that the death of a family member can cause disruption in the family equilibrium. Herz (1980) has listed four factors that seem to affect the degree of disruption:

1. *The timing of the death in the life cycle.* Was it a child or an elderly member? The most disruptive situations come when an individual dies in the prime of life.
2. *The nature of the death—sudden versus anticipated.* Death that is sudden may not be preceded by the debilitating period of financial and emotional drain, but it produces the greatest shock to the system.
3. *The openness of the family system.* Openness is the ability of the fam-

ily members to communicate thoughts and feelings without overreacting to one another.

4. *The position in the family held by the deceased member.* The more emotionally significant a family member was in the family, the greater the emotional impact when that member dies.

Herz feels that these factors all work together to produce an opportunity for families to grow together and become more cohesive or, when negative conditions persist, to disintegrate and become scattered.

UNIQUE CHARACTERISTICS OF FAMILY MEMBERS

Even though the nuclear family faces a unique problem in bereavement, extended families also meet with special difficulties just because each person within each family is unique. People do not grieve alike. And this difference sometimes causes disagreements because of the expectations people have for the others around them. Personalities differ, frustration tolerance fluctuates, and grief is expressed in varying ways. For example, death anxiety and denial sometimes look like lack of feeling.

In one case, a grown sibling, after the death of her father, showed no reaction at all. The other family members were highly critical of her throughout the funeral arrangements and rituals. They thought that she did not care as much for their father as she should have. When I talked with her later, she said that their attitude pained her almost as much as the death itself. She explained that when he died, she became so fearful that everyone was going to die and leave her that she could make little outward show of emotion. Her behavior became wooden and stiff. She could not cry. The family interpreted this reaction to mean that she did not really love her father. They were furious at her lack of response. It took months for the family to get back on good footing again, but not before she suffered tremendously for being excluded from the family support system.

Anger within the Family

The irritability connected with the stress of bereavement acts to infuse newly bereaved people with sudden outpourings of anger and hostility. This anger can be confusing to the bereaved themselves, who normally would not react so sharply or violently. In one situation in the Tampa study, a son took it upon himself to arrange for the funeral of his mother. He saw this task as an unpleasant one and attempted to shield his sisters and grandparents from having to do it. Yet the situation blew up when he was criticized, especially by the grandparents, for excluding them. He reacted in anger and lost his temper, saying things he had not intended to say. Unfortunately, this incident took place at the wake, where the entire family had gathered. He explained,

> I was very insulted, very embarrassed. . . . I never even raised my voice to her before. I had no reason to . . . but this one time, boy, if I hadn't, if I didn't know that I can control myself, my temper. . . . The first thing she does is she jumps up and runs out of the room to where my uncle was, then he comes running in there, wanting to go outside with me because I'm talking to his mother like I am. And a few of my aunts were in there and a few other people, and he came in there wanting to jump on me. . . .
>
> I said, "Before we go outside and do anything that we might regret later, let's sit down and at least let each other know what's on our minds." Then when I got through telling him what I had to say and he said what he had to say . . . well, he went back in there and kind of got on her. Because I hadn't done anything wrong. The main thing she was really upset about was [that] I didn't let my brothers and sisters pick out the casket. I didn't let her look at it. . . . I didn't notify them and let them know, or get their OK of all the arrangements that I went through. And that was the main gripe she had. I didn't get them to go with me to do all the arrangements. They were all pretty broken up about it [the death], and, of course, I imagine anybody that went through that would be. But I just didn't see any reason to take my two little sisters in there to pick out a damn casket. . . . it was enough for me to do it than to let them have to do it, too.

This family difficulty was compounded the day of the funeral when the son unthinkingly placed himself and his siblings in the lead limousine while the grandparents rode in the second one. The grandmother who was hurt by the earlier situation made another scene, which created lasting repercussions.

> Everybody was upset, but I don't hold a grudge against her for the way she acted. She carried on something terrible. I haven't been by her house since then. I've kind of stayed away from there. She asked my brother the other day why I haven't been by. And I just told him to tell her that I was going to wait till everyone cools off and everything gets back to normal and I'll go back to my routine of coming by and seeing the relatives when you're supposed to, I guess.

A year and a half later, this family still avoided each other. The son, in his desire to protect everyone, had not taken into account the fact that his grandparents were the bereaved parents of his mother and, as such, needed special consideration. This oversight could be related to inadequate anticipatory socialization. As mentioned earlier, people may be oversensitive during a bereavement. Feelings are more easily hurt. Families called together at a time of high stress will often experience a clashing of personalities. The combination of irritability and anger with oversensitivity produces a potentially volatile situation.

It is important for families to make decisions about funerals ahead of time (Pine, 1986). Most often, this planning involves some discussion of death. The more discussions of this nature that can be brought into the open, the better the family will deal with death when it occurs. Too, when discussions are introduced ahead of time, there will be more open sharing of personal feelings within the family group after a death. This advance planning is perhaps one of the most important things a family can do to guard against misunderstandings that often arise at the time of death.

JEALOUSIES

Elliot (1948) points out that jealousies arise when families refuse to accept the role of certain members under new conditions (Elliot, 1948; Koos, 1946). As a result, many times jealousies arise that are never resolved. In the Tampa study, a wife who had nursed her husband through a long terminal illness was so beset by jealousy that the bereavement was a most complicated one. When the husband was dying in the hospital, his two brothers and their wives arrived from another city and began making decisions without consulting the wife. She not only felt left out but also ostracized for the manner in which she had cared for her husband during his illness. The situation worsened after he died. The funeral was a standoff. Each side of the family wanted to make the final decisions, and the argument in the hospital carried over to the leave-taking rituals as well.

The wife, deeply affected by the criticism she had received, withdrew. It took months of counseling for her to work through her hurt, anger, and indignation. She was shaken and unsure of herself by the lack of support she received and by the usurping of her position as primary caregiver at the critical time of her husband's death. She told me that she had felt such jealousy, especially because the husband had warmly welcomed the brothers at the hospital, that she thought she would never get over it. This wife was left with no support at a critical time, but even worse, she was criticized when she was vulnerable. She had few defenses on which to rely, so she turned her anger inward, leaving no expression for it.

The family is considered a unit, and when this unit is disrupted because of the death of one of its members, the breach is difficult to repair. Because the family maintains its balance by lifelong behavioral interactions, when one member is no longer there, the disruption causes an imbalance. Time and energy are required to establish a new emotional equilibrium. Naturally, much of the adjustment depends on the closeness of the family. A well-integrated family may respond with considerable outward show of emotion but may adapt to the loss relatively quickly. On the other hand, a poorly integrated family may show little reaction when death occurs, looking for all the world like they are managing well, but they may respond later with emotional problems or physical illness.

EMOTIONAL SHOCK WAVES

After serious life events have occurred, a network of aftershocks take place, creating one problem after another. These aftershocks have been referred to as "emotional shock waves" (Bowen, 1976) and are seen as serious emotional events that can take place anywhere within the extended family system, particularly in the months or years following a death or serious illness of a significant family member. These occurrences are not usually seen by the survivors as directly related to grief reactions; instead, they are generally viewed as separate and distinct from the bereavement. The shock wave becomes the stimulus that triggers the process into activity.

CASE STUDY: RIPPLES FROM A DAUGHTER'S DEATH

In one situation, the emotional shock wave followed the aftermath of a grown daughter's death from cancer. The mother had spent 5 years during her daughter's illness traveling back and forth between her home and her daughter's. They lived a full day's drive apart, so that when the mother visited she would need to spend a few days or weeks away from her husband. The visits became longer as the disease progressed, until during the last year before the daughter's death, she was spending most of her time with her daughter.

Because her daughter had a 6-year-old child and a husband who worked long hours, the mother remained with them a few weeks after the death to manage the household tasks. However, this situation left the father of the deceased to fend for himself through the months of aftermath while his wife was away.

The mother had delayed her own grief because she had others depending on her. But when she was in her home once again, she allowed full vent to her emotions. Her husband had dealt with his own grief by intensifying his activity after the death so that he was on the go all the time. When she returned, he expected that she would again focus attention on him. He had difficulty understanding why she would sit by herself for long periods of time. As the mother said,

> You see, I went home and I, and that was another thing that bothered him. He said, "You don't do anything but sit on the couch," and I said, "I am grieving. I haven't gotten myself together yet. I'll get over it, and I'll get going again."
>
> But I didn't want to start anything. I don't want to go over and work on my printing press. I didn't want to do anything. . . . I was just dead center . . . and I couldn't budge.

She had been in a holding pattern up to now. What she needed at this time was nurturance and assurance from her husband. She added,

> He told me, "I don't know why you're sitting there doing nothing—get going." You see, he didn't understand. He didn't want to break down himself, but instead he was doing it another way.

Suddenly, her husband was forced to retire. Then he had two important losses with which to deal. He had to survive not only the death of his daughter, but the loss of his job, too.

Rather than appear depressed at the loss of his job, he intensified his activity even further. He was angry that his company forced retirement at 65 and set out to show them (and the world) that he could be as productive as ever. In no time, he had another job as vice president of a consulting firm, continuing to work hard. He still resented his wife's suggestions to slow down as well as her own inability to speed up. One day he became angry, said the marriage was not working and asked her to move out.

This request for a separation came out of the blue for her. She had no idea that he was even thinking of a separation. They had been married for 40 years and had been considered by their friends to have an ideal marriage. Yet he said he felt that she was holding him back in his work. She described the situation:

> He said, "How many boxes do you need, and I'll get you as many boxes as you need, but I want you out of here." My gosh, after 40 years that was a terrible blow.
>
> He had been closed mouthed, you know, quiet and withdrawn. And he felt that I didn't want him to work. Well, I didn't. But if he got rid of me, there wouldn't be anything standing in his way at all to go on and on and be gone all day and evening if he wanted to. He was just on a terrible run.

She said that she felt he was a different person. It was hard to understand where he was coming from, especially because she was extremely tired and grief stricken herself. It was difficult for her to gain a perspective on the family crisis because she was so deeply involved in the situation.

We were always the example of the perfect couple. So, I knew that there was something wrong with him . . . that . . . it was not really him speaking. But I began to put things in boxes. I was panicked myself.

When the emotional shock waves begin, the ripple effect goes in all directions. One family member can infuse another, who in turn infuses still another. When this ripple effect happens, it becomes difficult to slow or stop the process. In this case, the wife began an anxiety attack of her own by starting to pack. But before she went too far, she was able to think objectively before further damage was done. She explained:

And so then I thought, "Well, my goodness, what are you doing this for? Are you crazy?" So then I went to our minister and told him . . . and he wanted to see us both, but my husband wouldn't go. Anyhow, I didn't want to throw away 40 years of marriage, and I feel the guy is entitled to one mistake; he's always been just fine. So I rode it out. But the next thing I knew, he wanted to sell the house and move into a smaller place, so we did.

The wife was very unhappy in the smaller place, but tried to make the best of the situation. She realized that her husband was desperately trying to regain the balance that had been lost when their daughter had died and when he lost his position of many years. However, in an effort to regain the lost stability, he made demands both on himself and his wife that kept them off balance. Now the wife had lost her home of many years, which also meant losing the neighbors who had become personal friends.

This couple not only had to get their own lives in order, but also the lives of their daughter's husband and child, who were still trying to manage alone. Both of them had been ill during the year following the death. Then her husband developed asthma, but refused to believe that it could have come from the stress with which he had been living.

It took months before this family regained a sense of balance after the experience of losing an important family member. The son-in-law finally began dating someone who could relate to his daughter as well. The mother and father eventually worked through the many problems created by the emotional shock wave and regained some order in their lives.

SUMMARY

Regaining balance after the loss of a significant family member can take years. The tendency to overreact can cause extreme forms of behavior, which sometimes turn family members against one another (Elliot, 1932). Hurts, resentments, and hostilities perpetuate themselves. But along with these obvious forms of nonfunctional interactions, other events take place that are seemingly not associated with grief at all, such as illnesses, job losses, divorce, or even another death. These events carry with them new losses and subsequent griefs. However, just as a pebble tossed into a lake causes an ever widening circle of diminishing intensity, so too does the emotional and situational ripple diminish in strength until it no longer can be seen or felt. The effects of emotional shock waves are usually diminished the farther one moves away from the death.

CHILDREN'S BEREAVEMENT

Children are notoriously excluded from death in American families (Kübler-Ross, 1969). In the desire to protect them from unpleasant or morbid situations, we alienate children from life, for death is an important part of life. But equally important, by excluding them from the concept of death, we hinder their emotional growth (Bluebond-Langner, 1977).

Children, particularly young children, are often shipped off to friends during the ritual so that they are not exposed to funeral homes or talk of death. From this abandonment comes a feeling of separation from the family at a time when children need closer contact as well as answers and explanations from the parents. Fears arise about what happened to the lost family member and what may happen to them as well in the future (Kübler-Ross, 1983). Fortunately, there is a movement toward greater openness with children about death, but this movement is arriving slowly. Children need to know as many details as they are equipped to process. Naturally, this communication depends on the children's age as well as their relative inquisitiveness. They ask questions if they are interested and if they feel that the atmosphere is receptive and nonjudgmental.

Even beyond children's need to know is their need to grieve. There has been some concern in the past that children do not really grieve before they reach a certain age (Sullivan, 1956). This absence of feeling sometimes appears to be the case when small children ask only a few questions concerning a recent death and then race outside to join their playmates, seeming to forget the conversation. Children process information differently from adults, and small bits of information are all that can be adequately processed at any given moment (DeSpelder & Strickland, 1983). Adults must be patient with their questions, answering only those questions that the children need to know. This communication must be done in a warm, caring manner so that the door is always open to further conversations. So often children are left to themselves rather than encouraged to reveal and discover their responses to grief.

SIBLINGS' BEREAVEMENT

When a child dies, the survivors, both parents and remaining child or children, must adapt to a new reality. A complex family process begins, far more complicated than the sum of the individual responses of the survivors. The family is caught up in what is known as "survivor guilt," an agony experienced by those who feel responsible in some way for the death of another. The mother may experience extreme guilt for not having protected the child enough. The father may feel anger at the forces that robbed him of his child and now leave him powerless. The remaining siblings may feel their own guilt for having survived when their dead brother or sister did not. Generally, the child will try to match the climate created by the parents. If the circumstances of the tragedy are clear, children are in a better position to honestly deal with their own emotions. If the circumstances remain ambiguous, the atmosphere tense, and the climate hostile, then it will be difficult for the surviving child to sort out his or her involvement in the situation.

As mentioned, siblings often suffer survivor guilt for just being alive when their sister or brother is dead. This guilt stems at least in part from the wish most children have to be the only child. If this wish were true, then that child would have all the attention of the parents as well as all the toys and other material possessions. Most of us have, at one time or another, told our brother or sister to "drop dead." The comment was made only as a retort; in our wildest dreams, we never expected the sibling to do it. When death occurs, whether by accident or slow terminal illness, the remaining sibling is plagued with the awful memory of that comment or of similar retorts. Because such a thought is shameful, it is generally internalized and kept secret for fear that others will think the worst—the worst being that this child might have in some way caused the death. The guilt is kept inside to ferment, to grow, and often to cause behavioral problems later on in life.

Another source of guilt for siblings is that comments are made that lead the sibling to believe that the smartest child or the nicest one has died. The surviving sibling thinks that he or she does not really deserve to be alive (but unfortunately is).

OPEN VERSUS CLOSED FAMILIES

CLOSED FAMILIES

A word should be said about the family that maintains a good front for outsiders following a family death yet are not open to one another. These families maintain a conspiracy of silence for anyone not connected with the immediate unit. There is a feeling here that death is private and intruders will not be tolerated. Unfortunately, this approach is nonadaptive for at least two reasons. First, it prevents necessary social support from others. Friends and neighbors remain apart when they realize they are not wanted. Second, it perpetuates silence even within the family, for the lack of openness permeates throughout the family unit. Bereavement is a time when friends are a necessity. In the Tampa study, survivors most often cited family members as having been the greatest help in getting through their grief. When families are not open about death, they establish poor climates for dealing with death when it occurs.

OPEN FAMILIES

Families who are used to sharing their feelings and who remain nonreactive to the normal emotional intensity in the family can usually be just as open and accepting about their feelings when a death occurs (Herz, 1980). The more that families can communicate thoughts and feelings before a loss, the better the family will deal with death when it happens. Herz adds, "The longer and more intense the family stress, the more difficult it is for the family relationships to remain open and the more likely it is that dysfunction will develop" (p. 233). Remaining open is perhaps one of the most important things a family can learn to do in order to guard against misunderstandings that often arise at the time of death.

When a family system is open, when members can share thoughts or feelings without fear of rejection or abandonment—even when these thoughts and feelings are negative—there is a good probability that even the most intense grief can pull the family closer together than they were before.

CASE STUDY: AN OPEN FAMILY'S RESPONSE TO GRIEF

In one family in the Tampa study, a teenage daughter was killed in a car accident on the night of her graduation, but the family was able to stay close and even comfort the family of the young man who was driving the car. Kim, the oldest of their three children, was an accomplished pianist, had held scores of offices in her high school career and was also a popular and very lovely young woman. Her date was a friend whom she had been going with for several months, a likeable fellow who was a good athlete and a scholar also. However, on the night of graduation, he had enough to drink to cause him to be unsteady leaving the last party. Friends wanted him to let Kim drive, but he insisted that he was fine. On the way to Kim's house, he took a curve at high speed and the car rolled over, throwing Kim out. She was killed instantly. He did not receive a scratch.

The family was remarkable in the way that the members handled their grief, drawing even closer with daily powwows. They were able to process their shock and anger without being devastated by guilt. They ministered to the boy's parents and even brought the boy into their family circle as well. Their emotional style was not to overreact but to allow a very natural flow of honesty to take place, which was also coupled with a good measure of love. Apparently, this family had no hidden agenda. This is not to say that they did not suffer and grieve the loss of this wonderful family member. But what struck me was the diminished number of physical and emotional symptoms shown a year following the death. This finding was in direct opposition to the other families in the Tampa study that had lost a child; in those families one year later, the grief was intensifying.

The ability to remain open and receptive to each other during a time of severe emotional crisis is one of the primary factors in a positive outcome for families undergoing loss. Unfortunately, the time of crisis is not the optimal time to learn this pattern, which is why health care providers can offer a great service to bereaved families. Caregivers often function to bring the family into a closer relationship with each other by helping members to verbalize their feelings and to grieve openly. Even when the family refuses to be seen as a unit, if the caregiver can work with individual members, much can be done to encourage gradual participation in family interchanges. When anxiety is reduced by interaction with a sensitive, caring counselor or therapist, tension in the family is relaxed and the way is open for more honest communication of thoughts and feelings.

PART FOUR

COMPLICATED GRIEF

CHAPTER 13

Suicide, Homicide, and AIDS-Related Death

Like towards the last, you know, my husband, I don't know what was causing it, but he would get irritable, and it got to where he'd snap at me and I was on nervous edge, rushing him back and forth to the hospital. . . . I was nervous myself . . . plus, trying to get over the loss of my mother, one thing and the other. I remember that I used to snap at him . . . and I used to look pretty hateful. One time he said, "You hate me, don't you? I bet you wish I'd die, so you'd be free of me." And I let it go. I was just mad enough to be mean enough to let it go at that and not try to explain . . . and he died and I never got to tell him that I didn't mean it.

Widow, age 57

RIEF TAKES MANY FORMS. The differences in intensity and longevity are caused sometimes by personality factors, sometimes by situational or social factors, and other times by horrendous deaths or multiple or long-term debilitating illnesses. Whatever the reason, there are times when an individual does not follow the normal course of grief but instead responds in a manner that does not appear adaptive for that individual. Therese Rando, in her complete work on complicated mourning, states that it is more useful to look at complications in mourning processes than to focus on particular symptoms of complicated mourning. Yet many mental health workers who deal with these kinds of problems find little help in searching for a diagnostic category. At present, the Diagnostic and Statistical Manual of Mental Disorders (DSM-III-R; American Psychiatric Association, 1987) contains only the diagnostic category for uncomplicated bereavement (V62.82). This void leaves caregivers with little else to do but assign other diagnoses that have little clinical implications. I can only guess that the general thinking among the authors of the DMS-III-R is that complicated grief becomes something else—anxiety or depression, for example. Of course, this assumption may be true, but in leaving no other choice but to label grief as something else, this assumption avoids the obvious cause of bereavement.

The following are some of the terms used by writers and researchers to describe a complex emotional response to grief. "Pathological," (Freud, 1917; Raphael, 1978, 1975; Osterweis et al., 1984), "morbid" (Goalder, 1985; Schulz, 1978; Sullivan, 1956), "atypical" (Parkes, 1972), "complicated" (Worden, 1982), and "unresolved" (Rando, 1984; Zisook & Devaul, 1985), as well as other, more specific labels, such as "chronic," "delayed," or "disturbed."

All these terms imply that grief has taken an unusual course, which places the individual in what Raphael (1980) labeled "a high-risk bereavement pattern." She explains in this way: "When the emotions of grief are unduly inhibited, blocked, or suppressed, or when the normal process is blocked, partial, or absent, then the normal bereavement response may not occur" (p. 153).

Horowitz et al. (1980) term as *pathological* any severe grief intensification that results in maladaptive behavior. They describe it as such: "Pathological mourning involves processes that do not move progressively toward assimilation but, instead, lead to stereotyped repetitions or extensive interruptions of healing" (p. 1157).

Because of the many moderator variables that tend to exacerbate the grieving process, I have found that the term *complicated grief* has the greatest descriptive utility primarily because it summarizes the many social, situational, or personal variables that act to create additional problems in grief resolution. Not only do premorbid personality characteristics of the griever have an effect on bereavement outcome, but other moderator variables—either social or situational—act on bereavement as well, often creating a high-risk situation. In this light, the caregiver should give proper weight to the complication when determining treatment modalities rather than considering only personality variables and applying a stereotyping label, which has the connotation of personal pathology. This chapter examines various concepts of complicated bereavement.

What causes certain individuals to be at high risk following a significant loss? Certainly, enough research has been conducted aimed at ferreting out risk factors in bereavement to begin to identify individuals who are at special risk even before a bereavement takes place. However, the many factors implicated—such as lack of social support, illness before bereavement, poor ego strength, and so on—often interact concurrently to confound the main effect of bereavement. Too, it is in the quantity as well as the interaction of risk factors that the greatest complications in bereavement arise. The more risk factors within any given situation, the greater the complication in bereavement.

That bereavement carries with it an element of risk has been well documented (Helsing et al., 1981; Kraus & Lilienfeld, 1959; Maddison & Viola, 1968; Parkes, 1972; Stroebe et al., 1981; Young et al., 1963). Assessment of these factors and agreement among researchers and clinicians, however, does not always coincide. In order to provide the best intervention to those bereaved individuals who are potential victims of illness and death themselves, it is important to identify as many risk factors as possible that could interfere with the regeneration and renewal of the bereaved or prohibit them from continuing to live satisfying and fulfilling lives.

Erich Lindemann (1944), in his well-known study of survivors of the Coconut Grove nightclub fire in Boston, also used the concepts of delayed or distorted grief to describe what he termed as morbid grief reactions. Of the distorted version, he listed nine alterations in an individual's grief reaction that would indicate complicated grief:

1. Overactivity without a sense of loss.
2. Acquisition of symptoms belonging to the last illness of the deceased.
3. Psychosomatic conditions such as ulcerative colitis, rheumatoid arthritis, or asthma.
4. Alteration in relationship to friends and relatives.
5. Furious hostility against specific persons.
6. A wooden formal affectivity or conduct resembling schizophrenic reactions.
7. Lasting loss of patterns of social interaction.
8. Acting in unusual ways that are detrimental to social or economic existence.
9. Agitated depression with bitter self-accusation.

Lindemann feels that certain conditions, such as the loss of a child or a key person in a social system, produce complicated grief as well and do not necessarily depend on a former history of psychoneurotic reactions.

In Parkes's (1972) sample of bereaved widows, he noted that only two features—intense separation anxiety and avoidance of grief—were evident in cases of complicated bereavement. Those who suffered acute separation anxiety carried with them their preoccupation with the deceased years after the death had occurred. This chronic form of grief kept the griever agitated and grief stricken long past the time when other members of Parkes's sample had moved through a natural resolution. On the other hand, those who showed an avoidance of grief managed to delay the normal symptoms of grief for a considerable period of time and, in many cases, acted as if nothing had happened.

Parkes concludes that there are actually no particular symptoms that strikingly separate normal from pathological grief, but that (1) extreme expressions of guilt or identification symptoms and (2) delay of grief by more than 2 weeks duration could both be indicators that grief is taking a more severe course.

Horowitz and his group (1980) have outlined three patterns of pathological grief seen in bereaved patients. Those patterns were (1) a frighteningly sad response to loss, (2) out-of-control rage, and (3) a deflated or hibernative response. These responses were seen as a reemergence of latent self-images from childhood that had been held in check by the positive relationship with the deceased person. Loss of the relationship then opened the bereaved person to threats of instability and a worthless self-image that heretofore was balanced by the admiration and appreciation of the deceased. The writers conclude that the bereaved person must become able to revise unrealistic fantasies in order to be released from a pathological response.

What specific indicators can alert the caregiver either in the beginning or during treatment? Lazare (1979) has outlined 13 clues that he finds helpful in diagnosing complicated grief. He warns, however, that any one of these clues in and of itself would not necessarily be enough to determine a complicated grief reaction. It is important to look for clusters. He outlines the clues as follows:

1. A depressive syndrome of varying degrees of severity, beginning with the death.
2. A history of delayed or prolonged grief.
3. Symptoms of guilt, self-reproach, and panic attacks and somatic expressions of fear, such as choking sensations and breathing attacks.
4. Somatic symptoms representing identification with the dead person, often the symptoms of the terminal illness.
5. Physical distress under the upper half of the sternum accompanied by expressions such as "There is something stuck inside" or "I feel there is a demon inside of me."
6. Searching behavior.
7. Recurrence of depressive symptoms and searching behavior on specific dates, such as anniversaries of the death, birthdays of the deceased, and holidays, especially Christmas.
8. A feeling that the death occurred yesterday, even though the loss took place months or years ago.

9. Unwillingness to move the material possessions of the deceased.
10. Change in relationships following the death.
11. Diminished participation in religious and ritual activities.
12. The inability to discuss the deceased without crying or the voice cracking, particularly when the death occurred more than 1 year before the interview.
13. Themes of loss.

Several of the foregoing clues seen in the same individual would act as a flag to alert the caregiver to the complication in the situation and the possibility of a poor resolution.

SUICIDE

Life has become both more dear and more cheap. And if it can be taken by others it can also be thrown away by oneself. (Schneidman, 1971, p. 37)

Because of the survivor guilt that is extreme in families experiencing a suicide, this type of bereavement has been considered a most difficult one to endure (Osterweis et al., 1984). Clinical observations have indicated that suicide survivors may even experience exaggerated forms of bereavement unique to this particular form of loss (Cain & Fast, 1966; Bunch, 1972; Silverman, 1974, 1981). A study of suicide notes (Jacobs, 1967) found that often the perpetrator wrote a martyring type of note, indicating that the death was aimed at relieving or freeing the survivor.

In one study, Sheskin and Wallace (1976) examined case study data on 12 widows, each of whose spouse had committed suicide; the researchers then compared the data to 48 widows of nonsuicide deaths. It was found that the suicide widows needed more complete explanations of the death and suffered deeper guilt than did the nonsuicide widows.

Evidence is beginning to accumulate suggesting that people who experience the death of a friend or family member by suicide will likely experience a difficult, more complex grief reaction than will those in which the death was from natural causes or accidents (Allen, Calhoun, Cann, & Tedeschi, 1993; Van der Wal, 1989–1990; Calhoun, Selby, & Selby, 1982). Still, it is difficult to gather much information from suicide survivors, at least, to gather a sample large enough to be representative of the total population of those bereaved by suicide. Another difficulty lies in the absence of rated and reliable tools to measure data. Third, there is a certain discomfort by researchers to speak to survivors following a suicide because they fear that such questions would intensify or prolong the survivors' grief. However, beginning in the mid-1970s, there began a more open view about gathering research data with the result that more and better information is shedding some light on the needs of suicide survivors.

The latest research is divided into three major areas (Stillion, 1996). They are:

1. Attitudes toward survivors.
2. The experience of suicide survivors.
3. Postvention with suicide survivors.

The research carried out concerning the survivors of suicide has shown that respondents view suicide survivors more negatively than they do survivors of natural death or of accidents. In one report, respondents viewed the parents of the child portrayed as a suicide as less likeable, more blameworthy, and less psychologically healthy before the death than they viewed the parents of the same child who was portrayed as having died from illness. The same researchers repeated another bogus incident, portraying an apparent suicide and asking the respondents to describe their feelings upon hearing the story. Again, the respondents described the victim as psychologically disturbed and, in one case, portrayed the suicide survivor as one who could have done more to prevent the death.

In looking at the experience of suicide survivors, Reed and Greerwald (1991) conducted a large study of relatives of suicide and accidental death. They used questionnaires mailed to respondents approximately 9 months following the death of their relatives. Survivors of suicide deaths reported experiencing greater guilt, shame, and rejection than did survivors of accidental death. However, the researchers reported that suicide survivors reported less emotional distress and shock than did the accident survivors. A large percentage of suicide survivors disclosed that they had been given warning before the death.

Several studies have looked at grief of spouses of suicides. Saunders (1981) found that those spouses experienced greater rejection from friends as well as from the deceased mate's family. Increased health problems were found among spouses whose husbands had died from suicide or accident (Pennebaker & O'Heeron, 1984).

Although a number of studies indicate equivocal responses as to negative feedback by suicide families, a larger number of respondents report on the negative view that survivors face from a general population. People in society view survivors of suicide more negatively than they view other survivors, and even the survivors have negative views about themselves.

Postvention programs have been established by communities to help the professionals who work with suicide survivors (Shneidman, 1971). It has been found that well-planned and immediate reaction is important, especially when the potential suicide is an adolescent. Adolescents respond to what is called a cluster or copycat suicide more frequently than do older groups (Stillion & McDowell, 1996). Cluster suicides occur when a group of people living in the same geographic location commit suicide over a relatively short period of time. Both cluster and copycat suicides have been known to show a contagious effect in adolescent suicide (Carter & Brooks, 1990).

To help develop organized programs, Wenckstern and Leenaars (1991) posited eight principles of positive postvention:

1. Begin as soon as possible after the tragedy.
2. Expect resistance from some, but not all, survivors.
3. Be willing to explore negative emotions toward the victim when the time is right.
4. Provide ongoing reality testing for the survivors.
5. Be ready to refer when necessary.
6. Avoid clichés and banal optimism.
7. Be prepared to spend significant amounts of time (generally several months) in one school.
8. Develop the postvention program within a comprehensive health care setting that also includes prevention and intervention.

Although these principles were devised for school personnel, they would be applicable to community-based programs as well.

There are four categories of causal factors in suicidal behavior: biological, psychological, cognitive, and environmental. These roots contribute to the major areas of risk factors associated with suicidal ideation in human behavior.

BIOLOGIC RISK FACTORS

Suicidal behavior is closely aligned with depression. The research to study this approach has centered around brain function, genetic causes, and gender basis. Looking at risk factors associated with biologic functioning, studies have shown that depression is related to one neurotransmitter, serotonin, known to regulate emotion. Some researchers have suggested that a deficiency in serotonin could be implicated in depression and suicide attempts.

Genetic causes have held intriguing possibilities in attempts to correlate family history and suicide. One study on family history and genetics relating to suicide concluded that the incidence of suicide behavior is higher than in the general population. Another study reviewed 10 cases of identical twins that had committed suicide, and a third showed that half of the samples were psychiatric inpatients (Stillion, McDowell, & May, 1989).

Gender-based research has shown that in all developed countries, males complete suicide at higher rates than do females. A possible reason for this finding lies in the aggressive behavior of males, which has been highly correlated with suicidal behavior. More than three male deaths by suicide occur for every one female death by suicide.

Psychological factors contributing to suicidal ideation are depression, feelings of hopelessness and helplessness, low self-esteem, and poor coping behaviors. Studies have shown that of these factors, hopelessness could best predict the level of lethality of a suicide attempt (Wetzel, R., 1976; Goldney, R., 1981). The lack of healthy coping skills, along with the use of alcohol and drugs, is frequently seen in suicidal individuals.

Not all researchers see suicide survivors as being in high risk during bereavement. Shepherd and Barraclough (1974) felt that the outcome of bereavement was equally divided between "better off" and "worse off." Yet Stroebe and Stroebe (1987) questioned the validity of these findings because of the 44 spouses interviewed, 10 had died during bereavement. Although the sample size is small, the researchers pointed out, the number of deaths is excessive, indicating a significant risk for the suicide survivors.

FACTORS COMPLICATING GRIEF AFTER SUICIDE

1. The bereaved survivor must struggle with feelings of abandonment, humility, personal diminishment, and desertion.
2. Anger, guilt, and shame—strong feelings of betrayal—crescendo into rage, leaving the bereaved without a focus or target for emotional venting. Genuine sorrow is brushed aside to make space for the torturous self-blame. The bereaved feels a need to be punished in some way for the part he or she played in the suicide. A sense of personal rejection comes from the fact that the deceased chose to die, to give up life.
3. The bereaved searches endlessly to find a rational reason for such an impossible act. The unfinished business with the deceased remains just that, with no logical solution to the constant question of why.
4. Social stigmatization produces deeper and more complicating factors of social isolation. In a study done to compare the bereavement of suicide survivors with those whose loved one died of other causes,

Range and Calhoun (1990) showed that less community support was given to the suicide survivors than to other bereaved individuals.

The stigma of suicide puts a social strain on survivors. Investigations into the death are difficult. Publicity is demoralizing, and family interactions are divided. The lack of social support leaves the family feeling isolated and ashamed. The lack of systematic research attests to the fact that this type of bereavement represents a personal disaster that most people would prefer not to encounter. Yet given the meager data available, suicide survivors may represent a group that has an extremely high risk of illness and death.

HOMICIDE

The family was traveling in Europe for a summer vacation, stopping each night or two in small bed-and-breakfast facilities. In retelling the horrible trauma they experienced in one of the hotels, the parents become confused as to what night the murder actually occurred. The family dined together in a restaurant near their hotel that evening after walking around the little town and then decided to retire early. The two boys, 8 and 11, shared a room next door to the parents while the 15-year-old daughter had her own room on another floor. The parents didn't find her until the next morning when she wasn't at breakfast. After receiving no answer to their knocks at the door, they got the hotel manager to open the room. What they found was unimaginable. Their beautiful daughter dead, pierced with endless stab wounds—no sign of the murderer, no sign of a motive, no solution ever to this heinous crime. The family eventually was forced to leave the country and return to the United States without a resolution or answer of any kind.

Needless to say, this family was beyond devastation and suffered seemingly unending torture. A comprehensive study of the clinical and empirical literature related to the reactions of family survivors of homicide victims determined that this grief differs from the grief of other bereavements in the depth of horror, rage, and vengefulness. Lula Redmond (1996) writes about homicide, "There is no preparation for this sudden onslaught. There is no comprehension that death could come so swiftly, and in a violent, degrading, brutal means at the hands of another human being" (p. 54).

One of the main characteristics experienced by survivors is a state of cognitive dissonance. The death doesn't make sense. Nothing prepares a person for the psychological senselessness of such brutality. The mind is overloaded with a whirlwind of thoughts as the senses struggle, searching for something that would make sense. Cognitive dissonance may continue for months or years, creating delayed grief reactions that are interminable.

A second very difficult emotional reaction to contend with is the homicide survivor's intense anger and rage. Anger is a normal grief reaction, but for the homicide survivor, the rage intensifies to the level of wanting to violently destroy the murderers. Elaborate plans of torturous heinage are devised, usually more horrendous than what the deceased suffered. Knowing that these murderous fantasies are normal doesn't quiet the deep-seated rage that the bereaved is suffering. The bereaved feels that he or she is going crazy and struggles with the internal conflict caused by his or her own values, beliefs, and sense of justice. However, in venting and verbalizing the murderous impulses, the anger, rage, and desire for violence lose their intensity and power. The renewed sense of control can help the bereaved ease the murderous impulses. The most profound sense of power can be fueled by the energy of directed anger (Redmond, 1996, p. 56).

When a loved one has been murdered, the value placed on the belief that good people do not commit harm to one another is violated. The powerlessness creates a sick feeling of frustration that robs the bereaved of hope for any understanding of the world. The homicide becomes a personal violation of each survivor's values and belief system.

Finding someone to blame for this tragedy absorbs much emotional time as the bereaved attempts to gain a modicum of control over a senseless act. This blame can be shifted back and forth from oneself to others. Family members may accept unrealistic responsibilities or perhaps extend them. Communication among family members may become stilted as each member withdraws from the others in an attempt to either protect or to place blame on someone (anyone) else.

It has been estimated that 1 out of every 133 to 153 persons will die from homicide. This number is growing rapidly. The very thought of murder terrifies most people, even though a larger percentage of people are killed in traffic accidents.

Michalowski (1976), in writing of the social meanings of violent death, discusses the different responses to various forms of violent death. He writes, "It is the manner of dying, and not the death itself, that determines the social meaning of any death" (p. 83). He lists five distinct areas that make this form of violent death more salient than any other:

1. *Inevitability.* Homicide is not considered an accident. Traffic fatalities result from circumstances beyond human control, which is not true of homicides.
2. *Controllability.* Homicide is perceived as controllable in that it arises from the willful acts of individuals.

3. *Intent.* Homicide by definition involves intent.
4. *Deviance.* Homicide is illegal and considered abnormal, whereas a traffic fatality is perceived as less of a social problem.
5. *Social Utility.* Homicide provides no social utility; society will tolerate traffic deaths because the automobile does provide social utility. Death by homicide so sickens our society that, even though most deaths are by other means, homicide assumes prominence in our social world.

Grief following the murder of a loved one is long, extremely painful, and seemingly endless. The bereavement has been seen to be exaggerated, delayed, and filled with rage, shame, guilt, and emotional withdrawal. Bereavement following homicide has been likened to a form of post-traumatic stress disorder (PTSD) (Redmond, 1989; Rynearsom, 1978). Because the symptoms are so varied, emotions so intense, and chronology so elongated, the grieving person suffers through an endless nightmare of pain.

After working with numerous families surviving the homicide death of a family member, Lula Redmond (1996) discusses the confluence of bereavement and post-traumatic stress:

Homicide survivors may present symptomatic behaviors characteristic of PTSD up to five years following the murder of a loved one. This becomes a normal range of functioning for this distinct population. All homicide survivors with whom I have worked were assessed at intake with some characteristics of PTSD. Survivors present with a history of nightmares, flashbacks, fear of strangers, emotional withdrawal, eating and sleeping disturbances, constant intrusion of thoughts of the murder, case-related associations, irritability, angry outbursts, and avoidance of reminders. (p. 52)

Stigmatization follows the bereaved because they must deal with the public side of homicide. The family is avoided as if, by the avoidance, outsiders are protected from such a horrible event ever happening to them. There is a strange belief in our culture that the victim somehow was to blame. This protective shield is set up by others to somehow remove themselves from this tragedy. Families of victims must suffer the isolation and finger-pointing. The community seems to establish this isolation in order to assuage their own vulnerability. This response comforts people into believing that their own family is protected from such a horrible tragedy. This rationale perpetuates emotional distance and exclusion and leaves the survivors alone in their sorrow.

Feeling isolated by the community is only the beginning of the grief brought on by the stigmatization of homicide. Other systems are operating to discover the truth behind the crime. Law enforcement officers may be gentle and sensitive in their approach but the news they must impart to the survivors is heartbreaking. There is no gentle way those words can be spoken. The griever, in shock, confused, and shattered by the incongruency, strives to make sense out of the impossible truth. The trial itself not only puts the family through long hours of torturous testimony, but also forces them to confront the suspect in court. In spite of the horror of the trial, survivors should attend and actively participate in every phase of the criminal justice proceedings. Such participation appears to alleviate the conflicts of the tragedy.

Homicide survivors lose control of their lives; they feel that a part of themselves has been violated, leaving them powerless to do anything about it. As Redmond (1996) states,

> When a crime occurs, the victim survivor becomes frustrated and powerless and control of one's person, property or possessions is lost. A criminal takes command of the very personal and private right to control one's own life, possessions and lives of those whom one loves. (p. 69)

The therapist counselor must help the survivors build a bridge back to the living, must reconnect families and communities, must erase the stigmatization and replace it with security.

AIDS-RELATED DEATH

It has been known as the "Great Disenfranchiser" (Doka, 1989). AIDS is the plague of this century; it leaves death and grief strewn in its wake. Approximately 1 million people contracted human immunodeficiency virus (HIV) between April 1991 and January 1992, the greatest percentage of them through heterosexual intercourse. The total number infected worldwide is currently reaching 10 to 12 million persons; by the year 2000, 30 to 40 million individuals will have contracted the infection. These statistics make AIDS and HIV-related disease one of the leading causes of death in North America, Western Europe, and Southern Asia (Batchelor, 1984).

The nature of AIDS, together with its psychosocial meaning, puts both the patient and the survivors in a marginal place in society. The bereaved are isolated from others by the dreadfulness of the illness, which creates a typical case of disenfranchisement. The perceived communicability, the social stigma, and the general attitude of fault or blame brought about by society and loved ones leaves the AIDS patient suffering alone, with few supports (Klein & Fletcher, 1986).

AIDS survivors seem more likely to struggle with unresolved grief. Parents of AIDS victims might be at greater risk for developing the symptoms of complicated grief. Many people grieving the death of a loved one who died from AIDS may be automatically disenfranchised.

The following suggests five of the more likely issues that have been observed as powerful manifestations of this grief (Rosen, 1989).

1. Social stigma surrounds the disease. Many families are cut off from social supports as a consequence of either the family's self-imposed retreat and desire to remain private or the distancing imposed by relatives unwilling to have contact with the family.

2. The lack of social sanctions can have a strong effect, especially for homosexual relationships, by automatically disenfranchising the bereaved. Inadvertently, the deceased may have set up a difficult situation by invalidating the commonly accepted rights of survivorship.

3. Survivors suffer fear about their own health status. This fear represents a legitimate concern for the survivors who have had sexual contact with the deceased. Yet this fear of contamination has also been seen in survivors who have no reason to believe that they have been contaminated.

4. Families experience a need for secrecy together with shame and guilt. Secrecy almost always leads to feelings of guilt and to the inner turmoil of shame. By this behavior, families are creating a position for themselves that leaves them isolated and disenfranchised in their personal sorrow.

5. Conflicts exist within the surviving family. Families of AIDS victims cause themselves much sorrow, especially parents who feel a need to maintain secrecy about their son's homosexual relationship. The fact that the AIDS victim is often young and looking forward to life points to the unfairness of the disease. And the fact that the disease is often preventable escalates grief for the parents. The concurrent crises of the death itself and recognition of lifestyle differences can produce a form of bereavement overload (Kastenbaum, 1969).

Differences between parents were noted in a study done by Burnell and Burnell (1989) that saw mothers as overprotective, attentive, and forgiving. They readily offer their love and support. Fathers, on the other hand, showed great difficulty in overcoming the shame and stigma of the disease. Some fathers found it hard to even speak to their sons. As opposed to mothers, fathers found it difficult to forgive the hurt and rejection experienced because of the stigma of the disease.

Further conflicts arise when the patient's biologic family and chosen family interact with negative results. Frequently, the lifestyles of the two families are in disagreement, with the chosen family presenting a different approach to habitation. The two families may argue about funerary rituals or about who has the right to care for the deceased both before and after his death. The family might suffer a double loss, that of their physical son and that of the ideal son the parents had dreamed about. Resolving this conflict may take years, if indeed it ever is resolved.

Lloyd was a buyer at a large department store when he developed AIDS and suffered many complications (dementia, blindness) during a long period of illnesses. His family lived in a small western town in which his father was a Protestant minister. When Lloyd became sick enough to require hospice care, he went home to live with his family, fully expecting his longtime partner, Terry, to be there with him. Unfortunately, Terry was no longer recognized or accepted by the family. He was asked to leave the family's home, and Lloyd died there without further contact with his partner and good friend. At the funeral, Terry was neither recognized nor acknowledged by any member of Lloyd's family. Needless to say, Terry's grief, without any support, was prolonged and extremely difficult.

A significant issue for the homosexual community is multiple loss, or bereavement overload (Kastenbaum, 1969). This phenomenon constitutes a high risk factor for complicated bereavement patterns (Biller & Rice, 1990). The large number of actual and projected deaths brought on by the AIDS epidemic continues to grow as grief continues to present deeper and varying problems.

Several important studies have been undertaken to explore the grieving process of gay men who have lost loved ones to AIDS. A sizeable number of these studies have been qualitative in nature, examining the effect of AIDS-related multiple losses and attempting to identify processes, coping strategies, and affective behavior (Biller & Rice, 1990; Carmack, 1992; Martin, 1988; Sherr, Hedge, Steinhart, Davey, & Petrack, 1992; Viney, Henry, Walker, & Crooks, 1992). Martin found a positive relationship between the number of losses due to AIDS and symptoms of psychological distress. Neugehauer et al. (1992), using quantitative methods of data collection and analysis, examined the relationship between the actual number of losses and the intensity of the loss and examined the existing relationship between the social and demographic variables of the response to grief.

Jerry died of AIDS complications while on and off a respirator at a large hospital in Seattle. He experienced all the complications of AIDS because his illness occurred prior to today's protease inhibitor therapy. He had lived with his partner, George, for more than two years. During their relationship, the primary caregiver burden fell on George's shoulders. When Jerry was nearing the end of his life, many of his friends whom George had never met or seen before began to "come out of the woodwork" to offer assistance to George. At this point, George was so emotionally overwrought that he began to experience paranoia and felt that the friends were interfering and wanting to wrestle control from him concerning Jerry's care. George became abusive and indignant toward the friends, and little by little, they withdrew their support, leaving only one person to provide any help. During the course of Jerry's illness, George had no family help and only that minimal support of friends. As a result, no one assisted the couple in the last days of Jerry's illness. After some time, George did receive help from a hospice bereavement aftercare program, but not before he had suffered alone and with deep feelings of guilt and shame.

A total of 93 gay men who were either HIV negative or whose status was not known participated in the Grief Experience Inventory. The mean number of losses reported was 19.1. The largest number reported was 200. The Grief Experience Inventory (GEI) was chosen to measure the multidimensional components of the grief experience. The GEI consists of 135 true/false statements found to be frequently associated with grief and bereavements. Social support showed itself to be a critical factor in facilitating the bereavement process. Comparison revealed than those men with excellent support had significantly less anger than those with only some support. Men who were unemployed scored significantly higher on the anger/hostility and somatization subscales than did employed men.

Having a committed partner contributed heavily to the bereavement process; those subjects who were not in a committed relationship were subject to increased levels of despair and feelings of social isolation. The researchers wondered whether social isolation and high levels of despair in these individuals interfered in the development of an intimate and committed relationship or if bereavement responses were more intense because these individuals did not have the support of a committed relationship. The significant difference found between levels of support in four of the five subscales lends evidence to the importance of such support. The findings of this study show social support to be a critical factor in successful facilitation of the bereavement process (Lazare, 1979; Sanders, 1989; Zisook & Devaul, 1983). This study showed that the correlation between the high number of losses and intensity of grief was not significant. The researchers found it difficult to explain the lack of significance when, in other studies, the psychological distress afforded by multiple losses had been high (Martin, 1988; Martin & Dean, 1993).

As a possible explanation for the lack of significant findings in studying multiple losses, the researchers posited a theory of delayed or unresolved grief. Various forms of prolonged, absent, or delayed grief have been described in the literature and explained as occurring as a result of being stuck, unable to move through the grief process (Lindemann, 1944; Martocchio, 1985; Zisook & Devaul, 1983).

The researchers used Sanders's (1989) Integrative Theory of Grief as a means of conceptualizing the impact of multiple losses. It appears likely that multiple losses causing a prolonged grief reaction could establish a threshold of intensity of grief or an adaptive response. The individuals who suffered one loss after another found it nearly impossible to pull back and conserve the energy necessary to continue in the next two phases of grief, in which healing might occur.

Rosen (1989) has written compellingly about the movement of the AIDS patients and their families toward powerful feelings of spirituality. He states that this movement is not necessarily toward a single religious connection but toward one that is more ecumenical in nature, a more universal spirituality that includes broad elements of a variety of religious faiths. Rosen goes on to explain that it is not unusual for people in terminal stages of any illness to seek a closeness with their God, but in AIDS patients, the feelings seem more intense. Rosen describes a therapy session of persons with AIDS during which a conversation took place regarding their closeness to God, his unquestioning love for them, and the certainty of a better place after their death. Rosen added that the patients seemed to be speaking of a "kind of syncretism" (p. 308) that was, in its richest essence, the warming and most loving aspects of all religions. This conversation contained no declaration of any particular moral or ethical teachings.

In speculating on this event, Rosen likened it to the need for a life review process in which patients have the opportunity to go over their past moral behavior. Because many AIDS victims have dealt with disenfranchisement on several levels, they may have found it redeeming to experience spirituality as a way to find the love and acceptance denied them in their lives.

Although a great deal of the current research focuses on male homosexuals and AIDS, it is important to remember that AIDS is affecting every race, ethnicity, social stratum, occupation, and religious connection as well as every age and sexual orientation. People can contract the disease through a variety of means: homosexual and heterosexual activity, intravenous drug use, contaminated blood transfusion, accidental needle-stick, and prenatal infection.

PART FIVE

TYPES OF BEREAVEMENT

CHAPTER 14

The Death of a Child

The winds howl at night. I think of last winter. I will never accept it—cannot accept it—not like Daddy—which I knew would happen sometime. It is not a normal sorrow. Back of it is always "It need not have happened." And that is a torture. I suppose I can only swallow it whole. It will not be absorbed but will always be there, and always hurting, like something in your eyes. Nature does not absorb it but gradually provides a protective covering which numbs the sharp pain, but you are always conscious of it.

Anne Morrow Lindbergh (1973)

THE DEATH OF a child is an unbearable sorrow. For parents, the wound cuts deeply, ulcerates, and festers. Scar tissue is slow to form. For some, it never heals. Our society is not prepared to lose its offspring and rages at the unspeakable deprivation and misery caused by an untimely death.

Child death is now so rare in major sections of our populations, in contrast to previous times or other countries, that it is totally unexpected and consequently even more overwhelming a shock to the parents. Gorer (1965) was among the first to suggest that possibly the most distressing and long-lasting grief for most people is that of the loss of a grown child. Since that time, other researchers and writers have supported his position and even broadened it to include children of all ages (Clayton et al., 1968; Fish & Whitty, 1983; Levav, 1982; Osterweis et al., 1984; Rando, 1983; Sanders, 1979–1980; Singh & Raphael, 1981). The parents tend to define such a death as being against the very nature of things (Vernon, 1970).

FACTORS AFFECTING PARENTAL BEREAVEMENT

The Parent-Child Bond

When children are born, they are looked on as a way to personal fulfillment for the parents. No relationship in life is more important than the attachment between parent and child. The connection is more than one of
blood; there are deep emotional ties as well that bind the parents to the
child throughout life. The child represents a love object, which tends to
offer a unifying effect for the parents themselves, making them feel a part
of each other through their child. A child is a statement of a rite of passage
for the parents, a coming of age, as well as a source of power and adult autonomy. Perhaps of greatest importance is the fact that the bond between
parents and child is a fulfillment of deep-seated needs representing a serious narcissistic involvement for each parent (Furman, 1974). This explanation is similar to what Bowlby (1980) describes in his theory of attachment
behavior.

Besides the special bonding between parent and child, a child provides
psychic energy, which is the very fabric of the family formation. Family
unity is dependent on the child, who plays an important part in the developmental growth of the family. In an early study, Orbach (1959) uses a single case to explicate the multiple problems encountered in the family following the death of a child. He notes that the loss frequently reactivates
earlier disappointments or losses in the parents' lives, which affect the relationship to each other as well as to other key people. In the case reported,
the mother had attempted to maintain her relationship with her dead son
even after 5 years had passed. A continued denial of loss and an idealization of the boy impaired her relationships with others, including her husband, leaving her unable to resolve her grief.

Orbach did not present this case as typical, but he suggested that it underscores the importance of recognizing that grief can and does reactivate
earlier object losses. He, as well as others (Bozeman, Orbach, & Sutherland,
1955; Richmond & Waisman, 1955; Solnik & Green, 1959), noted that significant losses such as that of a child require reorientation as well as a familial
reorganization in order to further a positive bereavement resolution.
Orbach (1959) concluded,

> The work of mourning in the lives of some persons . . . not only involves the
> resolution of current attachments, but also a coming to terms with the reacti-
> vation of past losses which have been repaired in the current relationship. In
> addition, new adaptive techniques must be evolved to replace dependency
> upon the resources of the lost object. (p. 915)

The parent-child bond is one of multiple meanings that not only takes into account the parents' projections concerning the child, but the parents' identity as well. When the child dies, the parents feel the loss as if they themselves had also died.

IDENTIFICATION

Because children are physically of their parents' own flesh and blood, parents can see themselves in their child: their eyes, bodily contours, hair, gender. Even in cases of stepchildren or adoption, the mannerisms of the parent seen in the child are viewed as coming from the parent. The childhood years become a reliving of the parent's own childhood. As the child develops and grows, so does the narcissistic involvement of the parent. The child, in many ways, becomes the alter ego of the parent, and the parent tends to project her- or himself onto the child. Dependency, therefore, is a two-way street.

When a child dies, the parents grieve not only for the deprivation of being without their child but also for the lost aspects of themselves as well (Benedek, 1970; Furman, 1976). They now must learn to survive with only a part of themselves remaining, like learning to walk with one leg amputated. As such, the death of a child can be thought of as an invisible phantom limb agony. The parents are physically intact but emotionally fragmented, their sense of selves badly mutilated (Rando, 1984; Schwartz, 1977). Yet this is a loss with no prosthesis (Fish, 1986).

Identification is so personally experienced that parents often report actually either feeling the impact that killed their child or suffering the pain that accompanied the fatal illness. Identification continues to be experienced in psychological ways after the death, such as when parents either try to complete certain tasks that were started by their child or continue hobbies or interests of the child. This activity is helpful to the extent that it temporarily gives the parents a sense of purpose or meaning. However, it can act as a deterrent to grief resolution if it is carried on too long or too intently, for not only does it *not* facilitate the process of decathexis (letting go), but it can also direct attention away from other children in the family who need parental support.

IMMORTALITY

Children provide a future for the parents. Besides the hopes, dreams, and expectations that are developed with each child's birth, the future is also carried forth by the genes that protect the lineage of the family. One father in the Tampa study talked of his own feelings after his 6-year-old daughter had accidentally drowned in a neighbor's swimming pool:

> It's like leaving a piece of yourself behind or something. Like the only thing—People don't make their mark on the world, right? Not everybody becomes famous, not everybody has a book or something that people will read after they're gone. But children are a surefire way of leaving a piece of yourself behind. I won't have that now.

When a child dies, parents feel that their immortality has been tampered with, their future interrupted or stolen.

CHILDREN AS SOCIAL AGENTS

Not only is the child a physical part of the parents, but also the parents' social world is often arranged by the interaction with other parents or adults who come into contact with their child. Children are like personal emissaries when a family moves to a new community, putting parents in touch with other children and adults. As such, the child becomes a focal point for family planning and a major source of security and happiness for the parents.

When the child dies, the parents lose the connection between that child and the world. One mother told me that a year after the death of their only child, her husband was transferred to another city. They had an extremely difficult time making new friends or even wanting to. Neither of them had realized how they had relied on their daughter and her activities for their social involvement.

THE CHILD'S AGE

The age of the child does not seem to be a factor in determining parental grief reactions (Sanders, 1979–1980; Schiff, 1977). For the parents, the death will always be untimely (Raphael, 1984). Schatz (1986) reported on the tendency for bereaved mothers to think that no matter at what age the child died, it was a special age. Because this age was special for these mothers, it was a terrible time for their child to die, whether the child was an infant, preadolescent, teenager, or adult. In the Tampa study, whether the child was 6 days or 49 years old, the parents were devastated and inconsolable. The child represented life in so many ways. With the death, the forward projection of their lives ceased and the parents were forced to redesign their present circumstances to fit the ruins that were left.

PARENTAL RESPONSES TO BEREAVEMENT

DESPAIR

The bereaved parents in the Tampa study gave the appearance of individuals who had suffered a physical blow that left them with no strength or will to fight, hence they were totally vulnerable. *Despair* is the term that describes them most appropriately. Whether the death was caused by illness or accident made little difference in their response. The impossibility of surviving their child remained foremost in their thoughts. "Why?" was an obsessive rumination. Several spoke of moving through an unreal world—of life not making sense. Theirs was a raw, visible pain. In a well thought-out study in which 45 parents whose children died 6 months to 4 years earlier were assessed using the Grief Experience Inventory (GEI). It was found that parents of boys or children who died suddenly suffered more despair, anger, guilt and despair than did other parents (Hazzard, A., Weston, J., and Gutterres, C., 1992).

CONFUSION AND CONFLICT

Confusion in the early stages of grief is one of the most obvious reactions. When a child dies, confusion becomes extremely pronounced. The inability to concentrate has been described by many writers as one of the major symptoms of confusion (Rando, 1986b; Sanders, 1986; Schiff, 1977). The mind reels with a jumble of unintelligible thoughts, unable to take in the horrible tragedy. The usual modes of escaping reality, such as reading or watching television, are denied parents. Parents experience an intent alertness about anything concerning the lost child, but a complete disinterest in everything else. The amount of confusion experienced by the Tampa bereaved parents was exemplified in the problems they had making decisions.

One bereaved mother expressed these feelings after her newborn baby had died in the hospital hours after birth. She had gone directly from the hospital to her mother's house for a week or so to recuperate from the difficult delivery:

> I found that making decisions was for me extremely difficult. Normally, decisions are very simple and easy to do, something I don't think about. But now a decision of what to do tomorrow even was a trauma. And they would explain it to me how this is very common, and they said that you do one thing at a time and then you build up to your normal activity. But we were going to come back to our house, so I said, "Okay, let's go back on Thursday." Well, it was such a trauma for me to actually try and plan how I am going to pack up

my clothes, how I am going to put things in the bathroom in a box to get them back. I mean, these are normal things that wouldn't bother anybody, but for me it was just too hard. It was like the most difficult thing that I had ever tackled in my life. I couldn't.

So I finally got myself worked up to such a tizzy over just moving, I said to my husband, "I can't do it." So we took another 10 days, and then it was better.

Another bereaved mother, whose son died at age 49, expressed the same difficulty in decision making:

Well, I want to do this, then I'd get a notion, well, I think I'll bake a cake, and then, like I don't want to bake a cake. Then again I will. I can't make up my mind about anything. I think that's how I can do this [weeding the garden] because I know that I can stick my head down there and keep going.

The constant preoccupation with the lost child makes concentrating on anything impossible. Habitual tasks require immense effort. Simply starting the day for some can require too much effort, partly because trying to decide what to do is too exhausting. One mother told me that often she would try to get up and make breakfast for the family, realize she could not even decide what to prepare, and go back to bed in utter despair.

GUILT

For bereaved parents, the feelings of guilt run high (Fish, 1986; Friedman, 1974; McCollum, 1974; Miles, 1979). In our culture parents feel responsible for their children's welfare even before birth. Conception carries certain aspects of accountability with it. From that moment on, parents begin planning for their child, wondering what he will be like, what she will be when she grows up, who he will marry, how it will feel to be a grandparent. Their thinking is taken up in large part with forward projections and how they, as parents, will be facilitators of their child's future. If the child dies, whether by accident or illness, parents feel responsible (Miles & Demi, 1983–1984; Rando, 1984). Implicit in this guilt is the thought that if they had been doing their duty, had been more on guard, the death would never have happened. Granted, these feelings are irrational. However, they do explain the "if only" ruminations of bereaved parents: if only I had come home a few minutes earlier, if only I had refused him the car, if only I had taken her for a checkup when she complained of a headache, if only I had not waited so long to get help, if only . . . if only. . . . These circulating broodings are obsessive, leaving parents with only an empty "Why?"

In a well-thought-out model of parental bereavement guilt, Margaret

Miles and Alice Demi (1986) see guilt as arising from parents' deep sense of helplessness in not being able to prevent the death. Based on a significant study involving 63 parents whose child had died by accident or chronic illness death, these researchers outlined the following sources of guilt:

- *Death causation guilt.* When the parent believes that he or she either influenced the cause of death or failed to give adequate protection to the child.
- *Illness-related guilt.* Parental feelings that the parent did not give adequate care to the child either during the illness or at the time of death.
- *Parental role guilt.* Parental feelings that the parent did not meet societal or self-imposed expectations.
- *Moral guilt.* Parental feelings of being punished in some way for past transgressions of moral, ethical, or religious mores or practices.
- *Survival guilt.* Parental belief that it goes against the nature of things to survive one's child.
- *Grief guilt.* Parental belief that the parents did not behave in a proper and fitting way either at the time of death or during the bereavement process (e.g., did not behave in a way that society expected them to behave).

Parents often feel guilty that they did not say "I love you" often enough. One mother, whose 21-year-old son had been mysteriously killed in a boating accident, felt that she was at fault for not telling him this more often.

> I was discussing this with my daughter about 2 weeks ago. I had gone over to see her on the weekend and I had told her that I was so sorry that I didn't tell Bob that I loved him and she said, "Oh Mom, you didn't have to tell him that. He knew how much you loved him. You showed it to him all the time." And I said I felt that I should have at least said it.

She agonized over this omission for a long time until she could begin to forgive herself. It was as if this mode of thinking kept her from focusing on the tragic aspects of his death.

ANGER

Anger has been among the severest reactions of bereaved parents. Anger is understandable when one considers the amount of helplessness generated by losing a beloved child. Because parents are responsible for their children and have acted as problem solvers and caregivers, when a child dies, parents are left with a sense of powerlessness. There is nothing they can do to solve this problem. No matter what they do, they cannot bring their child back. This senseless frustration, this awful deprivation, leaves them with an intolerable rage but little on which to focus that rage.

In the Tampa study, anger was significantly higher for the bereaved group as compared to the controls. Other studies of parental bereavement have found similar results. Fish (1986) noted that mothers sustained greater anger than did fathers after 2 years, but mothers were seemingly unaware of their anger. On the other hand, Rando (1983) found that fathers appeared to be overtly more angry than their spouses. She also noted that as the length of their child's illness increased, so did the parents' anger. She suggested that as the illness progresses, disturbance in the parents grows stronger.

Anger pervaded many of the bereaved parents' thoughts as they dwelled on the injustice of surviving an untimely death. Many parents felt that more could have been done by the doctor, the hospital staff, the rescue team, anyone who was involved in the events surrounding the death. One mother whose son had died of internal injuries during a hospital stay thought that he might have fallen out of bed and that the hospital staff was covering it up. Another father was justifiably angry because his son's murderer had not been apprehended. He felt that because he had little clout, he was getting the runaround from the police force. He despaired that the murderer would never be caught and ruminated on this thought constantly. His wife had mixed feelings about convicting anyone. Although she felt that for society's sake, the murderer should be put away, she was not sure that she really wanted to know who did it—that the vindication would not bring back her son. The helplessness brought about by losing their child in such a senseless and violent manner was overwhelming.

From the Tampa study, six sources of anger have been recognized as acting to cause major despair and frustration in bereaved parents. These sources of anger, described in detail in Chapter 5, are confrontive anger, displaced anger, ambivalent anger, internalized anger, helpless anger, and appropriate anger.

Anger, like guilt, is best dealt with by verbalization. Professionals need to take a noncritical approach to accusations and outpourings of angry parents. Anger can be a facilitative emotional expression that, when encouraged in a positive and nonjudgmental manner, can help the bereaved parent actively move through the emotional phase of grief without dire consequences.

A source of anger for some in the Tampa study was the way in which they were told of their child's death by health care personnel. Understandably, this task must be a difficult one for any caregiver. In one case, the parents were called to the hospital after their 18-year-old son had been killed in a car accident. The mother described it this way:

But, see, they called us at 6:30 in the morning. I answered the phone and they asked was I his mother. They said they would like us to come down to Tampa General Hospital. There had been an accident. And I said, "Is he hurt bad, is he all right?" And she hesitated for at least 20 seconds and said, "Ah, you just better come down." So we got ready right away and went."

On our way down, we turned on the radio to [hear the] news, and they announced the news from the Thanksgiving weekend—how many were killed, 29, or something like that—and said however, a few minutes after midnight a young man had been killed on Toben Road. And I said to my husband, "Don't break any speed laws, he's gone." I knew it was him then.

They didn't tell us when we came in; we sat there for over an hour. Nobody came in, and finally my husband went out and asked if they couldn't please tell us something. They said the doctor is busy right now and he will be with you in a few minutes. And then I kind of got hope. I thought, well maybe it wasn't Bobby. Finally, this doctor came in and he said, "I didn't see your son. The doctor that saw him has left. But," he said, "he is dead," like that. But if I hadn't heard that on the radio that he was killed instantly.

This couple was bitter about the way they were told and felt that some kinder disclosure could have been offered in order to help them better process the tragic news.

The parents in the Tampa study seemed to follow a general pattern of attempting, for months after the death, to explain an apparent mystery that surrounded the circumstances of the death and that troubled them greatly —they sought some missing explanation that was needed to put the event in perspective. Two cases involved possible suicide, and one involved an unsolved murder. But even in cases in which the child died in a hospital of a chronic disease, parents had a need to have every minute accounted for, every detail explained. Many of the problems bereaved parents have following their child's death are caused by their being underinformed of the events surrounding the death or illness. There is a distinct need for health care providers to include parents and families in a postdeath conference that would provide more details. Even when no new evidence or information is available, it is often helpful for the parents to hear the details again from an authoritative source.

SOMATIC PROBLEMS

The large number of somatic problems among bereaved parents is an indication that survivors of the death of a child are undergoing a high degree of stress (Fish & Whitty, 1983; Rando, 1983; Sanders, 1979–1980). Investigators in the field of stress research have reported some of the adaptational techniques and coping strategies of parents of fatally ill children (Chodoff, Friedman, & Hamburg, 1964). Observed over a 2-year period, three coping mechanisms emerged that seemed to be pervasive with all parents in the study:

1. Isolation of affect toward the child's illness, as if they were dealing with the tragedy of another's family.
2. Denial that enabled many of the parents to maintain a certain degree of hope, overemphasizing favorable and minimizing unfavorable developments.
3. Motor activities used as defense mechanisms, such as long walks, sewing, or knitting, in an attempt to combat anxiety and to forget about their position.

Anticipatory mourning, first described by Lindemann (1944) as the gradual detachment of emotional investment, resulted in a muting of grief reactions among these parents. This action helped with the adoption of an attitude of philosophical resignation when death came.

Reporting also on the anticipatory grief of parents awaiting the death of their children, another group of researchers examined the corticosteroid excretion of the parents (Wolff, Friedman, Hofer, & Mason, 1964). During periods when the parents successfully defended themselves against acceptance of the precipitating loss, corticosteroid excretion was relatively low and stable. However, when grief was experienced, corticosteroid excretion was elevated. Apparently, this reaction is not just a function of increased activity, because when the mode of defense had involved a distracting agitation, a low corticosteroid excretion was still maintained. Yet when the child was close to death and the agitation was replaced by a quiet grief, corticosteroid excretion rose. The researchers pointed out that a high corticosteroid excretion correlates negatively with a strong immune system.

Bereaved parents should be encouraged to consult their physicians for a checkup. Other researchers support this view. It is their feeling that the caregiver has a responsibility not only to the dying child but to the entire family unit as well. It appears that the death of a child results in loss of emotional control, which exposes those survivors to greater vulnerability of external pathogens. This fact alone could explain the deep feelings of despair and alienation expressed by parents in the Tampa study whose child has died.

Marital Problems

It has been estimated that 75% to 90% of all married couples have serious problems following the death of a child (Schiff, 1977; Simpson, 1979). Although the death is their common pain, spouses have a difficult time helping each other, especially if communication is poor before the death (Binger, Ablin, Feurerstein, Kushner, Zager, & Mikkelsen, 1969; Miles & Crandell, 1983). For the most part, husbands seem to deal with their grief in a non-verbal manner, keeping their feelings to themselves, while wives want to talk about both the child and the death. Fish (1986) finds significant differences between spouses in his study, noting that they were out-of-sync (i.e., not synchronized) with each other much of the time, and neither was able to minister to the other.

RESPONSES OF EACH FAMILY MEMBER

GRIEF OF FATHERS

Part of the out-of-sync aspect stems from role differences that our society imposes on marital partners. Men are socialized to be strong, controlling, self-sufficient family protectors (Schatz, 1986). These factors work against open expression of emotions, thereby inhibiting the grief response. Loss of control over the death itself strips the father of his ego and sense of self, leaving him angry, guilty, and with a strong sense of personal failure. He often holds the mother responsible for the death, which further divides the couple.

A major problem with the father's remaining stoic during grief is that the mother thinks that he does not love the child (Schatz, 1986). So often, the name of the child is dropped from conversations at home because parents think that doing so will facilitate grief resolution. Even when the mother wants to talk about the child, the father often remains quiet and seemingly noncaring. This attitude is often caused by the many male roles a father has learned to adopt since early childhood. Schatz (1986) outlined six of the roles that can impede the father's positive grief resolution. These are:

- The role of being strong—a macho man who always controls his emotions.
- The role of competing, of winning in a crisis, and of being the best.
- The role of being the protector of family and possessions.
- The role of being the family provider.
- The role of being the problem solver—fixing things or finding someone who can.
- The role of being the controller—controlling actions and the environment.
- The role of being self-sufficient—standing on his own two feet. (p. 295)

When caregivers encourage fathers to talk about the dead child, about feelings that spring up during grief, not only the father but also the entire family will be helped to accept the reality of the death, while ensuring that no one is accused of forgetting the lost child or being unresponsive to grief.

One wife complained when her husband grieved more for his pet poodle.

> Well, he grieved more over our poodle that died, that got killed out here. He actually grieved more, in ways that showed, than he has [over] our son. Now figure that one out. I thought he was going to lose his mind when our other poodle died, thought he was going off his rocker.

But she also said that even though they did not grieve alike, she could understand his feelings a bit more clearly. She even commented that in some respects they were closer now than ever before. It seems that just seeing him grieve over something reassured her that he was not completely unfeeling and cold.

Grief of Mothers

A mother is socialized to fill a different role. She is expected to be the nurturer, the caregiver, the hub of the family; she communicates with each member and helps members communicate with each other. She is used to carrying the emotional burden of the family. For the most part, women have been socialized to believe that it is their place to create the family circle. When a child dies, the circle is broken. Grief freezes her into a shell, and she cannot function in the prescribed role as she once did. A 1986 study by Littlefield and Rushton found that mothers grieve more intensely than do fathers for the loss of a child. A mother grieves not only for her child, but also for the loss of the delicately balanced family system (Schatz, 1986). At this point, she needs the nurturance for herself more than she is able to give it to others. Turning to her husband for help, she instead finds him withdrawn and uncommunicative, which she often interprets as a lack of love for the child, or worse, for herself. Wishing to communicate but unable to, she instead finds herself locked in social isolation (Schatz, 1986). Even sexual expression, which had helped draw the couple together in the past, is impeded by the inability to feel close now. Fish's (1986) study of marital differences affected by a child's death indicates that 60% of the wives and 40% of the husbands were aware of sexual distress. He related it to their sense of alienation from each other.

CASE STUDY: ONE FAMILY'S TRAGEDY

A terrible sense of loss and despair was experienced by a family in the Tampa study when the middle child died. Although he was 12 years old, he was developmentally handicapped and had spent his life close at home and with his family. He was deeply loved by his brother and sister. His parents gave him much affection, and in many ways, his presence was like having a baby at home all the time because of the care he required. He was a nurturing object for the entire family as well as a source of unqualified love returned to them.

His death was a severe trauma to each family member. Both the father and mother cried openly during the initial interview, almost too heartbroken to describe their emotions. Six months later, at the second interview, their grief had not changed. However, they were beginning to observe problems with their 16-year-old son. He was working out his own hostilities at his brother's death, the parents realized, but he nevertheless was constantly getting into trouble at school and had recently been in a scrape with the police. The father was suffering considerable guilt over this situation, feeling somehow to blame but also feeling angry that he could do nothing to stop his son's acting out. The father said that he was now more bitter than he had ever been in his entire life. He felt that God had let him down, and he said, "Let Him do anything to me—I can take that—but leave my wife and children alone. They have never done anything to deserve this horrible mess."

The father began to feel that whenever he attended church, some awful calamity happened, so he stopped going. He wondered why he should do something that caused "a kick in the butt." Yet he still believed in an afterlife and in knowing that he would see his son again in another life, but he just could not reconcile the afflictions that he had suffered with a loving God. He said, "I feel as though God has it in for me personally."

For this father, grief seemed worse now than it had been in the beginning. For example, he would go to a business meeting in another city where associates did not know about the loss, and they would say such things as how lucky he was to have such an interesting job, how fortunate to be in an area of the country that he liked; but inside he would be thinking, "If you really knew how I felt and what I am living through, you would not think this." He felt stigmatized and different.

The wife rose every morning at 5 A.M. so that she could have some quiet time to think and be alone. Her faith in God was strengthened, she felt, but it was the slow process of letting go that she found so painful and difficult. She got a job in an office "just to get out of the house." She said that no one at work knew about her son's death, and she did not have to talk about it to anyone. When she was busy, she could block the memory for a while, which seemed to give her a small respite. But when she came home in the evening, she was exhausted and had to rest on the couch before she could prepare dinner. The father said that it made him angry when she fell asleep on the couch right after work and again after supper. He was ready to take a walk or stay up late, but she was "out on the couch."

He said that she was using sleep as an escape, but she said that she was tired after a full day's work. This situation was a constant source of bickering between them.

Two years later, at the follow-up interview, this couple said that they felt worse than they had at the beginning. They thought that they had aged 10 years in the process and were not too hopeful about feeling better in the future. There had been even more trouble with their older son. They felt an overwhelming fear of impending doom, worrying each time the phone rang or doorbell sounded. They still cried openly when they talked about their deceased son, and they felt that they would never get over the pain of losing him.

Too, they argued a good deal. When they weren't fighting, they said, they were silently withdrawn from one another. Life was changed, and the entire family was affected. They had even talked lately about separating for a while.

What can we learn from these bereaved parents? First, we sense the terrible emptiness of their lives since they lost their son, who was like a baby. Because he required 24-hour care, his death left a void that could not be filled. Because he was dependent and deeply attached to each family member, his death removed a source of love and purpose from each of their lives. They felt that their situation was unique, that no one could possibly know what they were living through; consequently, to seek solace from others was useless. Even other bereaved parents have not suffered exactly the same situation. The father talked about being with business cohorts and expressed the alienation with which he lived. He said that he spoke like a businessman, but inside he felt like a misfit. The mother took a job where no one knew her sorrow so that she could avoid the ambiguous position of being a bereaved parent, but she felt the emotional drain of maintaining her denial of feelings during work.

Yet, paradoxically, even though they had intentionally created isolation (and some insulation) in their jobs, they also felt isolated at home because their friends had stopped asking about their loss. Friends had ceased referring to their deceased son at all, leaving the parents bereft of all support. They felt stigmatized, recognizing that others did not know what to say to them.

Concomitant stresses produced by their teenage son's problems as well as the death of a beloved aunt added to their burden. Grief was begun anew in each of these situations. Yet a major bereavement is rarely experienced by itself. One grief brings on another, which triggers still another. For some people, the process seems to go on forever. These stresses can erode away coping ability, diminishing resiliency.

The father felt that he was being punished by God for some cosmic sin he did not commit. The catastrophic loss left him and his family vulnerable and exposed. His older son's misbehavior left him feeling powerless and frustrated. There appeared to be no respite from the emotional shock wave set into motion by their middle son's death. The father not only assumed responsibility for the death of his child but also for the pain suffered by his family in their bereavement.

In assuming a protective position, the husband denied his own right to grieve. The emotional aspect of grief was then left to the mother, which created a problem of its own because the two parents were not sharing at the same level. The wife got up an hour earlier each morning but fell asleep right after dinner. She inadvertently had created her own isolation. The husband felt that she was escaping and was angry because she was not there for him. Because parents grieve differently and on different schedules, this dissension may lead them to retreat further from one another.

GRIEF OF SIBLINGS

Guilt and ambivalence appear to be the most difficult emotions for the surviving sibling to deal with (Stephenson, 1986). Just as the child's mother feels that the child died at a "special" age, the surviving sibling feels that the deceased child was, in all senses, the "special" child: the brightest, funniest, and most attractive. Implicit in this survivor guilt is the fear of not being able to measure up to the parent's expectation now that they must carry more of the burden of responsibility. Siblings also feel guilt that they were in some manner responsible for the death (Brice, 1982).

As discussed in the previous chapter, ambivalence is present in all sibling relationships and is often acted out with admonishments to "drop dead" or other thoughtless quips. Ambivalence also plays a part in a sibling's private wish to be the sole center of parental attention. These competitive responses are natural and are usually outgrown. If, however, a sibling dies, the remaining child or children are left with the unfinished business of attempting to resolve the love-hate relationship. This ambivalence then turns into another source of guilt.

Caregivers can encourage family members to share their feelings and thoughts openly, thereby validating the child's feelings. This communication provides the siblings with an opportunity to work through the negative emotions without lasting implications.

FINDING MEANING IN THE LOSS

One of the most difficult tasks for parents (and for siblings), but one that is most important in grief resolution, is the search for some meaning in the child's death (Rando, 1984). Because of the incomprehensibility of the loss, parents need to find an explanation that will impart some degree of special significance or importance to their child's death. In their analysis of in-depth interviews with 145 bereaved parents, Cook and Wimberly (1983) found three types of religious commitment that provided a link between parents' explanations of their loss and the subsequent degree of comfort or distress experienced:

1. Reunion with the deceased child in heaven.
2. The child's own faith as an influence on many lives.
3. The child's death as a punishment for wrongdoing—usually encountered among fathers more than mothers; has less beneficial effect but validates a sense of guilt.

These writers found that religious beliefs of the parents grew stronger as a result of attempts to cope with the death. Along the same lines, Binger et al.'s 1969 study stated that parents were helped by religion only when they had found it supportive before the death.

Some bereaved parents find comfort in a more secular philosophical meaning by focusing on the people who are influenced or helped by their child's life, illness, or death (Miles & Crandell, 1983).

GRIEF OVER TIME

Of the three types of death studied in the Tampa investigation, the death of a child produced the highest intensities of grief. At follow-up 1½ to 2 years later, grief intensities had actually increased for some parents. This finding implies that parental grief goes on for years and that 2 years represents only the beginning of grief for many. William Fish (1986) found that the grief of mothers was more intense after 2 years than it was in the beginning, and it did not taper off until after 5 years. For fathers, he found the same rise in intensity up to 2 years, but with a steady tapering off after that. In Therese Rando's (1983) study of bereaved parents whose child had died of cancer, grief actually intensified during the third year. These findings do not begin to describe the time it would take to complete the bereavement process. There has been a vast underestimation of the length of time it takes to survive the death of a child. More studies in this area will undoubtedly increase our understanding of the dynamics of parental bereavement.

CHAPTER 15

The Death of a Spouse

On February 18 my wife and I were in an automobile accident in which she was crushed and I did not get a scratch. To this day, I am haunted by the lingering sense of shock, loss, and memory of her poor little limp body, broken and bleeding, lying in the wreck. That hundreds of others are going through this experience right now does not help me.

Daily, I go over a litany of a thousand "ifs," any one of which would have saved her life—a deadening treadmill. I was driving—thus a sense of guilt. When death is a murderer, there is no preparation for a shock like this. My hand-in-hand companion of 45 years, torn from me in one awful wrench. We were very close and sentimental. The loneliness is spiritually devastating.

We had no children; we have only acquaintances in this retirement community; our close friends are in other cities. We were solitaries, self-sufficient.

Daily, I count my blessings (and they are many, thanks to her esthetic temperament and practical forethought) and weigh them in the balance against my loss. Daily, I go over the details of that awful accident and regret that murderer death did not take me, too. We had always wanted to go together and here was the perfect opportunity. Daily, I calculate the value of survival and wonder if it is worth the effort. I have no transcendental beliefs. I search the light and dark corners of my mind and heart and can find no hope of ever seeing her again. Disembodied souls and spirits are chimeras. How could they mean anything outside our present environment? The absurdities of resurrection are too much for me to accept.

There are tricks of habit and memory which bring her close to me. [They are] beautiful to contemplate, but like moonlight, gossamer, are gone.

Often, in such a dark low moment, I get a letter from one of our dear friends with a great lift out of the shadow. I have heard a Christian Scientist say that desire is prayer. If so, I have prayed. And if the Lord has replied, it has been through the beautiful letters I have received.

But the spell is temporary; I do not look for time to assuage my grief. That is the tragedy of the elders; there isn't enough time left. Who lacks the courage to exercise his own option must go on like an automaton and leave the choice to death. Or like Dylan Thomas, "Rage! Rage!" or like Edna Millay, "bolt my door and put up a fight."

But they were young people.

Widower, age 72

How does a person survive a tragedy like this one? What impels a mourner even to want to continue alone each day in utter sadness and sorrow? That the death of a spouse is a stress of immense proportions has been documented by any number of researchers (Clayton et al., 1971; Glick et al., 1974; Helsing et al., 1981; Marris, 1968; Parkes, 1972; Parkes & Weiss, 1983; Raphael, 1984; Stroebe & Stroebe, 1983; Vachon, Rogers, et al., 1982a). It has been listed in a popular stress inventory as the number one stressor above all other losses (Holmes & Rahe, 1967). Yet unless a couple dies together, widowhood is the inevitable conclusion of all marriages that do not end in divorce. However, it still continues to be an event for which little or no preparation is made, adding further to the burden placed on bereaved spouses.

FACTORS AFFECTING BEREAVEMENT OF A SPOUSE

Marriage, particularly in this century, has shifted from a strictly contractual significance to a more personal matter (Saxton, 1968). As such, marriage becomes a compelling source of intimacy and personal need gratification. Marriage partners often become each other's best friend and companion. Even when the marriage is far from perfect, when it is only one of superficial need exchange, important bonds are still established. These bonds are based on expectation of various role requirements within the marital structure. Traditionally, the wife maintains the home and bears children. The husband provides and protects. Within these major areas lie a multitude of individual tasks that fall into place during the early part of the marriage, becoming habitual and usually taken for granted thereafter. When one of the partners dies, not only is physical support removed from the other, but also an assortment of tasks and needs that are left unattended. As a result, it is seldom clearly understood exactly what is lost (Parkes, 1972) or for what one is truly grieving. Filling those roles or learning to perform them oneself, alone and unsupported, can be an overwhelming task in itself. Redefinition of roles constitutes a major endeavor during the bereavement process. As Silverman and Cooperband (1974) state, "It is necessary to learn to be a widow as one learns to be a wife, or mother" (p. 10). Of course, this advice is equally appropriate for widowers.

The largest bulk of the bereavement literature has focused on the problems encountered as a sequel to the death of a spouse (Glick et al., 1974; Maddison & Viola, 1968; Marris, 1968; Parkes, 1965; Parkes, 1971a; Raphael, 1984). These writers give fairly detailed accounts of the psychological concomitants of grief as well as specific symptoms that accompany the process. Other writers have discussed the high mortality and morbidity rate of the bereaved spouse (Helsing et al., 1981; Jacobs & Ostfeld, 1980; Kraus & Lilienfeld, 1959; Mor, McHorney, & Sherwood, 1986; Rees & Lutkins, 1967; Stroebe & Stroebe, 1983; Vachon, 1976; Young et al., 1963). Each of these reports presents grief as a stressor of immense proportions, having debilitating effects on the survivor. Reactive depression has also been described (Blanchard et al., 1976; Clayton et al., 1972), although others have seen this symptom as the need to conserve energy rather than as clinical depression per se (Engel, 1962; Sanders, 1979–1980). Focusing on widowhood as a sociological problem, Berardo (1970) and Lopata (1973; 1979) see this time as a period of social isolation, impaired health, and general deprivation.

One of the first studies to direct attention solely to the loss of a spouse by death was done by Peter Marris (1968) in London. He interviewed 72 widows, approximately 2 years after the death, whose husbands had died in youth or middle age. Marris planned interviews around three topics: (1) income (introduced to show how well she managed), (2) problems she had to meet since her husband's death, and (3) emotional reactions. The interview was planned so as to move from practical matters to those of subjective personal feelings.

In 1968, Marris concluded that it may take 2 or more years to become reconciled to bereavement. Earlier, Lindemann (1944) had proposed anywhere from 8 to 10 weeks; later, Glick et al. (1974) estimated that it takes 5 or 6 years. Glick et al. noted many physical symptoms as well as psychosomatic illnesses. Marris also focused on the psychosocial aspects of loneliness and deprivation—both financial and social—that tend to alienate the widow during her bereavement. No previous author had given so detailed and systematic an account of the grief process. Since that time, a number of researchers examining conjugal bereavement have done extensive studies, producing supportive results.

Colin Murray Parkes has been one of the most prolific and influential researchers in the area of conjugal bereavement. His study of London widows

(1972) revealed that anger and irritability, two normal accompaniments to the grief syndrome, often lead the widow to seek medical attention. Later, he joined Glick and Weiss (1974) in a study of Boston bereaved spouses that contributed more information than previous studies. They found that three important variables affected bereavement outcome.

1. Low socioeconomic status, particularly identified by low income and occupation of the husband.
2. Lack of preparation for loss, often due to short duration of illness.
3. Preceding life crises—number as well as intensity of life crises experienced before the bereavement, such as infidelity, divorce, or loss of a job.

Other factors thought to affect bereavement outcome included large numbers of children under 6 years and alcoholism in the husband. As to the preparation for the loss, those wives whose husbands died quickly had a more difficult time during the first year of bereavement with respect to social withdrawal and self-reproach. Persisting preoccupation with the deceased was noted, which resulted in continued pining and yearning for the deceased. The third variable, preceding life crises, was seen as resulting in high ambivalence toward the deceased spouse and consequently heightened guilt and anxiety for the bereaved. Interestingly, the debilitating effects of ambivalence were seen most sharply in the group who had suffered through the long-term illnesses of their spouses. Although a long-term illness might better prepare the individual for the bereavement to come, it also provides a period of exhausting vigilance and care, which tends to encourage the spouse occasionally to wish for the end of the long ordeal.

Sanders (1980–1981), in looking at differences between younger and older bereaved spouses, finds that younger spouses initially showed greater shock, confusion, and personal death anxiety as well as guilt. They experienced feelings of disbelief as they tried to make the tragic event real. The older spouses showed a different trend. Denial seemed to be working as a suppressor variable, giving evidence of a more diminished emotional grief reaction. This suppression did not mean a lack of grief, however. Instead, denial appeared as determined optimism or, as Parkes (1972) labeled it, "compulsive self-reliance." At follow-up, older spouses showed exacerbated grief reactions. Despite their courage and faith, it became increasingly difficult to maintain an optimistic outlook for the future when (1) time was seen as running out, (2) physical health became tenuous, and (3) being alone not only meant deprivation but also fear for one's personal safety. Sadness and loneliness were evident in both groups, but it appeared that the younger spouses were motivated by hope, thereby resolving their problems gradually, while the older spouses were repelled by hopelessness, thereby exacerbating their symptoms.

RESPONSES TO BEREAVEMENT

SHOCK

The initial shock of death produces disbelief and numbness. Even when death is expected, no one quite expects it to be so final, so irreversible. The bereaved may attempt to forestall the impact by intellectual acceptance without the emotional component. This reaction is especially true if one has the responsibility of making funeral arrangements and of nurturing others. Quite soon, however, the protective veneer wears off and the bereaved is exposed to the raw awareness of the loss (Engel, 1962). Bereaved individuals in the Tampa study spoke of moving through an unreal world, of not feeling quite in touch with anything. It was difficult to put the event in perspective or even to believe it had happened. One widow whose husband had died of a heart attack said,

> I mean it was just . . . oh my, I would have never dreamed it. And I don't suppose he would have either because we hadn't had any sickness in our family. And the only thing he did was smoke. He didn't drink. But we never even had any idea that he had this kind of trouble. . . . It's just one of those things. It's kind of hard to comprehend that it really happened. Until I look at his picture, then I realize he is gone. He's never coming back. But it is still unreal—I can hardly believe it at times.

Other had different memories. When death takes place in an intensive care unit of a hospital, the life support equipment can leave a vivid impression. One widow described the terror surrounding her husband's death when she had to witness these circumstances:

> On the night he got sick, I called one hospital where he had been before and [I] asked for Dr. . . . , but he said well you could bring him over, but we don't have room. And that's so sad. Right at the time when you really need to be in a familiar place . . . there was no room there. So then I had to take him to St. Joseph's. He all of a sudden got this awful pain. . . . I suppose it was his kidneys. 'Cause they weren't very good.
> Well, he died the next morning, about noon. He never did want to go to the hospital, but when he started in with that awful pain, I knew I couldn't do anything for him and he had congestive heart failure and emphysema. . . . I knew something was drastically wrong.

This widow said that she had continuing thoughts about seeing her husband in the hospital. Although she knew that she could not do anything else but take him there when his pain became so intense, she nevertheless felt guilty about not being with him when he died, especially when he had wanted to be at home.

Because she was told little about his condition and what they were trying to do, she was angry at being so isolated. What angered her the most, however, was that the hospital staff had used deception to get her out of the room when he was dying. She said that she was too frightened to ask questions even if she had known what questions to ask.

Families of dying patients are at a disadvantage when the hospital staff leave them out of the communication pathway. Not knowing what is transpiring, not being familiar with the physical signs of impending death, the already anxious family members are left to cope alone in a strange place among unfamiliar people. The stress they are experiencing, compounded by the shock of death, places a physiological strain on the bereaved that is often not alleviated for months. Caregivers can be especially helpful at this time to assist families in recognizing the events as they take place. The process, then, leads them more gradually toward the reality of the situation.

The life-death transition is not made quickly for the bereaved. It takes time to grasp the event of death. Several spouses refused to allow an autopsy because they felt that their mates had already gone through enough. One widow said,

> I wouldn't let them do an autopsy, he'd been cut on too much. I just, you know, afterwards they asked if they could do it, but I said no because it wouldn't help him any, and it wouldn't be that I wouldn't want to help someone else; I just felt like I had seen him go through so much. Just the thought of them taking him, cutting . . . I just couldn't do it.

GUILT

Guilt was experienced in varying degrees by all spouses in the Tampa study. However, for some, it also produced lasting consequences that were hard to quell. For example, the helplessness that was experienced during the death, when nothing could be done to stop the process despite all efforts, left the bereaved feeling out of control of their world. Afterward, separation anxiety ripped at the bonds that held the couple together, and the spouse's longing for the deceased prompted a search for some indication that the emptiness was only temporary.

In one case, a widow was plagued with guilt for not sensing the seriousness of her husband's condition earlier. He had sustained asthma attacks before, but he was usually able to get to the hospital in plenty of time for a treatment. As a matter of fact, he had recently admitted to having lost his death anxiety because he was assured of reaching help in time. On this particular occasion, he awoke in the early morning hours, complaining of shortness of breath and saying that he needed to get to the hospital. His wife, however, having been through this dozens of times before, did not particularly hurry, even stopping to fix herself a cup of coffee. However, this time was different. On the way to the hospital, her husband stopped breathing and rolled over onto her shoulder. She had to drive the rest of the way knowing he was dead. She related it this way:

> It was awfully hard . . . like I say, if he had been in the hospital and passed away, it would have been just as hard to face you know. The loneliness would have been there . . . but it was a point that it was just a horrible thing . . . what it is to be driving with somebody dead on your shoulder . . . It seemed like I was forever getting there. And not a soul in sight. I just kept hoping I'd run into the rescue squad or something, that I could signal to stop and give assistance but . . .
>
> And do you know that I never looked at his face. I had to let him down when I got his body, real easy on the seat . . . and ran inside . . . and you know I was in such a hurry and shock . . . that I never looked at his face. To this day, I don't know what his expression was.

The picture crowded her mind and left little room for other things. She felt guilty that she did not stop to look at him as he was lying on the seat of the car. Somehow, she could not bring herself to do it, she said. Guilt was exacerbated, and memories were filled with distorted pictures of the last hours before death.

DEPRIVATIONS

A number of widows in the Tampa study were overwhelmed by the business end of family management. Financial matters such as the red tape involved in settling insurance claims or social security benefits were almost incomprehensible to some widows, especially coming at a time when their ability to concentrate or think things through was impaired. Widowers were not as disrupted by business matters because they had generally handled them before. Instead, they had greater difficulty with the practical issues of home care.

Deprivations were also felt in areas of service, particularly for widows who had to learn to manage household repairs. A widow explained her insecurity:

> If something breaks down . . . like in the house, I take it very hard now because I always had someone right there that I could count on and I felt secure. Now if something really happens that takes a lot of financing, like the car or something, that really bothers me.

Another widow talked about the worry of doing all the chores alone:

> Over a period of time, you get to thinking, you're alone more, see you have more problems to think about. Now my other problems here, I have so much housework . . . then there's things to do outside. I worry over the painting and have to worry about the lawn; there's so much around to worry about.

These widows were trying to manage their homes the way they always did, but without the help of someone to provide maintenance. A newly bereaved wife said this:

> Well, like something goes wrong with the plumbing, you know, and that makes me panic. Like if he was here he could handle it right away 'cause he was real handy at all these things. Good heavens, if something really big comes along, what would I do?

But widows were not the only ones who felt the deprivations of a lost partner. Widowers were equally lost when it came to such things as preparing meals or shopping. One widower told me that he was absolutely panicked at the thought of having to fix his own meals for the rest of his life. He said he had no idea of how to even start. He was relieved when his daughter bought him a microwave oven and then prepared a special meal for him each evening when he came home from work. She did this even though she lived halfway across town from him.

The widowers in the Tampa study seemed to receive more nurturance than did widows. They were invited out to dinner more often, or they had food brought into their homes for a longer period after the funeral than did the widows. In our society, men traditionally are not expected to take care of home care details the way women are. Yet, when a husband dies, there is not comparable assistance for widows in taking care of business or financial matters or household maintenance.

For widowers, the greatest deprivations were experienced in social isolation. Most were still working and were able to manage their days without focusing on grief. Some said they could go the entire day, if they were very busy, and almost forget that the death had occurred. But when evening came and they had to go home, they were bereft. In most cases, the wife had been the social organizer for the family, leaving the husbands without the ability to make contacts or to reach out to others.

One widower got through the early period of grief by having his son and daughter-in-law move in with him. However, when they later moved to another state, he became lonelier than ever. A year and a half after his wife's death, he was still alone, not able to socialize or arrange evenings out. He talked of wishing to have someone to share things with. His children were a comfort, but he recognized that he could not be pals with them, that he needed someone his own age to talk and be with. He said that it struck him the hardest when he visited his son at Christmas. He had never made a trip without his wife, and he was painfully aware of her absence. Everywhere they went, he thought about how he would have liked her to be with him. He said that he still thought about her almost all the time. Paradoxically, although he longed for a partner, he was afraid to get involved with anyone because she might come between him and his children, or he feared that he could never find anyone who would meet the same standards that his wife had met. He did not know how to enjoy himself because his job and household chores had always been his only outlet except for the things his wife planned for them.

SITUATIONAL VARIABLES AFFECTING BEREAVEMENT

SUPPORT SYSTEMS

The Tampa study showed that grievers got through the days following the death only with the help of friends and family. One widower proudly told me that 84 people had come to his house between the death and the funeral. Having many friends and family members to help during crises can be an enormous support to the bereaved. Walker, McBride, and Vachon (1977) described this support as a dense social network, noting that the more help that was offered, the better adjustment over time for the bereaved spouse. The bringing of food, flowers, anything, was a deep comfort to these bereaved spouses as they moved through a house that had been theirs but now was empty of one of them.

EATING ALONE

Eating alone was painful for many bereaved spouses. One widow told me that she had lost 20 pounds in 3 months following the death, and she felt it was partly because she could not bear to sit down at the table alone. Even when she brought dinner into the living room to eat in front of the television, she still remembered the times they had done that together. Very often, bereaved spouses ate standing at the kitchen counter or at the refrigerator, taking things out absentmindedly without much relish. When a wife is used to cooking for another, she feels unsatisfied when cooking only for herself. Too, it is difficult to learn to cook in single helpings. Quantities at the grocery store are not packaged for one person. Besides, when appetite is slight, why bother? These thoughts were expressed over and over, especially among the widows in the study. Widowers ate out more often or were invited to dinner. However, when they did eat at home, they were troubled by the loneliness of eating alone just as much as widows were.

SEXUAL GRATIFICATION

Lack of a sexual partner did not seem to be a major deprivation for most spouses in the Tampa study, especially during the early period of bereavement. Of greater concern was the sheer weight of loneliness and separation. Waking in the middle of the night to find oneself huddled alone in one corner of the bed, getting up in the morning with no one to say good morning to, and the long lonely evenings that were awaited with dread represented some of the empty events that constituted their lives. Raphael (1984) noted that the need for nurturance, either to give or to receive it, outweighed the need for sexual expression during bereavement. Many widows in the Tampa study expressed a longing just to be held again by someone who cared for them. Value seems to be in the little things that weave together the richness of relationships, but when taken away, they subtract the color from one's very existence.

SENSING THE PRESENCE OF THE DECEASED

The habits of a long marriage are not easily forgotten. Having a partner in the home, talking, eating, sleeping, all are taken for granted after years of being together. Perceptions of these experiences do not cease when one of the partners dies. These perceptions often become manifest through sensing the presence of the deceased. Parkes (1972) described these experiences as hypnagogic hallucinations, or more simply, illusions. Preoccupation with the deceased keeps these illusions alive and stems from the need of the bereaved to search for and find the lost person. They are rewarded by a sense or illusion of the deceased's presence. Parkes stated that it is a normal and common symptom of bereavement. Many of the Tampa spouses reported feeling the presence of the deceased in the house. One widow said,

> You know, the other morning, I got up and I could see him so plain, and I wondered, maybe I dreamed about him and didn't remember dreaming because he was so plain, like he was around me . . . he looked so good . . . like he was for real.

When the illness had been long and the mate had been in a certain bedroom during the illness, a spouse usually had a perception of the mate's presence associated with that area of the house. A 78-year-old widower talked of seeing his wife:

> I see her coming out of that back bedroom there. There are two bedrooms back there, she slept in one and me in the other for many years, and I can see her.
> It tears me up. I jumped out of bed one night and called to her when I saw her but she vanished. I've heard her call me too, loud enough to know that I knew it was her.

Most spouses who had this experience took comfort in the thought that their mates were nearby, offering consolation or trying to let them know that they were safe and unharmed. Other writers have concurred that these hallucinations of the deceased represent a common experience, that it is "hallucinatory wishful longing" and is maintained as a way of clinging to the lost person (MacDonald & Oden, 1977; Matchett, 1972). On the other hand, Hoyt's (1980–1981) case studies describe patients who related experiences in which they felt the presence of a deceased person. The "ghosts" appeared at the time of letting go and were associated with relinquishing attachments rather than clinging.

CARRYING OUT TASKS ACCOMPANYING THE DEATH OF A SPOUSE

Funerals

Funerals that had been prearranged gave the spouses in the Tampa study a feeling of carrying out orders from the deceased, which not only simplified things but also brought a measure of consolation to the remaining mate. One widow had promised her husband that she would only use a GI casket, but when she got into the selection room of the funeral home, she changed her mind.

> I had two real good friends with me and we were laughing afterwards because my husband insisted, "I want the GI casket. If it's good enough for Ike, it's good enough for me and I don't want you going into a lot of money and blah, blah, blah." So we saw what the normal GI casket was and I just couldn't do it.
>
> So I went $250.00 more for one that hermetically sealed and it was a very nice-looking casket. Then we were giggling . . . we would just see Ben going, "I told you not to, you know." But we got out, and when we were going back to the car, we looked up and said, "Sorry about that, Ben. We just couldn't do it. No way."

For this widow, humor brought a momentary relief to the shock and sadness experienced during bereavement. But to some, it also produced guilt feelings, in that they thought it was improper or disrespectful. Yet when people can experience moments of laughter or amusement without feeling guilt, they benefit by the reduction of tension. Humor can be one of the most therapeutic antidotes in grief.

Making arrangements at the funeral home was difficult for all the bereaved spouses in the Tampa study. Generally, the surviving spouse was accompanied by grown children, relatives, or friends who helped in the selection of various alternatives concerning the ritual itself. One widow described these feelings:

> I have a friend that works with me; she's worked with me a long time, and she went with me to pick out the casket and clothing, and that's hard, that's a hard job. . . . It really tears you up to pick out all these things. He had some clothes, but most of his were heavy, and so I just went ahead and bought him a new suit . . . like I wanted to.

There was a degree of comfort for this widow, knowing that she was able to provide nice clothing for the funeral when he would be seen by all his friends. But most of the Tampa spouses supplied something from the wardrobe of the deceased rather than purchasing a new dress or suit.

As mentioned, when prearrangements were made for the funeral, the surviving spouse had an easier time getting through the shock period of grief. Although making these arrangements before death occurred was not easy, spouses experienced a feeling of relief when it was done.

One widower whose wife died of cancer after many months of pain and sickness had, through her encouragement, made arrangements for the entire service. He explained,

> It was easier for me once we had finally talked about it, and I can't say who brought it up. We were both ready to talk about it, but she told me what she wanted and certain specifics . . . what she particularly did want and what she particularly didn't want and what she didn't care much about either way. With that, I went to a funeral director maybe 2 or 3 weeks before she died. Sat down and made complete arrangements for the whole thing. That was a relief. I knew it would be. I knew it after I walked out of his office. I kind of felt—there, that's done.

In this case, the widower knew beyond a doubt that his wife was dying and that these arrangements had to be made sooner or later. He chose to do it when he felt he could make rational decisions. But for some, making prior arrangements was impossible. In some cases, magical thinking suggested that if arrangements were made, it would bring on the death sooner. For others, these arrangements were just too final to do before death occurred.

DISPOSING OF CLOTHING

Tampa spouses found that disposing of clothing was one of the hardest things to be done. One widower, after a year and a half, had not removed any of his wife's things from the house. Even her cosmetics were as she had left them in the bathroom. He blamed his sister-in-law for this, saying that he thought it was a woman's job to do these things. In another case, it took a young widow a year before she felt that she was ready to part with her husband's clothing. But for most of the bereaved spouses, it was done within the first 6 months.

A traumatic experience for one widow left her wishing that she had not gotten rid of her husband's clothes the way she did.

> I gathered up some of his things. At the VFW, they had a rummage sale, and I took over some of his good things. They were washed and ironed, just ready to use . . . on hangers too. And I went out there to the rummage sale to contribute them because I'm a member of the auxiliary, but I never attend. And they had wall-to-wall junk. They had everything on tables. And it was all just real junk. And here I was bringing his good shirts and walking shorts. And I was supposed to throw them on the table with all the rest of the stuff. And that made me so depressed at the time.

They didn't have any racks, and I even had them on hangers. And they didn't have any racks to hang them on. So I just laid them on the table, across the table as fast as I could.

And I felt people grabbing and looking and then throwing it down like it was nothing. I was sorry that I did that, that I took those clothes out to that rummage sale. Because I'd rather go down on Central Avenue and find a bum and say, "Here." I'd know where they were going.

Clothing will often have stronger attachments than might be expected. Certain items were treasured more than others. For example, the deceased (1) wore the clothes the last day of life, (2) thought a great deal of that particular item of clothing, or (3) was given that shirt or belt on a special day. These objects may symbolically represent the deceased and act as linking objects for the bereaved (Volkan, 1970).

The one item that seemed to be kept most often was the wallet. Because of the personal aspects of various documents in a wallet, it was difficult to discard. Some said it was like throwing away the past of that person.

I kept his wallet . . . all his cards, everything, just like they handed it to me in the hospital . . . I have used some of that money to give his grandchildren . . . and I'll always say this is from Grandpa, you know? Whenever I buy something they especially want, I have gotten it from the money he had in his wallet and always tell them, this is from Grandpa.

Widow, age 63

I have his wallet upstairs. And I mean, I didn't just keep it for personal reasons, I guess. I mean, I just never have taken all the cards out of it. It's just up there.

Widow, age 60

Yes, he had a couple of wallets. . . . They're right here.

Widow, age 57

I kept it as it was when I found it on the dresser . . . all the cards, driver's license, even the money he had. I still have it just as it was.

Widow, age 29

I got rid of everything else of hers, her clothes and most of her jewelry, but somehow I couldn't get rid of her wallet. It's upstairs in a drawer . . . all her cards still in it.

Widower, age 63

That one item that we use so excessively every day and that, when examined, tells about our personal history was retained by most of the participants in the study. As one widow put it, "It was like throwing him out when I tried to dispose of it . . . so I didn't."

But items that belonged to the deceased were usually disposed of, bit by bit, until the house became the home of one owner. A young widow said,

> But I think . . . it's a funny thing. You keep them for a little while and gradually you let them go. Now some people go through it fast all at one time. I didn't do that. Gradually, as the time came . . . somehow or another it just came within itself. And I just felt free to do it. And then I hung on to other little things then, you see, I got rid of those. And then . . . it just went down. I didn't do it all at once. Just gradually.

ADDITIONAL FACTORS AFFECTING BEREAVEMENT

CHILDREN

Children of the bereaved in the Tampa study were either a help or a hindrance, and sometimes both. If children were minors and still at home, the parent had double concerns—personal grief and children's grief. In one case, the mother handled both griefs well. She prepared the children before death by explaining carefully the medical condition of their father. The two older ones were able to visit their father in the hospital and tell him they loved him, something that helped the children later on. On the day he died, the mother discussed his condition with them and told them that he would probably die very soon. During the services, she made sure that they understood what was going on and were allowed to express their grief. After the funeral, she overheard another person saying to her oldest boy that "he was now the man of the house and would have to take over." This remark upset the mother, who promptly took the boy aside and told him to take such comments with a grain of salt—that people just did not know what else to say.

She later gathered the children around her and told them they needed to share this loss together. They began doing things as a family without the normal divisions that the death of a parent causes. This is not to say that the family did not mourn, but that they openly shared their grief with one another.

She told me that one of the hardest things she had to do was accompany

the boys to Little League, where their father had always been active. On the first night, after they had won, one little player presented her with the ball signed by all the players. She said she had been fairly stoic up to then, but that gesture caused her to break down. Still, she would not have avoided that poignant reminder.

Grown children sometimes reversed roles with their parents during their parents' grief, becoming overly concerned that parents not become too depressed. A 59-year-old widower said he received a long, scathing letter from his son, "in which he ripped me up and down for going into a state of depression." He added, "He was, in a sense, right. He wrote things like, 'It isn't you,' and 'Pick yourself up and shake yourself. And let's get going again.' "

Asked how he reacted to the letter, the widower said, "Well, when I first read it, I had a negative reaction." But then he said he realized that his son was only trying to help. "Well, this was his way of helping, and this was his way of supporting. And among other things, he said, 'Is your hair cut or your shoes shined? If you're going out to sell, you need to watch these things.' I wrote back, 'Number one, I am not a Howard Hughes. I have not become a recluse.' And I said that I shined my shoes, and I even take a bath once in awhile."

In most cases, grown children were a large support for the bereaved parent, who described them as being helpful in surviving their grief. One close-knit family realized that they were hindering their mother's resolution of grief by doing everything for her. Before the death, she had often driven to visit relatives nearby, but afterward, she had stopped going out very much. After the death, she had "temporarily" moved in with a daughter who lived next door, but she had never moved back to her own house. When I interviewed them, she was in a recliner in which, I was told, she spent most of her time. After about 9 months, the family held a conference and decided that they should take a harder line with her for her own good. They insisted that she move back to her own home and begin driving her own car. She resisted at first, but they were firm, and eventually she was back to her usual schedule. They felt that if they had not taken that stand, she would have continued to decline.

Children were an important help to parents in getting through grief in the Tampa study, but when participants were asked what the most important aid had been throughout the bereavement process, the unanimous answer was "friends and family members." They particularly lauded friends who had stuck by them through the long, arduous months of bereavement—nurturing, listening, helping.

RELIGION

Religion was also a mainstay, providing hope to many when discouragement threatened to shake them loose from their foundations. However, they also felt anger toward God as they tried to work through the meaning of their impossible loss. A young widow expressed these feelings when she said,

> I was telling my neighbor, I said "It takes inner strength because I couldn't have done it by myself." And I'm Baptist and I believe in heaven and hell. It has helped quite a deal, yet there were times when I was bitter, you know, "Why, God? . . . why not take someone who had no desire to live?" because I've seen so many people who could just care less whether they lived or died. Just nothing . . . nothing to offer, and I said, "Why Joe, when he was so full of life and had so much to live for." I went through this period too.

Although faith in God was a strong support for most participants in the study, bereaved spouses appeared to be especially helped when they not only attended church but also had good family interaction, meaning that church activities would usually also involve social events in which close family members also participated. This combination reduced anger, depression, and feelings of isolation, and it increased optimism among bereaved spouses, even resulting in better physical health. This finding points not only to the negative effects of isolation during crises but also to the high intensity of psychological problems encountered as well. When people supply nurturance, grief is less intense.

LONELINESS

Loneliness is a major problem of bereaved spouses (Cumming & Henry, 1961; Lopata, 1969, 1974). As our culture becomes increasingly couple-companionate, single people have a difficult time fitting into places where they had been comfortable prior to the loss (Lopata, 1969). For some, the situation was frightening. One widow discussed her anxiety:

> When I thought my nephew was leaving and maybe I would be alone, I was desperate . . . I really was desperate . . . I was really afraid and I was desperate . . . And I'm not so much afraid of somebody coming in and hurting me or anything like that, as I am thinking, "I'm alone because there's nobody ever going to be with me ever again" . . . and going berserk. That's my fear. It isn't a fear of somebody coming in, because that doesn't bother me. It's the other part of being alone . . . there's nobody.

Lopata describes this feeling as loneliness anxiety (Lopata, 1973, 1974), which often leads the bereaved to undertake busywork as a means of avoiding loneliness.

The future loomed empty during the first year of bereavement for most of the Tampa spouses. Adding to the problem in many cases was the awkwardness of making new friends when they did not feel like reaching out to others. Old friends seemed safer, but spouses felt no longer a part of the couple-companionate society to which they had once comfortably belonged. As Lopata (1972, 1973) noted, those bereaved spouses who were already deeply immersed in close family and friends were the least lonely. Yet understandably, those individuals had the greatest difficulty in carving out a new life for themselves.

Contributing further misunderstanding to the bereavement process is the poorly understood function of the need to withdraw from others. This withdrawal was generally taken as a first step toward a breakdown—and therefore became a frightening element rather than a healing one. It is important for the bereaved and their loved ones to understand that the period of mourning is by and large a hibernation time, a holding pattern in which the natural function is to find meaning in the loss, to let go. If this step were more fully understood, the bereaved would feel far less fear and anxiety. Understanding the purpose of this withdrawal will not necessarily reduce the despair, sadness, and sorrow felt because of missing someone who is deeply loved, but it will supply a measure of faith and hope, which promises that healing will occur eventually.

REMARRIAGE

The intense pain of grief that was experienced during the early months after the death began to ease for many of the Tampa study participants after the first year. New attachments were beginning to form. Within the first year, two widows and four widowers had remarried. Some of those who had remarried did so with replacement in mind. One widower was candid from the beginning that he could not live alone, did not want to, and had no intention of trying it. He found a suitable companion and was married within 6 months. This man had had a happy marriage and recognized his own needs. A year and a half later, he still seemed quite content with his new life—not that he did not have times of sadness, but that the replacement had somehow filled a lonely gap in his life.

In another situation, a widower married a woman whom he had known for years and who was in his social circle. She had six children, four of whom were living at home. However, this ready-made family seemed to be no obstacle for the widower, who bought a larger home and incorporated the whole family. It was a happy decision for him also.

Of the 43 remaining spouses in the study, thoughts of remarriage ranged from "absolutely no" to "perhaps, if the right person came along." One widower had lost two wives to cancer and felt that he could not go through it again—either the marriage or the possible illness. "I might just as well tell you. I wouldn't be opposed to marriage, but I would never go into it . . . really, because of all that I've been through in the past 40 years."

This widower managed quite well by himself because he had taken responsibility for the cooking and shopping all through his wife's illness. When she died, he simply continued doing all the household chores as usual.

Another widower felt that he had gained a certain freedom and did not wish to tie himself down again.

I don't think I'll ever remarry. . . . I don't think so. I enjoy taking ladies out to dinner and stuff like this . . . as far as marriage is concerned, I don't think I want to get married. A lot of people think that . . . but right now I don't think I would. I enjoy the company of ladies, but as far as getting into a permanent marriage situation, it's not my plan.

At least half of the widows had not removed their wedding rings, either out of loyalty or as an indication that they still considered themselves married. A number felt that they would remain psychologically married for the rest of their lives, that they would feel guilty and disloyal if they did not.

For some, a year and a half was too soon to be thinking about a new relationship. This finding is supported by the Harvard Bereavement Study (Glick, Weiss, & Parkes, 1974), which found that bereaved spouses were not ready for a new relationship for several years. A 51-year-old widow who had made a good adjustment to living alone still hesitated when asked about remarriage.

I really haven't thought much about it. If I meet someone, I think it will probably be my belief in God had meant it to be that way. I don't know, even my husband had said when we were updating our will, he said that I "would probably remarry at some time." And I thought, "my goodness, what's he talking about?" And I think about that and I think he realized that maybe someone would come along. He said, "You're young enough to be married again." But anyhow, it hasn't really entered my mind.

There were some who had no doubt about their feelings concerning living alone. A 55-year-old widow had this to say:

If I thought I had to stay by myself the rest of my life . . . uh, uh . . . I'm not that type . . . I'm not a loner. I told my son, "all right, you're in the business world." I said, "I don't mean today or tomorrow . . . a little later you meet somebody your mama's age, you keep your mama in mind." He laughed. Course he knows his mama. In fact, he and I are just alike. He couldn't be alone either . . . no way . . . I can't. I'm just miserable.

The preceding comments, reflecting the feelings of the bereaved spouses, indicate that a year and a half is too soon to expect bereavement to be completed. Most are still in the phase of withdrawal or are beginning Phase 4, healing. Some had not made the decision as to whether they would want to readjust their lives to include a new mate even if one came along. The Harvard Bereavement Study (Glick, Weiss, & Parkes, 1974) concluded that it takes between 4 and 5 years to move on with a new life. Much depends on the age of the surviving spouse. The younger one is, the more optimistic the future appears. However, spouses who reach their 70s and 80s rarely talk about finding a new mate. People at that age realize that life will more or less spin itself out as it is being lived.

CHAPTER 16

The Death of a Parent

When it hit me, I just sat down there on the little deck, and I cried. I love an old chain swing, and I had gone and bought a swing and I got the post and the bolt, and everything, and I was going to do it myself, 'cause my husband was busy and he kept putting me off, and I got into it and was trying to drill holes, and this and that, and he still wouldn't help me. Finally, I got so exasperated, it dawned on me that my daddy had always been my right-hand fellow—that anything I wanted to do, no matter how little or how big, he was right there to help. All of a sudden, it just hit me that maybe Daddy had spoiled me in this way, because I could depend on him. I knew he would help me. No matter how little or how big it was . . . and I just sat there and cried because it dawned on me that Daddy was gone.

Bereaved daughter, age 53

OVERVIEW AND GENERAL DESCRIPTION

FOR MOST OF US, our parents will die when we are middle-aged. The remarkable success of medical science and positive health conditioning have contributed to the extension of life spans by eliminating childhood diseases on one end of the continuum and controlling many other killer diseases on the other. Ours has become a four- or five-generation society (Kastenbaum, 1977). Such longevity creates a picture of eternal life on earth, supporting a notion that one will be here forever, along with one's parents and children.

Yet, at some point in middle age, people realize that their parents are growing older. Because the adult years are busy, largely taken up with marital relationships, career goals, parent-adolescent conflicts, and self-

231

actualization needs, this realization sometimes comes as a surprise. Recently a friend said to me,

> I hadn't seen my mother and father for several months, and when they arrived at our beach cottage to spend the week, I was overjoyed that we would have time together. But halfway through the vacation, as I watched them set up their beach chairs on the sand, it dawned on me that my parents were growing old. They moved more slowly than they had before and didn't do as much. My parents were growing old, and I had real trouble processing this.

There was a note of fear in my friend's voice as she related this discovery to me. Could it be that she was recognizing that with the aging of her parents, she too was growing older? Was she also realizing that now that they were older, they could die, and with their death, the last buffer was removed against her own death (Moss & Moss, 1983–1984)? Both these emotions—anticipatory grief for parents' death and fears of one's own aging—contribute to the sense of loss one experiences as one's parents age. Although the death of an adult's parent can be regarded as meeting the natural order of universal dynamics, most people, especially if the parent is still active and not considered to be extremely old (Moss & Moss, 1983–1984), are still emotionally unprepared to release a parent when death occurs (Kastenbaum, 1977).

The death of a parent may have many meanings for an adult child. Freud himself was confused by his own reaction when his mother died in 1930.

> It has affected me in a peculiar way, this great event. No pain, no grief, which can be explained by the special circumstances—her great age, my pity for her helplessness toward the end; at the same time a feeling of liberation, of release, which I think I also understand. I was not free to die as long as she was alive, and now I am. (Freud, 1960, p. 400)

This reaction is the same "developmental push" that Osterweis, Solomon, and Green (1984) speak of when a role change takes place after a parent dies. The death propels many adult children into a more responsible stance within the family, especially when the parent is no longer there to fall back on (Pincus, 1974).

Compared to the number of studies of bereavement reactions in general, relatively few studies have focused on the nonpathological variants of the grief of an adult child (Anderson, 1980; Horowitz, Daniel, et al., 1984; Kaltreider, Becker, & Horowitz, 1984; Malinak, Hoyt, & Patterson, 1979; Moss & Moss, 1983–1984; Owen, Fulton, & Markusen, 1982–1983; Sanders, 1979–1980; Schlentz, 1978). Much of the lack of attention is because the death of an adult's parent has lower intensities of grief than do other types of death. Of the three types of death studied in the Tampa study (the death of a child, a spouse, and a parent), the death of a parent showed the lowest levels of grief intensities across all scales. Sanders noted that adult children have most often redirected their attachments to other individuals, such as spouse or children. Their lives were busy and involved.

Owen, Fulton, and Markusen (1982–1983) supported these findings in a similar study in which the three types of death were investigated. They reported that these survivors had little preoccupation with the memory of the deceased and fewer physical complaints than did the other groups. They detected less disruption and less emotionality during the postdeath adjustment. Interpreting their findings in terms of sociological changes seen in smaller nuclear families, these researchers pointed to the impact of institutionalization of the dying and professionalization of their care as providing the families with a protection from responsibility.

Yet, the parent-child relationship represents the longest tie of one's life—the very prototype of the attachment bond (Moss & Moss, 1983–1984). A genetic link forms the core of this relationship. The early established bond between parent and child creates an attachment that endures well into old age. Besides, few loves are as unconditional as that of a devoted parent. Faced with the loss of this unconditional love, the adult child can feel greatly deprived when forced to give up the attachment.

One bereaved daughter, age 55, described her feelings this way:

> Someone of greatest importance had suddenly gone from me. I was completely bereft, stunned as I never anticipated it. The only one who ever truly loved me was gone from this world. The world felt empty, and I lonely.

FACTORS AFFECTING BEREAVEMENT

AGE OF THE ADULT CHILD

The younger the adult child, the stronger is the attachment. Childhood memories of dependency and neediness are fresher in the minds of young adults than in those of older, mature adults. Too, the younger adult child has fewer significant others to draw from for support during grief. The urgent demand for comfort from the one person who has always presented nurturance leaves the bereaved in an insecure and sadly deprived state. One daughter in the Tampa study was only 19 years old when her father died. She was the only child living at home. Two older siblings were married and living in another part of the city. Her father's death was the first one she had ever experienced. When he had a massive heart attack, her first reaction was one of anger and denial. She said,

> I screamed out, protesting that he just could not be dead. It seemed like one of the most impossible things that could ever happen. I felt guilty about not letting him know how much I really loved him. I have a very empty feeling that our home would never be the same. I wanted him so much to be alive. I felt very burdened and lost.

This response supports the study done by Horowitz, Daniel, and others (1984), in which they found that the death of a father led to dramatic reactions. The bereaved immediately experienced as a shocking initial realization either the perceived loss of safety or the potential idealized praise the father might have offered in the future.

The loss of a parent when one is young, particularly when the parent has been a strong support, leaves the survivor with the realization that he or she must now fend for themselves. A 21-year-old daughter, after her mother died, said:

> When she was gone, I knew that I had to grow up, start accepting responsibility without leaning on her. Many of the times, I didn't actually go to her for help, but I knew she was there if I needed her. All that changed. I must see things through myself now.

CASE STUDY: IDENTIFICATION IN EARLY ADULTHOOD

For one 18-year-old daughter, resolution of grief was slow and painful. Although the family knew that the mother had metastatic cancer, the daughter never let herself believe that she would die. Instead, the daughter maintained a positive stance, even when the mother had indicated that she wished to discuss her condition. When asked what her reactions were to the death, she replied:

> Complete shock and disbelief. I realized that I had not ever seriously considered her death until it happened. I was actually unable to think about it for very long or in any detail.

She showed excellent insight when later she realized how much she had been denying her feelings:

> I spent very little time with her because it was too painful. I really feel that I was employing a defense mechanism by avoiding her or not responding to her in conversations when she chose to talk about death.

Grief was difficult, and she spent much time ruminating over the thought that she had abandoned her mother at the end. A year later, she told me,

> The pain is still strong, both emotionally and physically. There is both an internal and an external yearning to be held by my mother. Life lost its meaning for quite a while after my mother's death, and actually only recently did I feel any enthusiasm for life. Even now, it still fluctuates radically at times.

When a parent dies, the bereaved also loses the family of origin in a direct way. The tie to a personal past is dimmed. No one can account for the beginning of the bereaved's life or has access to the unknowns of early life. It is, perhaps, the ultimate blow for one's internalized child (Moss & Moss, 1983–1984).

IDENTIFICATION

The attachment between parent and child reflects a bond, even when the relationship has not been ideal. Some degree of identification normally takes place simply as a result of early socialization. In the Tampa study, mannerisms and behaviors were often mimicked, especially between mothers and daughters. These mannerisms, generally begun early, become enduring responses lasting throughout their lives. Although the mannerisms are not always evident to the individuals themselves, they often become more apparent after one or the other has gone. The same 18-year-old respondent commented on this phenomenon after her mother's death.

> I find myself not only mimicking a lot of behavioral acts, but defending certain types of behavior that I detested while my mother was still alive. I am justifying everything that I used to feel was unjustified. Also, this involves defending her beliefs that I used to argue against.

In this case, identification was revealed in continued feelings of the presence of her mother. She sensed her mother's nearness often. During this time, she had difficulty separating her own feelings about something from those her mother might have felt had she been there. It was almost as though she had become her mother in various attitudes. When she enlisted in military service and went through officer candidate training, she began to distance herself from her deceased mother. Yet she was uncomfortable about it and said,

> My mother's presence was very strong for a good year after she died. The

strength of that feeling has waned considerably lately, so much so that it almost frightens me that I feel so distant.

This daughter still missed her mother and still regretted that she did not talk more openly to her when she was going through her last illness, but she also felt more comfortable by this time and felt that she had released her mother. Too, she had been able to separate her own thoughts from those she had projected as her mother's. She felt that she was, at last, beginning to live her own life.

Identification sometimes intensifies after a death and can actually facilitate grief in the early phases. The opportunity to internalize good feelings and thoughts of the lost one creates an ameliorative effect that seems to comfort and sustain the bereaved. It is as if the bereaved can more easily maintain loyalty and keep the memory alive. However, unresolved ambivalence leads to negative feelings that can inhibit the grief process, causing the bereaved individual to be stuck in one phase or another, unable to let go or to move on to other love objects. Still other grievers have been able to let go to the extent that they use terms such as *former parent* to describe the severed bond between the bereaved and the deceased parent (Taggartt, 1980).

Tandem Losses

There is no guarantee that an individual will suffer only one loss at a time. If that were so, a person might have time to recover from even the most difficult grief before another trauma occurs. However, in tandem losses, one grief intrudes upon another, combining emotions so that the effects cannot be separated.

CASE STUDY: LOSING TWO PARENTS

In one case, a 25-year-old married daughter lost both her parents within 1 year's time. First, her mother died of cancer. This loss was the daughter's first death experience, and she described it as the worst thing that had ever happened to her. She grieved for more than 6 months, thinking of her mother daily and crying frequently. Tears still came to her eyes when the final interview took place a year and a half later. She still misses her, thinking of the things in life they will never share again. She said,

> Every daughter looks forward to the time when she can become friends with her mother, you know, past the time when the mother-daughter role is maintained.

Usually this comes when the daughter has children of her own and can fully realize what the mother has experienced.

Well, my sisters had both reached this point, but I never did. I think now of the friend I missed having.

Her father had cared for her mother throughout the illness with undaunted vigilance. Her death must have represented both enormous loss as well as a personal defeat for him. He held up well during the funeral but later withdrew from everyone.

In the meantime, the daughter had moved to Florida and could not be near him. Her two sisters were nearby and did what they could to help him through his despair. Eventually, however, her father began staying in the house all the time. The neighbors would buy buns for him and put them on his porch every morning. If the buns were taken in, they knew he was okay. The neighbors said he would spend his evenings just sitting in the dark.

One day, the father did not take the buns in from the porch. A neighbor who had a key went in and found him dead of a heart attack. He had neither the will nor the desire to live without his wife. The daughter's first thoughts, after learning of the death, were "Well, now you are where you wanted to be, Dad." He had often said, when visiting his wife's grave (which was often), "Soon, I'll be with you."

It is understandably difficult for the daughter to separate the two deaths clearly. Obviously, they had a confounding effect. She told me that she tries not to think about it and keeps very busy with her job, yet the sadness of losing both parents within a short time and under such tragic conditions has its effect.

CASE STUDY: LOSING A SPOUSE AND A PARENT

In another case, a woman was widowed 2 years before she lost her mother. She had trouble sorting out the feelings she had for each grief. With her mother, she had 20 days warning when a stroke incapacitated her and she was forced to put her in a nursing home. With her husband, death was sudden and unexpected. Both deaths were quick in onset, but she did not feel as much personal deprivation with the loss of her mother, for she had been living apart from her for years. As she said,

I didn't experience as many of these feelings when my mother died as I did when my husband died. I mean with her, she was 82, and she had lived a good life. I missed her terribly but I wasn't angry. I was grateful that she didn't last that long to experience what I had seen in other people who had had strokes and lingered for a long time. That I wouldn't have wanted under any circumstances. So I wasn't angry; I was relieved, for her and for me. When my husband died, I was angry all the way through—angry and hurt.

The grief for her mother was actually over before our first visit at 2 months, but the grief for her husband still persisted.

CHRONIC-ILLNESS DEATH

The death itself was not always what brought about the greatest grief in adult children. Sometimes just watching a parent deteriorate from a physical or psychological impairment brought a feeling of powerlessness as well as horror. When a parent has always been pictured as strong and capable, the downhill trajectory of death can be a time of extreme sorrow and regret to the family. In some cases, children felt actual relief when the death occurred, because the parent no longer had the quality of life that he or she once had. This relief was articulated by a 63-year-old daughter who had cared for her mother for 5 years prior to her death.

> The bereavement was greatest when I knew she was never going to walk again and I saw her going down. That was just horrible. It was a shock certainly, but the greatest shock was having her bedridden. When death came, I was relieved.
>
> I am very thankful it happened the way it did because my mother knew nothing . . . she had no pain . . . she died in her sleep. The only difficult thing about the stroke . . . she had a tube and that was not painful for her, I could tell; it was just hard for me. I had always prayed that she would go in her sleep and she did.

It was easier for this daughter to let her mother go than to hang onto her as sick as she was. This attitude is in keeping with the work on anticipatory grief, which has found that some expectancy of the death prepares one better and leads to a less intense form of grief than does a sudden death (Fulton & Fulton, 1971; Glick et al., 1974; Raphael & Maddison, 1976; Vachon et al., 1976).

Some participants in the Tampa study expressed their grief more strongly than others, but for the most part, these adult children were engulfed in their own busy worlds. They had families, jobs, and daily responsibilities that allowed them little time to dwell on the deceased parent.

DEATH PREPAREDNESS OF DECEASED

The bereaved are sometimes better prepared for the death of a parent if the parent appears to be ready and prepared for death. If death has been openly discussed in the family, if perhaps even burial plans and arrangements have been made, the survivors experience less trauma.

CASE STUDY: A WELL-PREPARED DEATH

The situation of a mother and daughter in the Tampa study illustrates well the benefits of death preparedness. The two had never been close, but after the father had died 10 years before, the mother had transferred her dependency onto her daughter, even living with her for several years.

Her mother had always been fairly decisive about what her funeral would be like. During her growing-up years, the daughter remembers seeing lists made as to what objects would be left to what people in case of her death. Her mother would tag certain dresses from time to time as to the one she would be buried in. The "funeral dress" would shift as fashion and mood would. This situation was not a morbid one to her mother, but one of planning for an important celebration.

> All my life since I've been about 16, my mother was planning her funeral. You would find a dress hanging in her closet and she would say, "This is my funeral dress." She would talk about who was to do her hair and so forth. She was very serious about this.
>
> Besides that, she had all her little wants about her funeral written on notes. They would be everywhere. You would find a little note here and it'd say, "If I die, call so and so." This death thing was big with her.

As her mother's health deteriorated and she needed more individual care, they decided together that she would go to a retirement home. Even there, she would keep current on what her funeral dress was going to be. As her daughter recounted:

> So right after Christmas, not this past one, the Christmas before, she said she'd like a couple of long-sleeve dresses because her arms were getting all these marks, which I also inherited from her. So I bought her two dresses, and one of them was a beautiful light blue dress. It had a little lace around a high neck, and when she opened the box, I knew immediately that that was the new funeral dress. I mean, I just sat there and I knew. So I kept asking her about it and I would say to her, "Mother, why don't you wear that blue dress?" She would say, "Well, I'll wear it one of these days." So along around summer, I said to her, "How come you don't wear the new blue dress?" and she just said, "Well." And I said, "It's the funeral dress, isn't it?" And then she laughed and said, "Yes."

She later contracted metastatic bone cancer, and even though she knew she was dying, she was as much in charge as ever. Both her daughter and grandson were with her on that last day.

She said, "I'm going to die today . . . no tonight." And it was like somebody be-hind her telling her to say that. It was. But she was as happy as a clam.

John would say to her, "Granny, do you know who I am?" "Of course." Then he would say, "Who am I?" and she said, "You're John Boy." But her voice [had] changed. It was like she was young again.

She said, "I've got to go," and John would say, "Where are you going, Granny?" "I'm going downtown." "What are you going to do downtown?" "I'm going to shop." And she would be quiet for a little while . . . then she would say, "Have you got my dress?" And it was like she was slipping in and out, and I said, "What dress, mother?" "I can't go downtown in this," she would say. She just slept away, and John said, "Momma, I've got to go get the priest" and I said, "Well, nobody here will give me any information, and besides I think she has had the last sacraments 20 times." But I said, "See if you can get Father Higgin" because mother didn't hold with these foreigners. And I said, "See if you can get him."

So pretty soon Father Higgin comes in with his blue jeans and she recog-nized him. . . . He said, "Do you remember me?" She said, "Yes." He said, "Who am I?" She said, "Father Higgin." By this time, her tongue was kind of thick. Then as soon as he gave her the last drink, she slipped into a coma. And it was like she was waiting for us to bring her a proper priest.

Yes, things should be done in a proper way. I know she had had last rites from several of these Spanish priests, but that was no good. As soon as Father Higgin left, she slipped into a coma, and she just slept away. And it was a beautiful, peaceful death.

She explained that she was able to find peace in her mother's death and ab-solve herself of the guilt because she had simply fulfilled her mother's wishes con-cerning the services. She felt that if her mother had died 20 years earlier, she would have had more problems with guilt because she had never lived up to her mother's expectations. In the past few years, she had become more comfortable with the situation. Yet, she still had trouble with certain things, such as her mother's belongings. As she said,

Just for instance, right now, I have a whole room full of boxes of her things. I have 32 boxes of glassware in storage. I wish they would deliver it, and I wish they wouldn't. I've got another closet full . . . she was very very involved with her possessions. She didn't want me to get rid of anything. She'd say, "Don't throw away this lamp because it is very valuable," and it would be a piece of junk, I thought.

So to me, that's where the conflict is. You're sitting there with your mother's things, thinking, "You know, I really ought to give it to somebody that would ap-preciate it!" But she probably wouldn't like the person I gave it to.

So while you are not grieving in the emotional sense, you are still tied to your mother's possessions just as she was. I am all right, but I think grief has taken its place in these things.

The daughter was asked if she remembered a difference between the way she grieved for her father and the way she grieved for her mother.

There is a difference, I don't care what anybody says, there is a difference. Now as I said before, my father and I were very close. I think I was supposed to be a boy but the genes got messed up because I am a very good mechanic. I'm very much like my mother in many respects, but I was daddy's girl and I like to do mechanics and all this sort of thing. I have my dad's toolbox and I use it every once in awhile. I'll need a screwdriver or wrench or something and every time I use it, I feel very close to him. I have other things of his, but I don't feel that way about them.

Now with my mother's things, I don't have this feeling because I used to . . . when she was going on about these ceramic angels and about how valuable they were, I'm thinking they are kind of dumb looking . . . and to me they look like ceramic. I don't know what is so valuable about two ceramic angels. But we had a big ceremony, you know, whenever we took down the drapes. We had to take down these angels and lay them very carefully so that nothing would harm these two little angels. Now, I thought they were dumb then, and I think they are dumb now. And yet I would have very much difficulty in giving these angels to anybody.

It was apparent that the mother was in control of her own death from the beginning. She knew what she wanted. Recognizing that she would die that night, she made sure that the funeral dress was ready and that last rites were properly administered.

Good insight was shown by the daughter when she recognized that she had displaced the grief for her mother onto the 32 boxes of glassware. What she did not see, however, was the difference between the father's toolbox and her mother's ceramic angels. The toolbox had taken on the sentimental quality of a linking object, but the mother's possessions had actually become her own belongings. Although she hated them, she could not part with them because of the strong identification that connected her to her mother.

DEATH ANXIETY

Even when death is expected by the family, when a parent dies, an intense degree of death anxiety accompanies the reaction. This anxiety can be generated from the conscious or unconscious realization that when a parent dies, the children move up to become next in line (Moss & Moss, 1983–1984). This anxiety can also be seen as the developmental push described earlier in the chapter (Osterweis et al., 1984). Death anxiety can also come from simply being exposed to death itself, particularly when one has been largely sheltered from dying people. Primarily, death anxiety emerges in the awareness that, as adult children, the number of years already lived are greater than the number of years remaining to live. The death of a parent is a reminder of personal mortality.

CASE STUDY: REALIZING PERSONAL MORTALITY

The concept of personal mortality was well expressed by a man whose mother had died from cancer. He said,

> My mother lived 12 years beyond the 70 we are promised. Anything over 70 is like a bonus, and she lived life actively and fully. I am 52 [years old], which is now past midway. Since Mother died, I have been thinking what I will do with my 17 or 18 years that I have left. I am thinking in terms of time left, whereas I didn't think this way before the death.

He told me that the time before her death was actually the most difficult for him because he had to watch the deterioration take place. His mother had always been active and involved in family and community matters until a year before her death.

> At 81, she was mobile enough so that she would get down on the floor with the children and play with them and things like that. She had a very active life . . . but when a person gets into something like cancer and you lose your mobility, it's . . . there are some things worse than death, you know.

Disease onset began with a lump in the breast. After a mastectomy, the cancer metastasized to the lungs, spine, and finally to the brain. Although she had no pain, she did suffer cognitive disability. Seeing her deteriorate over the last 3 weeks in the hospital was extremely painful for him, and he felt that he did most of his grieving them. He cried then, especially during periods when he thought she was dying.

> I cried more before the funeral than I did after the funeral . . . going down to the hospital, you know, it was harder then, as far as I was concerned. I said goodbye to Mother about 10 times. About 3 or 4 times, we didn't think we would see her again. She was that bad.
> You look at a person and you say, "There's got to be something better than this . . . because you remember the person at their strongest, their best moments and then you see them now in their worst moments and you don't like to. You wouldn't . . . say if an animal was hurt, your dog or cat or something was run over, you would try to save them, but if you could see it couldn't be saved, you wouldn't want them to suffer either. Sometimes, we treat our animals better than we do our people.

This man took a philosophical view in saying that he recognized that he is not grieving as he would if a younger person had died. He feels that his mother had a long, full life. He reiterated several times, however, the notion that he is more aware of the possibility of his own death now, that he is thinking in terms of time left to live.

One thing that may have contributed to the reduction of grief after the death, he thought, was the fact that the funeral arrangements had been made prior to the death. Making these arrangements was not an easy task to accomplish, but once it had been done, he had an easier mind. He described the events that led up to the decision to contact the funeral home:

> My wife and I knew it was coming to an end because we went down to the hospital every day, twice a day, and we could see that they had removed the artificial breathing system.
>
> So we took a day off from work and just went over to the funeral home and made the arrangements. It's not something that's done with any ease, that's for sure. Both my wife and I are pretty well educated, so we try to look at things in a logical manner, but it's not that easy sometimes. Still, making the arrangements then made it easier for us later. We are glad we did it.

At a follow-up a year and a half later, the greatest change in this man was in the reduction of death anxiety, which would indicate that movement farther from the event lessens the personal death anxiety. People have a tendency to repress the unpleasant side effects of loss and focus on the necessary requirements of living. However, he did say that he now thinks of his mother more in a reflective, contemplative manner than he did earlier. He said that he is now beginning to identify with her as to seniority and place in the family.

Grief for a parent seemed to be ameliorated if one had a supportive spouse at hand, especially if the marriage had been a long one and the couple had been close. The two were able to take the shock of death with greater fortitude than when the survivor was unmarried or widowed.

DIFFERENT GRIEF FOR DIFFERENT DECEASED

Several respondents in the Tampa study reported that they dreamed more of their family members since the death of a parent than they had at any time in their lives. A 62-year-old man who had lost both parents said,

> You know, since you were last here, I have dreamed more about my family [father, mother, and brother] than I ever did before. All of these people are dead. It is strange, and I don't know if it means anything, but I never used to dream of them, but now I have, not regularly, but more than I have in my whole life. I never used to dream, but I have lately.

As we discussed the various losses that he had experienced during his life, he commented on the differences and types of grief he felt after each of these deaths. He said that although each death generated a grief all its own, the situations surrounding the deaths did make a difference in his reactions:

My brother committed suicide some time after my father died, so I still had my mother left and had been taking care of her for about 10 years. My mother told me before she died that until you lose your mate, as opposed to a mother, father, brother, et cetera, you don't know what it is like to experience deep grief. She may be right; I don't know.

His further comment about grief illustrates the variety of reactions that can be generated by a significant loss.

You asked me if I had noticed any difference in the type of grief I felt when my mother, father, or brother died. When my mother died, I felt a loss but did not feel any deep pain, as she had been quite ill these last 3 years. I had time to adjust and to realize that she was suffering and that the only way the suffering would end would be when she died. Having watched her decline over a period of time helped me adjust to her death. But it was interesting that the greatest pain concerning a death that I ever felt was not with my father, brother, or mother, but was when our dog died. I went out into the middle of the street in front of the house. I was holding him in my arms and could feel his heart under my hand beating rapidly. Then it skipped a beat, then beat more rapidly again, then started missing more and more until it finally quit totally.

His voice quivered when he was telling of this incident. For the first time in the series of interviews he showed an outward, emotional sense of loss. "So you asked me if I noticed any differences, the only thing I can say is that I honestly believe that it hurt more to lose that dog than it has any member of my family."

SUMMARY

How can a person say what event will trigger the deepest grief in one's life? So much depends on the type and quality of the relationship and on the strength of the attachment shared with others. It seems natural to shift dependency needs from parents to spouse and, perhaps, to children when moving into and through adulthood. As families require time and attention, a person gradually disengages from the activities that were previously shared with parents. However, some people have relationships in which strong attachments are maintained and ongoing needs are still reciprocal. When these variables are operating, the death of a parent is met with feelings of enormous deprivation and, consequently, a sense of deep personal loss.

In spite of people's differences, some feelings occur universally when a parent dies:

1. Significant death anxiety is brought about by the knowledge that one is next in line. An individual becomes more aware of his or her own vulnerability and mortality.
2. With the parent gone, the bereaved is no longer anyone's child. While a parent lived, a person always had someone to relate to in terms of personal history. In other words, people had persons in the world who had always known them, who could share with them the memories of the past. With those persons gone, they feel orphaned.

The death of a parent represents a significant loss in many respects. Yet, when the funeral is over, our society expects survivors to pick up exactly as things were before. People rarely inquire into the personal feelings of the bereaved or acknowledge the grief after a week or two. People are impatient with the grief of a bereaved adult child, as though it does not require much attention or long-term reaction. Like the man, described in an earlier chapter, who wished that he could wear an armband to signify to others that he was still mourning his mother's death, these "adult orphaned children" must keep their feelings to themselves and mourn in secret.

PART SIX

RITUALS OF LOSS

CHAPTER 17

Rites of Passage

RITUALS AND RITES of passage are traditionally among the most powerfully sanctioned methods available to offer symbolic guidance to the human spirit. As such, they have always been important parts of the human experience. Historically, rituals provided direction for regulating people's lives. Information describing the rituals of cave dwellers have been recorded with rich inspiration—behavior that ranges from gathering food to burying the dead. Rituals transmit the combined wisdom of previous generations with the hope that this same wisdom may help the present generation deal with similar problems. Apparently, both the capacity and the need for ritual expression are built into the human psyche and act as shapers and guides for social structures. Although based on inner urgencies for social baselines, myths appear alongside these demonstrations. Myths are not only born of human experience, they also tend to shape it once they have been given verbal form and embodied in ritual. Myths then become both cause and effect of cultural reality. And rituals continue to reflect the emergent images of the myths passed on from generation to generation. Joseph Campbell was asked, "How do we go about creating myths?" He answered, "You don't create myths. Myths come like dreams. You have to wait for them." But he also added, "Each of us must recognize and make explicit the myths that do come, and the myths we live by. For we all live by a myth of some kind" (Campbell, 1988, p. 22).

The dreams that bring our myths and the recognition of our myths empower our self-generating rituals and, in turn, generate important strength from which we survive our personal losses and tragedies. Today, our mythology is neither uniform nor stable. We are between a time in the past in which the myths were passed on by a single shaman around a campfire and a modern world in which news and technology are spelled out for us on a worldwide web of confusion and disorientation.

As Virginia Hine (1978) wrote, "It would not be surprising then to find ourselves at this point in time witnessing the emergence of new myths and new rituals meaningful in a new age and supportive of values." She later adds, "I believe we are looking at the process by which ritual becomes traditional" (p. 83).

Rituals have been an integral element of life since the beginning of human existence. Once we recognize that our cultural myths represent our most basic beliefs, then we can understand how a life-sustaining power such as a strong myth can move us through the dreadful uncertainty of the radical changes brought about by the illness and death of a loved one. Myths represent the deep belief system, the worldview, that shapes the structure of any culture. Through myth, order can be retained and can therefore contribute meaning in life. In other words, behavior is to rituals what belief is to myths. And through our ritual behaviors, the cultural myths become a part of our rituals.

The need for ritual in our lives is based on the function of myth—of supplying a deeper meaning to life. Through myths the stories of the universe are shared; they explain the nature of the cosmos, the role of human behavior, and an explanation of why life unfolds as it does. Once these explanations are shared by a large group, the participants are able to experience the most impossible tragedy, the deepest hurts and agonies, making it possible for us to experience these dreadful disasters creatively. Individuals can live through the most difficult grief because there is meaning in the tragedy.

Human experience is the mother of cultural myths offering shape once given verbal form. Laurel Van der Post, in his study of the bush people of Africa, discussed the need for Western individuals to open their minds to the creation of myth. He did not necessarily advocate the release of old forms of mythical roots but instead the incorporation of new myths representing shifts on a transcendental level.

Also supporting the need for transcendental shifts in myths, Joseph Campbell spoke from the source of individual experience. Or as he writes, "Creative mythology springs not like theology, from the dicta of authors, but from the insights, sentiments, thoughts and visions of an adequate individual loyal to his own experience of value" (Campbell, 1988).

The vast social changes in the past 100 years in America have scattered the population, separating families and homes from each other. People used to grow up, live their lives, and finally die within a fairly small radius. When individuals in a community suffered a loss or even a gain, enough family, friends, and relatives were close by to support, help, or celebrate. Individuals who were feeling isolated or alone benefited from traditions of society that were carried out with well-worn guidelines. And the community knew what those traditions were and how to participate in them.

However, one set of conceptual tools has to do with the basic functions of ritual in any sociocultural system. Most rituals help facilitate a passage in the lives of individuals, whether beginning a marriage or ending a life. A culture has rituals for helping the passage from childhood into adulthood, rituals surrounding pregnancy and birth, rites for retirement or divorce, rituals for the dying and the grieving. These rituals are separation events. Other rituals function primarily to reinforce social cohesion, resolve conflicts, and re-create group harmony. These rituals are called rites of intensification. According to classical anthropological analyses, rites of intensification are those rituals through which the community reinforces social cohesion and reestablishes social harmony. In preindustrial societies, these rituals were based on connections drawn from each cultural group and its environment and made use of natural events such as solstices, equinoxes, and new and full moons.

In postmodern times, political rallies, elections, or even large religious revivals have served as ways that groups can join together with feelings of like mind to achieve social harmony and cohesion. Oftentimes these events, such as the Woodstock music festival, can further an entirely new basis for social cohesion.

Nathan Kollar (1989) outlines the many functions of rituals. He states that rituals as patterns of activity involve both social and personal habits. As such, they cover a wide assortment of social interactions, from worship services to war games, from athletic events to funerals. Certainly rituals are an integral part of our lives; they provide us with a blueprint for our daily existence as well as our entire life cycle. Rituals provide the pattern that holds life together. Whether we acknowledge it or not, rituals enter into every area of our lives.

Rituals are communal in nature but not necessarily done in a group. Although good ritual builds community, ritual done alone can have a different effect. Because rituals have many different meanings, they can be interpreted in many different ways. A marriage ritual might be performed with one set of expectations and celebrations, but the same couple might, several years later, choose to celebrate their divorce with a different set of expectations and emotions. Nevertheless, both these events carry with them a step forward toward meeting a new life. The ritual, whether formal or casual, helps create a constructive channel to help meet the new needs. Yet each of these rituals is a rite of passage or intensification.

THE NEED FOR RITUALS

Traditional cultures had some form of permission built into the ritual repertoire. For example, at a certain age approval was given to the young man or
woman who desired to become an adult. A ritual of passage marked that
transition. The ritual itself contained implicit understanding of the changes
being made. Today, in modern culture, formal rituals have diminished.
Families no longer live near one another, and it is rare to meet adults who
presently live in the area in which they grew up. The transitions in life must
be handled alone, without guidelines, community backing, sanctions, or
permissions. As a result, new guidelines are being developed today to give
expression to the transition of life. There is a small quickening of interest in
self-made rituals to fit various occasions. The event of a divorce has had a
history of painful litigation, ending in a complete separation of the couple
and division of children. Today we see the beginnings of a mediation approach in which the couple works through the painful details of the disso-
lution and manages to part as friends. Or as Feinstein and Mayo observe in
their book, *Rituals for Living & Dying* (1990), "Rock concerts mobilized
around causes such as peace, poverty, and human rights have become powerful vehicles around ritualistic activity in modern societies." These writers
noted that the 1960s and 1970s saw a gaining popularity of temporary
groups, such as encounter groups and workshops for personal development. These groups may have served the same functions that rituals and
rites of passage served in earlier cultures. Studies of the elaborate rituals devised by ancient societies have found that three steps emerge over and over
in these rites of passage:

Severance.   That part of the ritual that represents a separation, either real
      or symbolic, from a past state or a stepping out of the normal con-
      text of life.
Transition.   That phase that represents the gradual change from one
      state to another; often called *linial,* from the Latin word meaning
      threshold; a period very different from the individual's former or fu-
      ture states.
Reincorporation.   The acknowledgment of a reentry into a new life; a
      new beginning; a celebration of a return to the norm; a joining or
      reentry into life, incorporating the change.

William Bridges, in his book *Transitions: Making Sense of Life's Changes,*
suggests that we must consciously recognize this three-phase process in our
lives if we are to create effective rituals:

People sometimes bewail the fact that we lack rituals and suggest that we ought to create some. Clearly the rites of passage were terribly important ways of validating and facilitating development. But our own situation cannot be remedied by rituals when we have lost our understanding of what rituals dramatize. Before rituals can have any real meaning for us we must recover our understanding of respect for and willingness to experience this process of death, liminality, and renewal.

For all of us have natural cycles of regeneration though each of them requires a little death, a small winter, a subtle crucifixion. I don't suppose we can recapture the primeval rhythm in our society at large, but individually and in small groups we can. (p. 88)

RITES OF PASSAGE

Providing some type of ceremony will help alleviate the terrible loss one experiences in the death of a loved one. Several options are available. The ceremony selected will, in itself, be a form of memorial that provides an opportunity to offer respect to the deceased. The more personally meaningful the ritual, the more important it becomes to the bereaved. Rando (1984) points out that whether a religious or nonreligious ceremony (one with no religious connotations but simply a gathering of families and friends supporting one another) is selected, the important issue is that the ceremony be personally meaningful to the survivors. Without that element, the therapeutic value is lost.

No matter what type of body disposition the family chooses, the action nevertheless offers an acknowledgment that the death has occurred. This step, in turn, allows the bereaved to move forward in their grief. Generally the type of final disposition selected will have been determined before the death occurs. Here are some of the options:

Cremation offers the family the opportunity of holding the memorial service at any time. A memorial service may be offered shortly after the death occurs, or the family may wish to wait until a later time when more of the family can be together. The urn containing the ashes may be placed in a grave or columbarium, a mausoleum designed for holding cremated remains. Or, on the other hand, the ashes may be scattered by a family member or group of family and friends who will offer a memorial at the same time.

Entombment describes the burial in which the body is placed in a casket that is then placed in a mausoleum. The funeral or memorial service can be held in a church or funeral home, or the service can take place on-site at the mausoleum. The advantage of this type of burial is that some families are reticent to have the deceased buried in the ground and can have the comfort of a disposition that is aboveground.

Earth burial is the most common form of body disposition in America. Most often, the funeral service is held in a church or funeral home a few days after the death. Following this service, the body will be transported to a cemetery for earth burial. Most often, a short ritual to mark this second service will be held before the family and guests depart.

Our final rite of passage usually comes after we have experienced and gone through many other passages in life, including baptism, puberty, mid-life crisis, dealing with an empty nest, leaving home, having children, divorce, illness, and finally, death. Not all these events will be experienced by every person; however, this partial list shows the wide range of events in our lives that need rituals. These events are all life passages, and some form of ritual can help us move through the difficult transitions that each one produces.

Our society offers little with which to bridge the empty months and even years that follow a major loss. It ignores cessation of grief, that period of reincorporation that is so important for mobilizing the bereaved into a new life. Instead, society leaves the bereaved with little support or even acknowledgment that a loss had actually taken place. Few people share the period of reentry.

Some specific religions do offer help to the mourner, to at least get them through the period of shock and awareness of their grief. The Jewish religion suggests that ritual plays a vital role in helping the griever move through the first year of loss. Beginning with shivah, the first seven days of intensive mourning following the funeral, the mourner remains at home receiving a continuous flow of condolence calls. Although sometimes painful, the constant visitation by friends and loved ones helps to keep the bereaved engaged and mentally active. To further aid the bereaved in their focus on the deeply spiritual nature of the time, a shivah candle is lit and remains burning for the entire seven days. Then for a prolonged period (depending on what family member died), the Kaddish prayer is read daily to commemorate the memory. These rituals enforce both the reality of death and the affirmation of life.

THERAPEUTIC PROPERTIES OF RITUAL

Rituals give form, structure, and meaning to our feelings at a time when we are feeling decentralized and devoid of direction. At a time of severe loss, we need outlets for appropriate personal acting out as well as the opportunity to share with others. Because loss presents us with such a marked period of confusion and fear, the order offered by rituals provides structure and direction to a scattered mental state. At the same time, we have an implicit need to overcome feelings of powerlessness and to gain a stronger sense of control and competence. Being given permission to engage in our own emotional expression provides a channel for pent-up feelings. And indeed, rituals can provide this type of outlet.

Hine and Foster, in their book entitled *A Guide for Rites of Passage for Our Time: A Guide for Creating Ritual* (n.d.), cites numerous evocative descriptions of what ritual does "for the individual, for society, for the natural environment." Here are some of those descriptions:

Ritual is a way of moving into nonordinary levels of awareness.
Ritual links two orders of reality.
Ritual taps a source of power and energy.
Ritual sets human beings into archetypal situations, performing archetypal acts, which releases the transforming power of the Collective Unconscious, of the Higher Self, of God.
Ritual renews and regenerates.
Ritual is a way of lifting up a life crisis instead of just going through it.
Ritual is a way to both generate and reinforce commitment.
Ritual enshrines and enables.
Ritual gives form to human life, not in mere surface arrangements, but in depth.
Ritual, like love, is a force for negentropy.
Ritual is participation in the workings of the universe.

Ritual provides us a safe haven in which to ponder and feel, a haven beyond our present state and in our unconscious. This transmutation allows us the spiritual strength needed for the psychological changes necessary to fill the awful void left by the loss of a dear one. The ritual must be linked to a mythology that offers meaning to the experience of the moment or else it lacks the depth that ritual is designed to offer.

THE POWER OF SELF-GENERATED RITUALS

More people today are supplementing the current mourning rituals with self-made rituals that ease them across the empty time after the funeral and memorial service. Because our society offers little with which to bridge the empty months and even years following a death, this ability to design new rituals at various anniversary periods fills a definite need.

Bereavements contain anniversaries and specific periods that are extremely painful. Mourners approach those dates with fear and dread, worrying that they won't make it through the day. Planning a small ritual, confronting the fear, and acknowledging the day actually makes the situation smoother and easier to handle. For example, one mourner shared a birthday anniversary with family and a few friends by asking each one to read something that held a reminder of the deceased and to then light a candle to represent the spiritual connection. The tools that are used, and when or how they are used, really don't matter. A ritual planned ahead of time directs attention toward the expectations for a positive outcome.

SYMBOLIC TOOLS FOR RITUAL BUILDING

Rituals can be built with a wide variety of tools. The following list offers a few examples:

Music.   Melodies and rhythm speak directly to the intuitive level of awareness. They evoke a deep emotional response and move one at the deepest level of the unconscious.

Invocation.   Self-generated rituals often include some form of calling on a source of energy, such as a higher power or some other divine force, to be present. An invocation focuses the awareness of the participants on the memorialized person and also on a common source of power.

Silence.   Participants can often employ silence as a method of tuning in to each other in a particularly meaningful way. Silence may involve meditation or contemplation and is often used as an opening to the ritual experience.

Incense and smoke.   These ascending symbols have long been viewed as a way to make contact with the world of the spirit. Smoke is symbolic of transcending and purification.

Feasting.   The sharing of food and drink is a universal symbol of agreement or mutual commitment. It is used traditionally at the end of all rituals to indicate the joining of the community in love and support.

Rituals require us to surrender ourselves to the process that has been set into motion. They don't have to be elaborate. However, they should incorporate several of the tools listed here. And further, preplanning is very important to extend the unified focus central to the commemoration. "These personal rituals are internal rites of passage designed to modify and revitalize beliefs, attitudes, and patterns of behavior. They guide you toward fresh contact with the core of your being" (Feinstein & Mayo, 1990, p. 43).

PART SEVEN

PRACTICAL APPLICATIONS

CHAPTER 18

Therapeutic Approaches

T HE PREVIOUS CHAPTERS have underscored that no one special intervention or treatment modality will fit all bereaved people. Much depends on the phase of grief in which they are when intervention was
begun as well as many other moderator variables, such as personality of the
bereaved, death surroundings, attachment to the deceased, and a whole
host of extenuating factors. For this reason, the caregiver must know a great
deal not only about the bereavement process, but about the bereaved person as well.

WHO NEEDS INTERVENTION?

A number of researchers have repeatedly emphasized that bereavement
counseling or psychotherapy is not needed by all bereaved persons (Parkes,
1985; Raphael, 1984). The bereaved usually know what their needs are.
Silverman and Cooperband (1974), in follow-up interviews conducted 3
years after the death, found that widows who had not expressed a need for
help at the time of death had assessed their situation accurately and did not
need help during bereavement. In the Tampa study, only a small percentage
of bereaved were considered to be at risk, either through complications in
the relationship (guilt, ambivalence) or through complications with the
death situation (sudden unexpected death, death of a child, lack of social
support). Even in those high-risk cases, only five individuals sought professional counseling. Others managed to survive one way or another so that
at follow-up 18 months to 2 years later, levels of grief had diminished to the

degree that they were able to pick up loose ends and move on with their lives. As a matter of fact, some lives were actually improved by the death.

CASE STUDY: A LIBERATING DEATH

For example, the first participant who was interviewed in the Tampa study was a 75-year-old widower. He and his wife of 45 years had moved to Florida 10 years before, when he retired from the post office as a letter carrier. He said he had been so looking forward to retirement all those years so that he could do all the things he was interested in, such as lawn bowl, play duplicate bridge, and work in his workshop. They moved to a retirement community in which all these outlets were available. But once moved, his wife refused to let him engage in social activities because she said she wanted him with her. To enforce this desire, she managed to acquire one psychosomatic illness after another. When she died suddenly after volunteer surgery, he was surprised and then relieved.

When I called on him 6 weeks postdeath, I was unaware of the circumstances and was prepared to offer condolences and sympathy. Instead, I was greeted at the door by a spry and cheerful man who was only too happy to share his story.

It seemed that now that his wife was gone, he had no restrictions and could begin to live his life as he had always fantasized. He joined a lawn bowling group, found several bridge groups, and in a relatively short time had launched himself on a new course, meeting new people and proceeding to fulfill his dreams.

Later, when I described this situation to a close minister friend, he said that the term used in his trade for situations like that was a "God-given divorce." Obviously, this widower needed no intervention; he possessed the social skills necessary to acquire the support he needed. Actually, intervention may have interfered with his coping skills, especially if a caregiver had attempted to bring out the ambivalence or guilt, which certainly may have been there at an unconscious level. Follow-up at 2 years found the man just as content and spry; he was now dating.

Admittedly, this case was unusual. For most people, a significant loss leaves them deeply saddened, with greater physical and social adjustments to make. Yet nearly half the participants in the Tampa study (49%) were in the normal, grief-contained category and only 8% were in the disturbed category; these statistics point out how important it is that caregivers initially listen and support only. Decision to seek professional intervention should be made by the bereaved and by their families.

MUTUAL SUPPORT GROUPS

Although not every person going through a bereavement process needs professional intervention, everyone needs support and social contact as they deal with the frightening aspects of grief. Loss leaves the individual feeling small and empty. Social support can help rebuild the person again. As Melanie Klein stated as early as 1940,

> If the mourner has people whom he loves and who share his grief, and if he can accept their sympathy, the restoration of the harmony in his inner world is promoted, and his fears and distress are more quickly reduced. (p. 329)

Self-help groups can offer this support, especially when the family structure is diminished or disengaged from one another. Segal, Fletcher, and Meekison (1986) found in their survey of bereaved parents that the most consistently preferred source of support was another parent or couple whose child had died. This conclusion is in line with Silverman's (1987) findings in which she saw that the best type of help for the widowed is another widow. The widow can legitimize her feelings in a way that only someone who has experienced such a death can fully understand. Dr. Silverman states, "They are made up of people having similar problems and who are willing to share their experiences and concerns."

Outlining levels of support, Stroebe and Stroebe (1987) list three basic areas in which others can perform important functions for the bereaved:

1. *Instrumental support.* Tasks associated with the funeral, advice on financial matters, or help with household or other personal tasks are probably the first type of support needed.
2. *Emotional support.* This support encourages grief work, particularly by an empathetic listener who will not lose patience or disappear. The bereaved often need help in accepting the reality of the death. Being able to repeat their accounts of the death over and over will help to crystallize the reality.
3. *Validational support.* Being able to normalize grief can assuage the fears many bereaved have that they are "going crazy." They need to know that the bereavement process is longer than realized and that the usual symptoms and experiences in grief are to be expected.

The bereaved will experience a sense of relief by having supporters nearby who can continue to offer help in a nonjudgmental manner. Because bereavement reactions cover such a wide and diverse latitude, symptoms vary from person to person. Yet some general reactions and responses are felt by nearly everyone in one degree or another.

Osterweis et al. (1984) have listed a number of similar elements that mutual support groups can offer members:

- Person-to-person exchange based on identification and reciprocity.
- Access to a body of specialized information.
- Opportunity to share coping techniques, based on realistic expectations for optimal functioning.
- Increased sense of personal worth, obtained by focusing on how similar members are to others confronting the same situation.
- Reinforcement for positive change and maintenance of effort toward change through feedback on performance.
- Arena for advocacy and social change.
- Opportunity for education, not only of other persons with similar problems, but also of professionals and the public.
- Help for the helpers who themselves are aided by assisting others and by activism toward shared goals.

Phyllis Silverman, a pioneer in the study and formation of widow-to-widow groups, refers to the friendships formed in these groups as "linking relationships" that act as a bridge between the past and the future. Members act as role models for newly bereaved widows, offering guidance and a fresh perspective on feelings and behaviors (Silverman & Cooperband, 1974). A study by Vachon et al. (1980) found that widows helped by mutual support groups had benefited psychologically as opposed to widows who received no such support. Various widow-to-widow programs throughout the country are now offering support to bereaved spouses.

Compassionate Friends is a support group for bereaved parents that has chapters throughout this country as well as in England (where it began). Videka-Sherman (1982) found, in her study of bereaved parents' coping ability following the death of their child, that participation in Compassionate Friends provided the opportunity for parents to shift coping styles from preoccupation with the deceased child to altruistic outreach. It was found that reinvestment of one's interest and love preceded reduction in depressions as long as the investment was not a replacement for the lost child. Mutual support groups can act as a monitor for the bereaved in providing a reality check against premature attempts to form replacements without reaching the healing and renewal phases of bereavements. Burnell and Burnell (1989) point out that, whereas relatives and friends offer temporary emotional support, groups such as Compassionate Friends provide a longer-lasting resource that can effectively help bereaved parents through the long, difficult phases of grief.

Perhaps one of the most important and prolific movements anywhere is the hospice program. As late as 1974, just one hospice program existed in the United States; it had only a handful of patients and was unknown to not only the medical community but to the lay public as well. By 1987, the number had swelled to 1,683 recognized hospice programs taking care of more than 170,000 patients and their families (Parker, 1988). Hospice programs have expanded as the concept grows in service and aptitude. The degree of hospice service has fanned out to not only help patients during the illness but also help survivors after the death. Bereavement follow-up programs offer a dramatic change to how grieving families are considered.

Founded in London in 1961 by Dr. Cicely Saunders, the hospice movement spread rapidly across England and the United States, representing a change in social policy and a revolution in health care, especially in the support of the terminally ill and their families.

Hospice, at least in North America, is a secular movement, a nondenominational, non-church-related institution under community support (Stoddard, 1978). The religious and spiritual values fostered by hospice allow it to open its doors to serving the patient and the family. The spiritual community has helped allay some of the enormous burden borne by AIDS survivors.

Caregivers need to maintain an active list of local support groups for referral resources. Self-help groups can be a valuable adjunct to psychotherapy or, alone, a rich source of social support, information, and general sharing of common problems and concerns.

NEEDS OF THE BEREAVED

Perhaps even before the tasks of grief are undertaken, certain needs of the bereaved must be met. Because the shock of death places an individual in a vulnerable position, comfort and support are a necessary ingredient to the early phase of bereavement. At this point, the bereaved are analogous to what Maslow (1954) has referred to as "growth deficient"—a condition in which most needs on the Maslowan hierarchy remain unsatisfied. His theory outlines a ladder of basic needs, with physiological needs at the base, safety needs next, then belongingness and love, then esteem needs, and finally—an optimum condition—self-actualization needs such as needs for knowledge and beauty.

The needs of the bereaved are comparable to Maslow's hierarchy of needs, but they relate specifically to the needs encountered as one moves through the phases of bereavement. Each rung of the ladder equates with a new phase of bereavement. The needs of the bereaved are illustrated in Figure 18.1.

If mourners can be supplied the nurturance and comfort they require in the beginning of bereavement, resources necessary to move on and gain renewal can be obtained more readily (Raphael, 1984). If, however, safety

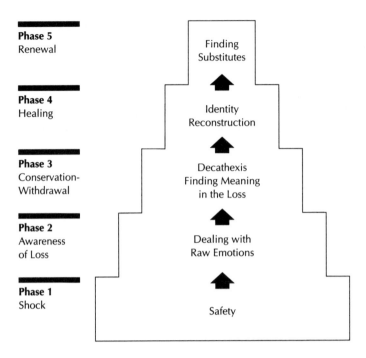

Figure 18.1 The needs of the bereaved.

needs are not met, there is clear evidence of deficiency motivation. This deficiency was seen in older widows (Sanders, 1980–1981), who lived with an absence of gratifiers and who felt that the future looked hopeless. Caregivers can supply an important element of safety simply by being there in a listening, nonjudgmental manner and gently guiding the bereaved toward acquisition of support through available social networks. Once the bereaved begins to experience a modicum of safety, it is possible to allow ventilation of emotions. At this point the bereaved does not feel complete safety. That security may not be fully attained until the top of the ladder is reached. A modicum of safety simply means that a small window of trust has been cracked just enough to begin restoration of physical and psychological resources.

As the bereaved build a stronger base by satisfying their basic needs, they are better able to work through the phases of bereavement. Like the tasks of the bereaved, the needs of the bereaved are in the form of a developmental process that permits growth through acquisition of the previous levels.

Needs will vary greatly between the first phase and the last one.

Getting through the rituals and the first few months after the death will take all the energy and strength one can manage. Rest is imperative but also impossible. The sympathetic nervous system is at an all-time high as fear becomes primary. The bereaved need all the comfort and nurturance they can receive to help ease the anxiety and fear. Their world has just exploded and the sheer helplessness of the loss brings on the feelings of a child needing the safety of a strong parent.

As the numbness wears off, the bereaved will feel their separation anxiety more intensely. Because it is necessary to feel the emotions fully, the needs during the second phase will focus on giving permission to the bereaved to fully experience the anger, guilt, shame, or tears. The second phase is still governed by the sympathetic nervous system, keeping the bereaved anxious and frightened.

As the exhaustion of the heightened activity begins to have its effect, the bereaved shift to a quieter period. Different needs are called for by the bereaved as they move up the rung of the ladder to Phase 3, conservation-withdrawal. The bereaved need to pull back, to begin reenergizing through rest and recuperation. Many supporters, as well as many bereaved themselves, mistakenly see this withdrawal as a period of depression instead of an adaptive period of rest. Although the bereaved definitely need to rest, they do not need to be completely alone. They still need help to process the events surrounding the death, but life must be kept simple. A quieter form of grief work occurs at this time through good friends who allow this process to take place. With help the bereaved will begin to move on to the next phase, that of healing.

Phase 4 sees the bereaved gaining in strength but in an on-again, off-again cycle. The bereaved still need to share memories, to continue to process their grief over and over again. However, as hope begins to gain a stronger foothold, the bereaved need opportunities to exercise their new-found confidence.

As confidence grows, the needs of the bereaved become less apparent; however, they maintain, as always, a deep need to be cared for and supported by family and friends. Their new self-awareness becomes more evident as they gather the sense of personal competency that allows them to accept responsibility for their new life. Stability is beginning to return. The bereaved are ready to reach out to others as they begin their new life.

REVIEW OF INTERVENTION STUDIES

Previous evaluation of psychotherapeutic efforts have focused (1) primarily on short-term treatment effects and (2) on outcome rather than process (Osterweis et al., 1984). Results have been equivocal as to positive differences found when intervention was used.

One study that focused on family coping (Polak, Egan, Vanderbergh, & Williams, 1975) found no noted differences between bereaved and controls at either 6 or 18 months postbereavement. Help may have been offered too soon—in some cases, within hours after the sudden death of a family member—and the family was still too shocked and numb for intervention to have positive effects. Intervention would have been more appropriate if the family had been given more time to acknowledge the event of death.

On the other hand, Horowitz, Marmar, Weiss, DeWitt, and Rosenbaum (1984) examined process and outcome of brief individual psychotherapy following the death of a parent or spouse. Treatment was a 12-session time-limited, once-a-week program using dynamic psychotherapy for stress response syndrome. The authors found significant improvement in all symptomatic outcome variables when pretherapy scores were compared with follow-up data. Those patients rated as having a more stable and better developed self-concept before treatment understandably showed better outcome in work and interpersonal functioning.

In a later study using eight psychologically vulnerable patients (Krupick & Horowitz, 1985), the same treatment modality failed to yield such positive results. However, the authors did feel that treatment helped prepare and motivate vulnerable patients to become involved in a more extended treatment program. Analyzing their study of 35 bereaved patients experiencing the death of a parent, Horowitz, Marmar, Weiss, Kaltreider, and Wilmer (1986) concluded that brief dynamic psychotherapy promotes a restabilization of individuals who have suffered trauma following a significant loss. These patients did not necessarily make vast improvements in self-concept or interpersonal functioning; those changes generally take longer than the 3-month period allocated these patients. They did experience an improvement in general stress symptomatology, however.

Raphael (1977) looked among bereaved women whose husbands had recently died to find a group that she defined as being at high risk. Widows in this group were identified as having a lack of social support as well as having had ambivalent feelings in their marital relationships. The high-risk group was further randomly subdivided into preventive intervention and nonintervention groups. The high-risk intervention group was offered supportive therapy for an average of four 2-hour sessions. Low-risk widows who were perceived as having adequate social support made up the control group. Assessment was made 13 months following bereavement, at which time the high-risk intervention group looked like the low-risk group. The high-risk nonintervention group indicated a substantial health impairment. Therapy had made a significant difference in level of risk.

In a study designed to find an effective method for helping bereaved patients who appeared to be stuck in one phase or another, Mawson, Marks,

Ramm, and Stern (1981) used what they termed a *guided mourning* approach. The authors divided their subjects into two groups of bereaved individuals. To the guided-mourner group they offered therapy in which the individuals were encouraged to say good-bye to the deceased by writing or by visiting the cemetery. Painful memories were relived and expressed until the distress was diminished. In the other group, the authors downplayed grief and encouraged the bereaved to avoid thinking of the deceased and to get on with their lives. The reaction was equated with a phobic avoidance response. Results showed the guided-mourning group to be significantly improved at follow-up whereas the control group of bereaved either deteriorated or showed no change.

Several studies have been undertaken to assess the efficacy of intervention with bereaved parents. Because parental bereavement is so much more severe than other forms, it was felt that parents would benefit most from the therapeutic treatment. Working with parents of stillborn infants, Forest, Standish, and Baum (1982) found no significant differences at 14 months between the group that had been given intervention and the control group, even though the experimental group had shown earlier improvement at 6 months. Another study (Videka-Sherman & Lieberman, 1985) obtained similar results when comparing those bereaved parents who received psychotherapy with those who were affiliated with Compassionate Friends but who received no individual therapy. Although the researchers found no systematic effects of participation in self-help groups or psychotherapy, they did note that at least neither source of intervention led to deterioration.

The foregoing studies offer a pessimistic view of the effects of intervention with bereaved individuals. However, it is important to remember that carefully controlled studies, especially ones in which vulnerable participants are involved, often have psychometric failings that produce artifacts destined to confound the results. Perhaps controlled studies of specific approaches, such as the Mawson et al. (1981) study of guided mourning, will demonstrate the more effective intervention modalities for helping the vulnerable bereaved.

PROBLEMS IN RESEARCH METHODOLOGY

SAMPLING TECHNIQUES

Stereotypes such as "pathological grief" or "bad grief" are often based on anecdotal information or poorly designed research. One of the major problems arising from bereavement studies comes from sampling techniques. Because bereavement reactions were initially studied within the confines of psychiatric institutions, the early approach to grief was focused on psychopathology. Consequently, the emphasis on pathological bereavement took undue precedence in investigations. However, even when this imbalance was recognized, researchers continued to make use of available hospital samples and generalize to all bereaved people, thereby excluding home deaths, accidents, or deaths occurring in places other than the hospital, without correcting for this factor (Clayton et al., 1968).

A sampling problem occurs in selecting participants for bereavement studies. Even with randomly selected samples, the experimenter is still governed by substantial information because age has been found to be a contributing factor toward stressful life situations. For that reason, it becomes imperative to include controls matched as closely as possible on as many variables as are tenable but that are as clearly different from the main effect being examined as can be arranged.

MEASURING INSTRUMENTS

The lack of standardized measuring instruments has presented a large obstacle toward replication of results. Objective instruments in bereavement are limited in number. Studies, for the most part, have used symptom checklists not specifically oriented to the area of bereavement but based primarily on past studies in which those symptoms have been indicated as contributory toward the bereavement syndrome, such as anxiety, depression, or guilt. Therefore, setting up the symptom may produce a self-fulfilling prophecy and may incorrectly show that effect. Two well-known instruments that have seen good validity and reliability are the Grief Experience Inventory (Sanders et al., 1977) and the Texas Inventory of Grief (Faschingbauer et al., 1977).

EXPERIMENTER BIAS

Another important methodological aspect associated with the possible confounding of results is experimenter bias. Previous studies have often shown results consistent with the experimenter's own bias. When an outcome was predicted, the results supported it, a possible self-fulfilling prophecy. Subjective measuring devices were used, and statistical analyses were weak or not employed at all. With objective questionnaires, systematic data collection, and rigorous statistical analyses, a study is more likely to generate unbiased, reliable results.

An experimenter bias is possible when the examiner's personality, gender, or approach may be viewed as intimidating to the participant. Too, an intervention bias can occur, especially in bereavement research, because participants may be vulnerable or especially needy of emotional support. Again, the use of an objective research instrument may partially balance this effect if information can be generated by the respondent rather than by leading questions from the examiner. It would also be helpful to balance the sample by having a male and a female examiner randomly assigned to each of two halves of the sample. This way, the gender effect could be balanced out statistically.

The preceding situations represent only a few of the biasing effects that could confound interpretations of bereavement results. Persons working in this area need to acquaint themselves with as many of the biasing effects as possible so that they can judge the efficacy of reported research data and correctly interpret the results.

INTERVENTION STRATEGIES

Because the grief process is supported by a number of theories, the type of psychotherapy used will depend on the particular training and orientation of the therapist. Yet with any of the theoretical foundations, the caregiver must recognize that grief is a process rather than a state. It is not a linear process, however, because grief has so many culs-de-sac, swoops, and pauses. In many cases, the bereaved can be stuck in one phase or another for an extended period, feeling unable ever to move on. Nonetheless, the object of psychotherapy is to make the process as progressive as possible so that the bereaved moves in the desired direction despite the regressions or delays encountered along the way.

Seen in this light, the caregiver can apply the dynamics of human growth, much like Erickson's stages of life, when it becomes necessary to bridge one level of growth before moving on to the next. Grief requires a particular kind of growth that demands confrontation with and formulation of personal identity (Kennedy, 1977). This growth is generally acquired against a backdrop of relationships with persons who are either supporting or impeding personal growth, but who are all necessary in helping the bereaved person recognize and carve out the new identity.

In the beginning of grief, however, it is unlikely that the bereaved can see the situation as anything but intense pain, severe deprivation, and probably the worst tragedy that could ever befall them. In this early grief, the therapist does well to offer nonjudgmental support, compassion, and most particularly, sensitive and sympathetic listening. Each bereaved person, from within a personal cocoon of misery, needs to be heard over and over. Only this repetition can make real the very unreal events of the tragedy.

The following represent a composite of suggested techniques and concepts selected from a variety of established therapeutic modalities. Recognizing that no one therapeutic approach would be appropriate in working with individual bereavement cases, the caregiver needs to take a more eclectic approach. A variety of techniques should be tailored to the individual needs of the bereaved. Too, no technique or therapeutic approach should ever be employed routinely without considering alternative methods of accomplishing the needs of the bereaved.

The techniques suggested here are arranged in a hierarchy to match the phases of bereavement outlined in the preceding chapters. In other words, client-centered and psychoanalytic therapies would be most suited to Phase 1, shock, and Phase 2, awareness of loss; existential-humanistic therapies to Phase 3, conservation-withdrawal; and Gestalt and behavior therapy to Phase 4, healing, and Phase 5, renewal. The bereaved is moved gradually from external support to internal self-awareness.

CLIENT-CENTERED THERAPY

Central to this approach is the relationship of the caregiver to the bereaved, a relationship with genuineness, nonpossessive warmth, acceptance, and accurate empathy. Because the griever's world has proven unsafe and the griever has few people in whom to trust, the caregiver needs to be with the bereaved on a moment-to-moment experiential basis, offering subjective understanding of the bereaved. This approach is the basis of nurturance and works well in the first two phases of bereavement, when safety needs are unmet and raw feelings are overwhelming.

PSYCHOANALYTIC APPROACH

The most helpful aspect of this approach rests in the concept of transference. Transference in the early phases of bereavement allows the bereaved to attribute to the therapist certain unfinished business in the mourned relationship. In this way, the caregiver becomes a temporary substitute for the deceased while the bereaved works through guilt or ambivalent feelings that are blocking the way to resolution. Countertransference should be carefully watched so that feelings of the caregiver do not intrude on the therapeutic alliance. Early loss experiences are also an important element of this approach, and they should be handled if they are seen as a confounding variable in the present bereavement.

EXISTENTIAL-HUMANISTIC APPROACH

As the bereaved moves toward Phase 3, he or she needs to accept greater responsibility for the outcome of grief. The existential-humanistic model, while more an attitude than a system of techniques, stresses self-awareness, a striving toward purpose in life, and an awareness of a need for community even in one's own aloneness. Choice is the basis of therapy. Emphasis for the caregiver is on a shared journey with the bereaved. Appropriate to the third phase of bereavement is the search for meaning, when the bereaved asks such questions as, "Why am I here? What can give my life purpose? What meaning is there for me in the loss?" The caregiver's task is to trust the capacity of the bereaved to discover an internally derived value system that provides a meaningful life. The caregiver then translates to the bereaved the need to trust in his or her own capacity to discover meaning even in the suffering.

GESTALT APPROACH

The Gestalt approach is an extension of existential therapy. The central task of the caregiver is to help the bereaved focus on the present moment. The past is behind, and the future not yet arrived. As such, the concepts of the Gestalt approach are particularly suitable to Phases 4 and 5 of bereavement. A central therapeutic aim is to challenge the bereaved to move from dependency on others to dependency on self. A key concept is unfinished business, which involves letting go of the past and moving on to new growth. The empty-chair technique, essentially one of role-playing, is done by having the bereaved sit in one chair and face an empty one while imagining the deceased sitting in it. The bereaved is then directed to convey to the deceased all the things that need to be said in order to complete the unfinished business. Through this technique, the bereaved can stop the internalized, badgering self-torture that may have gone on previously.

BEHAVIOR THERAPY APPROACH

Behavior therapy is aimed at goals of acquiring new behavior, eliminating maladaptive behavior, and strengthening and maintaining desirable behavior. Therefore, behavioral techniques are useful in dealing with complicated bereavement patterns and include such methods as desensitization for acute anxieties or implosive therapy or aversion therapy to break down denial or evoke the affect of grief. Guided mourning (Lieberman, 1978; Mawson et al., 1981) is a behavioral technique in which an individual who is avoiding grief responses is encouraged to confront the avoided and painful memories, both in imagination and in reality. The bereaved is asked to describe the memories over and over as well as to say good-bye to the deceased by writing letters and visiting the cemetery. This approach has shown some success in that improvement was noted in follow-up of bereaved, especially for phobic avoidance (Mawson et al., 1981). Although behavior therapy might be helpful in specific instances of complicated bereavement, it does not offer aid in the broader areas of personal and social adjustment that are so necessary to the fourth and fifth phases of bereavement.

Regrief Therapy

This mode of therapy was developed by Volkan (Volkan, 1971; Volkan & Showalter, 1968) and is used when the grieving person has not been able to complete the bereavement process. Volkan makes use of what he terms "linking objects"—those objects the bereaved used as symbols of and/or contact with the deceased. Volkan requests that the bereaved bring them to sessions in order to stimulate and reawaken blocked emotions. The bereaved is then helped to form boundaries demarcating self from the deceased, and emotional release is encouraged. The bereaved is seen for 3 months, in three or four sessions each week. The intensity of the therapeutic work is a motivating force that works to shake the bereaved loose from the obsessional grip of grief. This approach is similar to the "parting rituals" of van der Hart (1983), in which the bereaved individual is asked to collect and make materials symbolic of the relationship with the deceased. The therapist and bereaved then bury or burn the objects in a farewell ceremony, after which the bereaved joins his or her family and friends, signaling a turning point toward a new life.

Self-Hypnosis

When the bereaved is obsessively preoccupied with thoughts of the deceased, self-hypnosis has been used to break this pattern, allowing the bereaved to move on toward new love objects (Fromm & Eisen, 1982). Fromm and Eisen feel that the altered state of self-hypnosis, through primary process imaging, stimulates affective rather than intellectual responses. These responses unblock the problem areas and allow the mourner to move to a new set of expectations and realities that no longer include the deceased. The authors present a case study utilizing this method and showing that as the bereaved is able to accept the idea that the deceased is really gone, former life goals and priorities based on the deceased can now be reorganized, changed, or even discarded in favor of new ones.

MEDICATIONS

The use of psychopharmacological drugs has been found to be useful in the early phases of grief when shock is intense and pain acute (Jacobs & Ostfeld, 1980). There is no indication that a mild antianxiety medication will retard the grieving process; such medication can have positive clinical value in the reduction of symptoms of anxiety, fear, extreme tension, or psychic pain (Osterweis et al., 1984). Hypnotics (sleeping pills) are useful in relieving periods of insomnia or in breaking up patterns of sleeplessness. Particularly in complicated bereavement, caution should be used that the bereaved does not develop patterns of habitual use or that hypnotics are not prescribed if suicidal potential is suspected.

Antidepressants are contraindicated in the relief of normal grief symptoms (Worden, 1982). Many bereaved people show depressionlike symptoms such as sadness, hopelessness, insomnia, and feelings of diminished self-worth without having a full-blown clinical depression. Instead, these normal grief responses should be dealt with as part of working through the process of bereavement.

Medications that are used to relieve acute anxiety and distress in a crisis can provide a therapeutic service to the bereaved by slowing central nervous system activity and providing a temporary respite from severe psychic pain. As Green and Goldberg (1986) state, "By providing the patient with a sense of greater emotional control, these drugs actually facilitate grieving in some instances" (p. 190).

CHAPTER 19

Care of the Caregiver

WORKING WITH THE BEREAVED is stressful. Because of the complex feelings surrounding loss and bereavement, caregivers are often unaware of the subtle interplay between their feelings and the feelings of others. Caregivers have a tendency to take on the moods and feelings of the griever—the frustration, anxiety, guilt, sadness, helplessness, and anger. This tendency can result in what Kastenbaum (1969) refers to as "bereavement overload." The concept of "burnout" (Kalish, 1981) has been defined as a syndrome made up of emotional, physical, and occupational exhaustion, occurring when people become saturated with having many close associations with others while in a helping capacity (Maslach & Jackson, 1979). Caregivers will need to evaluate objectively the symbolic and displaced expressions of emotions, both within themselves and in the bereaved.

Contact with bereavement will normally reawaken every prior loss the caregiver has ever experienced. Of course, prior experiences with bereavement will enhance the empathetic capability of the caregiver if those bereavements have been resolved earlier. Although no one can know exactly what another griever is experiencing, it is nevertheless helpful to have been a survivor. Prior loss, however, is *not* a criterion for an empathetic caregiver. Of much greater importance are patience, gentleness, and the ability to listen carefully to what is said, both verbally and symbolically.

What usually constitutes the greatest potential for stress in helping relationships is the caregiver's desire to rescue the bereaved. In the attempt to make them feel better or to try to solve their problems, the caregiver may attempt to do the work of grief for the bereaved. These strategies are doomed

276

to failure and can only result in the caregiver feeling inadequate and over-burdened. The work of grief is the sole responsibility of the bereaved. Any preempting of this responsibility will result in a delay or postponement of bereavement resolution.

LaGrand (1980) suggests a fourfold approach to dealing with stress when it arises: (1) cognitive modification, (2) exercise outlets and "time-outs," (3) relaxation techniques, and (4) stimulus control.

COGNITIVE MODIFICATION

We can choose to interpret the stressor differently and thereby change the stressful situation. Expecting a negative result activates the self-fulfilling prophecy in the wrong direction, yielding negative results. Group support offsets and normalizes a stressful period and avoids what LaGrand (1980) calls the "depletion syndrome." The group releases emotional pressure by acting as a mirror, reflecting nonadaptive coping styles. Relationships remind us of our humanness and our personal needs for nurturance.

EXERCISE OUTLETS AND OTHER "TIME-OUTS"

Physical exercise provides us with a natural antianxiety component. It acts to offset somatic complaints of stress, such as headaches, backaches, and gastrointestinal problems. Muscles need to be exercised through their full range of motion. Exercise also allows needed time-outs from work, although these breaks do not have to be connected with exercise. A time-out can be simply taking a mental-health day to do something removed from any form of work, such as visiting a museum, going to an afternoon movie, taking a walk in the park. At any rate, the bereaved needs to plan for and incorporate some type of systematic exercise program into a personal lifestyle as a basic means of preventive medicine.

RELAXATION TECHNIQUES

Benefits from deep relaxation have been identified by numerous authors (Benson, 1975; Jacobson, 1938, 1970). Actually, therapeutic use of deep relaxation has been used for some time, in conjunction with visualization techniques, as an adjunct to chemotherapy and radiation for treatment of cancer (Simonton & Simonton, 1975). Relaxation provides the body with release of neuromuscular hypertension (LaGrand, 1980). As such, it provides greater restfulness, calmness, and general feelings of well-being. Meditation, hypnosis, yoga, biofeedback training, or autogenic training, when used on a regular basis, will help an individual learn to maintain a low arousal state of neurophysiological functioning (Pelletier, 1977), which is a guarantee against the overstimulation of stress.

STIMULUS CONTROL

Learning to control or change external factors that are major sources of stress is a necessary part of adaptive functioning, as is learning to experience reasonable control. Activities that can be controlled include managing time, changing jobs if the present one is unsatisfactory, moving if conditions of residence are unmanageable, and confronting a source of anxiety in order to work toward positive alternatives.

Caregivers who deal regularly with loss and bereavement will need to build in stress-management techniques as a way of life. Preventive health programs require planning but result in deeper feelings of well-being, greater job satisfaction, and a personal life that provides joy, good health, and renewal.

CHAPTER 20

The Lessons of Grief

W E HAVE MANY lessons to be learned before we can approach a place of transcendence. In the early phases of grief, when we are grappling with disappointment, anger, and loss, life's lessons may not be what we have chosen to learn. However, I firmly believe everything that comes our way is material for our growth. I have a hard time accepting that loss comes to us only to teach us, but I believe that when we suffer a loss we are presented with challenges that enhance our growth—if we are willing to see them that way.

When life is good, we have a tendency to become complacent about our surroundings. We are prone to take things for granted. John, a 55-year-old widower, said that he wished he could live his marriage over again. "I would have complimented Josie more, done things for her, seen all the places we had dreamed about together. . . . Now it's too late. She's gone." Our appreciation of the true values of living gets lost in our rush to get through the busy days of our lives.

LESSONS TO BE LEARNED

What can we learn from those who have suffered severe losses? What can help us as we must prepare to face losses of our own? In the Tampa study, when participants were asked what was the greatest help in getting through bereavement, they overwhelmingly answered, "friends and family," not "my work" or "my possessions." Relationships were valued the most. As discussed earlier, this is in line with what Selye (1974) has told us after his years of working with stress research. He advocates developing "altruistic egotism," or earning your neighbors' love. Selye advises that persons who invest in this philosophy will never be alone; they will have, instead, a large return on investment in the form of many friends and supporters.

THE VALUE OF LIVING IN THE PRESENT

Grief teaches us the importance of living in the present. We realize, after losing someone dear, the value of every precious moment. Living in the present means that we let go of the past and all its hurts, but it also means that we must not live in the future. Keeping control, trying to plan the outcome of all our events, only leaves us tied up in our own ego and defenses. Time is not on our side, and we need to experience life as it is presented to us. When we become willing to enjoy the moment, we find hidden treasures everywhere—the thrilled expression on a child's face while watching a kite ascend, or a flower in full bloom, or the rarefied colors of a summer sunrise as the sky opalesces from pale pink to brilliant gold. These treasures are worth searching for, but we must be willing to be here, in the present moment, to truly experience their wonder.

THE JOY OF SPONTANEITY

Grief teaches us the joy of spontaneity. We are aware more than ever of the need to take advantage of opportunities to play or relax. We learn that we must not waste chances to have lighthearted fun. If we keep to a rigid schedule, we miss the serendipity that is all around us. Life may be predictable when lived that way, but it becomes stagnant and boring. We need to accept the freedom of spontaneity as our right and privilege.

THE VALUE OF TIME

Life has a sweet beauty about it that we all try to grasp and hold on to. We feel the need, from time to time, to go back over the innocent moments of our lives. We want to deal with the questions of life and love—and even of death. We promise ourselves that we will do some soul searching when we have time. Then we keep busy with constant daily distractions so that we can excuse ourselves for putting off any opportunity for learning to center ourselves. What we come to realize only later is that these questions are answered for us in many hidden ways if we would only take the time to find them. Valuable insights are buried in the give and take of daily life; if we could slow ourselves down, we could find them. We all need what I call "hammock time"—experiences of daydreaming and fantasy. We need time to share our feelings with one another, but first we need to know what our feelings are. Grief teaches us that there is much to know about ourselves and our world, but that kind of knowledge requires a slower perception. We get hints of the wonders that are possible when we have occasional peak experiences. Slowing our lives would offer us many more of those wonders.

THE NEED FOR SIMPLICITY

Only after we have something taken from us do we realize its true value. We usually find that, because we spend so much energy trying to take care of the details of living, we miss many of life's smaller but important transactions. Ann realized, only after she had lost her husband, how much time she had wasted every day constantly prodding her husband to keep the house neat. Now it didn't matter how the house looked. She wished she had spent her time enjoying him rather than cleaning all the time. Grief teaches us that we need to simplify our lives so that more time is available for sharing with those we love.

We get caught up in daily distractions that take too much energy. To do things perfectly, we complicate our lives and add needless stress. Our perfectionism is a function of our egos and has no place in the world of love. Learning to live more simply frees our energies to be truly creative. In a world full of stimulation, it is necessary to divest ourselves of as many needless tasks as we can. Generally, we become more efficient in order to get more tasks accomplished in a day. What if we were to simplify everything as much as we could, and then used that time to be more creative? How our souls would be regenerated and our spirits uplifted!

THE BENEFITS OF CHANGE

Without change, we wither and die. Roger felt locked into a job he hated. Being a highly responsible person, he thought his first duty was to provide for his family. Secretly, he dreamed of quitting his miserable job and starting a lawn service, which would allow him to be outside all the time. He thought about it incessantly but could never figure out how to do it. He couldn't even bring himself to talk to his wife about it. Instead, he stuck with his job for 23 years, growing more lifeless with each year.

When Roger got colon cancer, he had a lot of time to review his life. He vowed that, if he could get strong again, he would start his little business. Even thinking about it made him feel freer. He didn't care how he did it; he knew he would be a success.

Recovery after surgery was slow, but gradually he was able to put his plan into operation. He contracted for only a couple of yards to start with; as he gained strength, he was able to add more. The last time I talked with Roger, he had no sign of the cancer and was happier than he had ever been.

Either we grow or we regress. There is no in-between, no status quo in life. Yet we continue to resist change with all the strength we can muster. It has been said that we go kicking and screaming to our growth. Facing change is one of the hardest lessons of grief. Who wants loss? We didn't want it and we haven't asked for it. But it has come to us, and somehow we must deal with it. We don't have many choices: either we keep on or we give up. If we give up, our soul dies. If we keep on, we roll with the changes, whatever they may be, and try to keep faith that we will come through. Grief teaches us that we must trust our higher power to lead us on the right path, to give us perfect guidance even when we lose sight of it or reject its effects.

THE VALUE OF PATIENCE

How frustrated we become when we must wait for something to happen. We like to have control over our world, to make things happen when we want them to happen, rather than leaving life to another set of rules. Grief teaches us that life can't be hurried if we expect to get out of it the best it offers. Patience helps us to seek out an understanding of each other, to wait good-humoredly when others must catch up. Grief also teaches us that we must be patient with ourselves, allowing the grieving process to take place in whatever manner it is supposed to. If life becomes hurried, we miss the best part—the quiet, uneventful, deeply meaningful moments we can know alone or with those we love.

THE PLEASURE OF LAUGHTER

In this book *Anatomy of an Illness* (1979), Norman Cousins describes how he cured his fatal illness with laughter. Doctors told him there was little or no treatment for his disease. He had noticed that, if he watched a funny program on TV, he slept better that night and had less pain. Cousins immediately set about to locate old movies and TV shows that made him laugh: *Candid Camera*, Marx Brothers films, episodes of *I Love Lucy*. He literally laughed himself back to health.

Norman Cousins's book contains an important lesson. When we laugh, our bodies are recharged and every cell is affected. The full, relaxing response of a wonderful belly laugh derives from a powerful physiological reaction that surges throughout the body. We come alive both emotionally and physically.

During grief, we often feel disloyal or guilty when we laugh; it doesn't seem appropriate at such a sad and somber time. Yet, grief is an emotionally charged period. When we laugh, we allow the tension to escape like steam from a simmering tea kettle. Laughter becomes a safety valve against explosion; it ensures better health because it releases some of the tension locked within our bodies.

Choosing to see the funny side as well as the serious side of life heals our pain and encourages wellness. Because it is habit-forming and contagious, laughter shared with others can heal them as well as ourselves.

THE NEED TO BELONG

Our need to belong to someone or something is as old as time itself. Our sense of belonging to the human race and our recognition of the importance of our kinship to each other enhance our quality of life. Grief teaches us that we need others. Over and over, bereaved people have told me that having friends near, feeling a closeness to them, being a part of a group, were all sustaining forces when they faced their personal tragedies. We need a sense of belonging—to the neighborhood, the folks who work with us, the group we call our friends. Knowing that we belong helps us feel more secure, more a part of the human race.

One of the wonderful things about bereavement support groups is that our pain can be shared with people who know what we are feeling. I heard one man say at a Compassionate Friends meeting, "I know when I come here I belong—no one will judge me ... we're all in the same boat." Knowing that others have survived equally devastating experiences gives us courage and hope. Suffering softens us and helps us to feel more compassion toward one another. Grief teaches us that we need to be more connected with others in our world. We learn the importance of keeping those connections alive.

THE VALUE OF SHARING

One of grief's lessons is the importance of being open, of candidly sharing our thoughts and feelings. As a therapist dealing with bereaved people, I often hear the phrase "I wish I had been able to say 'I love you'" or "Dad never knew I had forgiven him. I was waiting for the right time to talk with him." There may be things we need to say, appreciations we should express, separations that we should close. Grief teaches us that we have only *now* to let other persons know we love them. Families that stay open and share their feelings, whether hot or cold, trust each other more readily and survive losses with less guilt or ambivalence than do families living with barriers.

There is magic in sharing ourselves with someone else. Each of us profits from hearing another's story. We need to recognize and celebrate our bond with others. Mother Teresa reminds us of the importance in her wonderful book *The Joy in Loving* (1996).

If we haven't been as open as we'd like, one phone call can begin rectifying the situation. When we become more open and share ourselves honestly with others, they begin to follow suit. Sharing is as contagious as laughter.

THE NEED TO EXPAND OUR
FAMILY OF CHOICE

As we get older, we find ourselves in an ever diminishing circle of family and friends, particularly after our children are grown. We seem to have fewer opportunities to form new relationships. Our children were often emissaries who brought new friends (and their parents) into our lives.

As we begin to lose our dearest friends through death or distances and we see our own families diminish in number, we have an increasing need to gather in new "family members" of our own choice.

We can adopt new family members any time we find nonrelated kin— those special people who come into our lives as strangers but seem to have been friends all our lives.

I love a story Isabella Taves tells in her book *Love Must Not Be Wasted* (1974). David was three when his grandfather died. His grandmother told him Gramps had gone to heaven and was happy with the angels. A few weeks later, he told his mother that he would like to go over to his grandmother's and see whether Gramps was back from heaven.

David's mother, who had never approved of the heaven concept, tried to explain that Gramps was dead and buried and could not return. David wanted to know if that would happen to Grandma, too. His mother explained that all of us die. David went down a long list of people in the family, asking if each one would die. Then he asked about his beloved collie. Finally, he said, "And you, Mommy?" His mother said yes, she would die too, but not for a long time, not until David was grown up.

David thought a minute before announcing, "Then I guess I'll have to get me a new set of people."

Grief teaches us that we need to keep reaching out to others, to get a new set of people when we find our own set growing smaller. If we do, we will never be lonely or feel excluded from life.

THE WORTH OF RELATIONSHIPS

We hear a lot of talk about the risk involved in loving. For anyone who loves and therefore risks forming a connection with another person, suffering is guaranteed. But only when we love will we find a fullness of life and a personal experience of tremendous satisfaction.

Grief teaches us that relationships can never be taken for granted. People come into our lives to teach us, and each person is a special gift to be treasured and never taken for granted. Some people seem to be placed into our lives as comforters who help us to get through: special friends, resource people, family members who weren't close or available before. When we finally reach the other side of grief and are on our way to a new life, we may find strangers who become like family. We can only find them if we stay open to other people.

The next section draws heavily from the material of John Brantner (1977), who developed Selye's philosophy even further when he outlined three lessons that are "protection against separation and cures for loneliness" (p. 296). He cautioned that the first lesson is extremely difficult and perhaps only 1 out of 10,000 persons are good at it: the ability to have an intimate relationship with our own inner self. Learned through contemplative techniques such as meditation, retreats, psychotherapy, or study, achieving this lesson is arriving at the fullness of introversion at its healthiest. He added that if we master this relationship, we need never fear being shut off from other people.

The second lesson is easier, and maybe one person in five can do it: learning to develop an intimate relationship with one or more people. Brantner described this as "a love-based, mutual, sexual, rejoicing in the other—completing in the other" (p. 197). Learning this lesson means never feeling alienated or being lonely.

Brantner wrote that the third lesson is quite easy. It involves learning to relate to strangers quickly, to risk being a more open person to numerous others, and to enjoy the differences as well as the similarities that we find in people. He described this ability as being a "successful traveler" in the world. And too, if this lesson is well learned, a person never again is lonely in a crowd. Brantner also assured us that there are plenty of strangers in the world—approximately 4 billion on whom to practice.

But what can the bereaved and the caregivers teach us to enhance our own lives? The bereaved teach us, probably better than anyone else, the value of relationships. But not just any relationship—it is the quality, not the quantity, that matters most. Relationships that are intense and openly sharing are more valuable by far than the numerous, watered-down varieties.

The bereaved teach us the importance of open sharing of thoughts and feelings. In working with bereaved people, I often have heard phrases such as "I wish I had told him I loved him" or "I wish we could have resolved our differences earlier." There are things that we need to say, appreciations that need to be expressed, distances to bridge. The bereaved teach us that love is a gift to be given and received over and over—a commodity that needs to have constant attention. Loving and being loved is not just something that happens to us. It is a creative art that must be worked at in a variety of ways. And behind it all is the initial need to love oneself. Until this lesson is learned, one cannot truly go about the business of loving others. Yet it is important, too, to realize that we can get started this minute if we are willing to give up the crippling fears of rejection and self-consciousness and reach out lovingly, trustingly to others.

Brantner (1977) sums it up so well when he writes,

> Therefore, we must seek now, here, as large a number of relationships as we can stand; seek ever diverse and varied relationships; seek with at least one other an intense, intimate, love-based, mutual, sexual, generative, and vulnerable relationship; seek a knowing and vulnerable relationship with our own inner self; aware that all of these relationships begin with strangers, and that they all end in death, separation, grieving, and suffering; but also aware that these alone give life its meaning, these alone make life extraordinarily precious and these alone make life worth living. (p. 304)

References

Agee, J. (1957). A *death in the family*. New York: McDowell & Obelensky.

Alarcon, R. D. (1984). Personality disorder as a pathogenic factor in bereavement. *Journal of Nervous and Mental Disease, 172*(1), 45–47.

Allen, B. G., Calhoun, L. D., Cann, A., & Tedeschi, R. G. (1993). The effect of cause of death on responses to the bereaved: Suicide compared to accident and natural causes. *Omega, 28*(1), 39–48.

American Psychiatric Association. (1987). *Diagnostic and statistical manual of mental disorders* (3rd ed., rev.); *DSM-III-R*. Washington, DC: Author.

Anderson, H. (1980). The death of a parent: Its impact on middle-aged sons and daughters. *Pastoral Psychology, 28*, 151–167.

Atchley, R. C. (1975). Dimensions of widowhood in later life. *The Gerontologist, 15*, 176–178.

Attig, T. (1991). The importance of conceiving of grief as an active process. *Death Studies, 15*, 385–393.

Averill, J. R. (1968). Grief: Its nature and significance. *Psychological Bulletin, 70*(6), 721–748.

Ball, J. F. (1977). Widow's grief: The impact of age and mode of death. *Omega, 7*, 307–333.

Bartrop, R. W., Luckhurst, E., Lajarus, H., Kiloh, L., & Penny, R. (1977). Depressed lymphocyte function after bereavement. *Lancet, 1*, 834–835.

Batchelor, W. F. (1984). AIDS: A public health and psychological emergency. *American Psychologist, 39*(11), 1283.

Benedek, T. (1970). Parenthood during the life cycle. In E. J. Anthony & T. Benedek (Eds.), *Parenthood: Its psychology and psychopathology*. Boston: Little, Brown.

Benson, H. (1975). *The relaxation response*. New York: Morrow.

Berardo, F. M. (1970). Survivorship and social isolation. The case of the aged widower. *The Family Coordinator, 19*, 11–25.

287

Biller, R., & Rice, S. (1990). Experiencing multiple loss of persons with AIDS: Grief and bereavement issues. *Health and Social Work, 15,* 283–290.

Binger, C. M., Ablin, A. R., Feurerstein, R. C., Kushner, J. H., Zoger, S., & Mikkelsen, C. (1969). Childhood leukemia: Emotional impact on patient and family. *New England Journal of Medicine, 280,* 414–418.

Blanchard, C. G., Blanchard, E. B., & Becker, J. V. (1976). The young widow: Depression symptomatology throughout the grief process. *Psychiatry, 39*(Nov.), 394–399.

Blankfield, A. (1982–1983). Grief and alcohol. *American Journal of Drug and Alcohol Abuse, 9,* 435–446.

Bluebond-Langner, J. (1977). Meanings of death to children. In H. Feifel (Ed.), *New meanings of death.* New York: McGraw-Hill.

Book, P. (1996). How does the family narrative influence the individual's ability to communicate about death? *Omega, 33*(4), 323–341.

Bowen, M. (1976). Family reactions to death. In P. Guerin (Ed.), *Family therapy.* New York: Gardner Press.

Bowlby, J. (1953). Some pathological processes set in training by early mother-child separation. *Journal of Mental Science, 99,* 265–272.

Bowlby, J. (1960a). Separation anxiety. *International Journal of Psychoanalysis, 16,* 2–3; *41,* 89–113.

Bowlby, J. (1960b). Grief and mourning in infancy and early childhood. *Psychoanalytic Study of the Child, 15*(5), 9–52.

Bowlby, J. (1961). Process of mourning. *International Journal of Psychoanalysis, 42,* 317–340.

Bowlby, J. (1980). *Attachment and loss: Loss, sadness and depression* (Vol. 3). New York: Basic Books.

Bowlby, J. (1982). Attachment and loss: Retrospect and prospect. *American Journal of Orthopsychiatry, 52*(4), 664–678.

Bozeman, M. F., Orbach, C. E., & Sutherland, A. M. (1955). Psychological impact of cancer and its treatment: III. The adaptation of mothers to the threatened loss of their children through leukemia (Part I). *Cancer, 8,* 1–19.

Brantner, J. (1977). Positive approaches to dying. *Death Education, 1*(3), 293–304.

Brice, C. W. (1982). Mourning throughout the life cycle. *American Journal of Psychoanalysis, 42*(4), 315–325.

Bridges, W. (1983). *Transitions: Making sense of life's changes.* Reading, MA: Addison-Wesley.

Bridges, W. (1990). *Transitions: Making sense of life's changes* (Rev. ed.). Reading, PA: Addison-Wesley Publishing.

Briscoe, C. W., & Smith, J. B. (1975, April). Depression in bereavement and divorce. *Archives of General Psychiatry, 32,* 439–443.

Brown, J. T., & Stoudemire, G. A. (1983). Normal and pathological grief. *JAMA, 250*(3), 378–382.

Brown, N. O. (1959). *Life against death.* New York: Random House.

Brown, R. G. (1960). Family structure and social isolation. *Journal of Gerontology, 15,* 170–174.

Bugen, L. A. (1977). Human grief: A model for prediction and intervention. *American Journal of Orthopsychiatry, 47*(2), 196–206.

Burnell, G. M., & Burnell, A. L. (1989). The Compassionate Friends: A support group for bereaved parents. *The Journal of Family Practice, 22*(3), 295–296.

Cain, A. C., & Cain, B. S. (1964). On replacing a child. *Journal of the American Academy of Child Psychiatrists, 3,* 443–456.

Cain, A., & Fast, I. (1966). The legacy of suicide: Observations in the pathogenic impact of suicide upon marital partners. In A. Cain (Ed.), *Survivors of suicide.* Springfield, IL: Charles C Thomas.

Calhoun, L., Selby, J. W., & Selby, L. E. (1982). The psychological aftermath of suicide: An analysis of current evidence. *Clinical Psychology Review, 1,* 409–420.

Campbell, J. (1988). *The power of myth.* New York: Doubleday.

Cannon, W. B. (1929). *Bodily changes in pain, hunger, fear and rage* (2nd ed.). London: Appleton.

Carey, R. G. (1979). Weathering widowhood: Problems and adjustment of the widowed during the first year. *Omega, 10,* 163–174.

Carmack, B. (1992). Balancing engagement/detachment in AIDS-related multiple losses. *Image: Journal of Nursing Scholarship, 24,* 9–14.

Carter, B. F., & Brooks, A. (1990, May). Suicide postvention: Crisis or opportunity? *The School Counselor, 37,* 378–389.

Caserta, M., & Lund, D. (1992). Bereavement stress and coping among adults: Expectations versus the actual experience. *Omega, 25,* 33–45.

Cattell, R. B., Eber, H. W., & Tatsuoka, M. M. (1970). *Handbook for the 16 personality factor questionnaire.* Champaign, IL: Institute for Personality and Ability Testing.

Chenoweth, R., Tonge, J. I., & Armstrong, J. (1980). Suicide in Brisbane, a retrospective psychosocial study. *Australian and New Zealand Journal of Psychiatry, 14,* 37–45.

Chodoff, P., Friedman, S. B., & Hamburg, D. A. (1964). Stress, defenses, and coping behavior: Observations in parents of children with malignant disease. *American Journal of Psychiatry, 120,* 743–749.

Clayton, P. J. (1974). Mortality and morbidity in the first year of bereavement. *Archives of General Psychiatry, 30,* 747–750.

Clayton, P. J. (1980). Bereavement and its management. In E. S. Paykel (Ed.), *Handbook of affective disorders.* Edinburgh: Churchill Livingstone.

Clayton, P. J., Desmarais, L., & Winokur, G. (1968). Study of normal bereavement. *American Journal of Psychiatry, 125*(2), 64–74, 168–178.

Clayton, P. J., Halikes, J. A., & Maurice, W. L. (1971). The bereavement of the widowed. *Diseases of the Nervous System, 32*(9), 597–604.

Clayton, P. J., Halikes, J. D., & Maurice, W. L. (1972). The depression of widowhood. *British Journal of Psychiatry, 121,* 71–78.

Cook, J. A., & Wimberly, D. W. (1983). If I should die before I wake: Religious commitment and adjustment to the death of a child. *Journal for the Scientific Study of Religion, 22*(3), 222–238.

Corey, G. (1977). *Theory and practice of counseling and psychotherapy.* Monterey, CA: Brooks/Cole.

Corr, C., Nabe, C., & Corr, D. (1994). *Death and dying, life and living.* Pacific Grove, CA: Brooks/Cole.

Cousins, N. (1979). *Anatomy of an illness as perceived by the patient: Reflections on healing and regeneration.* New York: Norton.

Cumming, E., & Henry, W. E. (1961). *Growing old.* New York: Basic Books.

Darwin, C. (1872). *The expression of the emotions in man and animals.* London: Murray.

DeSpelder, L. A., & Strickland, A. L. (1983). *The last dance: Encountering death and dying.* Palo Alto, CA: Mayfield.

Deutsch, H. (1937). Absence of grief. *Psychoanalytic Quarterly, 6,* 12–22.

Doka, K. (1989). *Disenfranchised Grief.* Lexington, MA: Lexington Books.

Dubin, W. R., & Sarnoff, J. R. (1986). Sudden, unexpected death: Intervention with the survivors. *Annals of Emergency Medicine, 15*(1), 54–57.

Eggert, D. (1983). Eysenck-Persönlichkeits—Inventar Göttingen: Hogrefe.

Elliot, T. D. (1932). The bereaved family. *Annals of the American Academy of Political and Social Science, 160,* 184–190.

Elliot, T. D. (1948). Bereavement: Inevitable but not insurmountable. In H. Becker & R. Hill (Eds.), *Family, marriage, and parenthood.* Lexington, MA: D. C. Heath.

Engel, G. L. (1961). Is grief a disease? A challenge for medical research. *Psychosomatic Medicine, 23,* 18–23.

Engel, G. L. (1962). Anxiety and depression-withdrawal: The primary affects of unpleasure. *International Journal of Psychoanalysis, 18*(Parts 2–3), 89–97; *43,* 87–89.

Engel, G. L. (1967, June). A psychological setting of somatic disease: The giving up-given up complex. *Proceedings of the Royal Society of Medicine, 60,* 553–555.

Engel, G. L. (1971). Sudden and rapid death during psychological stress, folklore or folkwisdom? *Annals of Internal Medicine, 74,* 771–782.

Engel, G. L. (1972). Grief and grieving. In L. Schwartz & S. Schwartz (Eds.), *The psychodynamics of patient care.* New York: Prentice Hall.

Excell, J. (1980). A child's perception of death. In R. Lonetto (Ed.), *Children's conceptions of death* (pp. 87–103). New York: Springer.

Faschingbauer, T. R., Devaul, R. D., & Zisook, S. (1977). Development of the Texas Inventory of Grief. *American Journal of Psychiatry, 134,* 696–698.

Federn, P. (1952). *Ego psychology and the psychoses.* New York: Basic Books.

Feinstein, D., & Mayo, P. (1990). *Rituals for living and dying.* New York: HarperCollins.

Fenichel, O. (1945). *The psychoanalytic theory of neurosis.* New York: Norton.

Firth, R. (Ed.). (1957). *Man and culture.* London: Routledge & Kegan Paul.

Fish, W. C. (1986). Differences in grief intensity in bereaved parents. In T. A. Rando (Ed.), *Parental loss of a child.* Champaign, IL: Research Press.

Fish, W. C., & Whitty, S. M. (1983). Challenging conventional wisdom about parental bereavement. *Forum Newsletter: Forum for Death Education & Counseling, 5*(8), 4.

Fleming, S., & Balmer, L. (1980). *Group intervention with bereaved children.* New York: Springer.

Forest, G. C., Standish, E., & Baum, J. D. (1982). Support after perinatal death: A study of support and counseling after perinatal bereavement. *British Medical Journal, 285,* 1475–1479.

Frankl, V. (1959). *Man's search for meaning.* New York: Washington Square Press.

Fredrick, J. F. (1976–1977). Grief as a disease process. *Omega, 7*(4), 297–305.

Fredrick, J. F. (1982–1983). Biochemistry of bereavement. *Omega, 13*(4), 295–303.

Freeman, G. L. (1948). *The energetics of human behavior.* Ithaca, NY: Cornell University Press.

Freud, A. (1965). *Normality and pathology in childhood.* New York: International Universities Press.

Freud, S. (1917). Mourning and melancholia. In *A general selection from the works of Sigmund Freud.* New York: Doubleday Anchor Books.

Freud, S. (1929). Letter to Binswanger. In *Letters of Sigmund Freud.* London: Hogarth.

Freud, S. (1941). On narcissism: An introduction. In *The complete psychological works of Sigmund Freud.* London: Hogarth Press. (Original work published 1924)

Freud, S. (1960). Letter to Sandor Ferenczi. In *Letters of Sigmund Freud.* New York: Basic Books.

Friedman, S. B. (1974). Psychological aspects of sudden unexpected death in infants and children. *Pediatric Clinics of North America, 21,* 103–116.

Fromm, E., & Eisen, M. (1982). Self-hypnosis as a therapeutic aid in the mourning process. *American Journal of Clinical Hypnosis, 25*(1) 3–14.

Fulton, R., & Fulton, J. (1971). Psychosocial aspects of terminal care: Anticipatory grief. *Omega, 2,* 91–99.

Furman, E. (1974). *A child's parent dies: Studies in childhood bereavement.* New York: John Wiley & Sons.

Furman, E. (1976). Comment on J. Kennell and M. Klaus, "Caring for the parents of an infant who dies." In M. Klaus & J. Kennell (Eds.), *Maternal-infant bonding.* St. Louis: C. V. Mosby.

Gilbert, K. (1996). "We've had the same loss, why don't we have the same grief?" Loss and differential grief in families. *Death Studies, 20,* 269–283.

Glick, I. O., Weiss, R., & Parkes, C. M. (1974). *The first year of bereavement.* New York: John Wiley & Sons.

Goalder, J. S. (1985). Morbid grief reaction: A social systems perspective. *Professional Psychology: Research and Practice, 16*(6), 833–842.

Goldberg, D. P. (1972). *Manual of the general health questionnaire.* Windsor: NFER.

Goldney, R. D. (1981). Attempted suicide in young women. Correlate of lethality. *British Journal of Psychiatry, 40*(1), 71–74.

Goleman, D. (1979, Nov.). Positive denial: The case for not facing reality. *Psychology Today, 13,* 44–60.

Gorer, G. D. (1965). *Death, grief and mourning.* New York: Doubleday.

Green, S. A., & Goldberg, R. L. (1986). Management of acute grief. *American Family Physician, 23*(2), 185–190.

Harvey, C. D., & Bahr, H. M. (1974). Widowhood, morale and affiliation. *Journal of Marriage and the Family, 36,* 97–106.

Hathaway, S. R., & McKinley, J. C. (1951). *The Minnesota multiphasic personality inventory manual.* New York: The Psychological Quarterly.

Hazzard, A., Weston, J., & Guterres, L. (1992). After a child's death: Factors related to parental bereavement. *Journal of Developmental and Behavioral Pediatrics, 13,* 24–30.

Helsing, K. J., Szklo, M., & Comstock, C. W. (1981). Factors associated with mortality after widowhood. *American Journal of Public Health, 71,* 802–809.

Helsing, K. J., Comstock, G. N., & Szklo, M. (1982). Causes of death in a widowed population. *American Journal of Epidemiology, 116,* 524–532.

Herz, F. (1980). The impact of death and serious illness on the family life cycle. In E. Carter & M. McGoldrick (Eds.), *The family life cycle.* New York: Gardner.

Heyman, O. K., & Gianturco, D. T. (1973). Long-term adaptation by the elderly to bereavement. *Journal of Gerontology, 28,* 359–362.

Hine, V. H. (1978). *The pearl of great price.* Unpublished manuscript.

Hine, V., & Foster, J. (n.d.) *A guide for rites of passage for our time: A guide for creating ritual.* Unpublished manuscript.

Hinton, J. (1967). *Dying.* Middlesex, England: Penguin Books.

Holmes, T. H., & Rahe, R. H. (1967). Social readjustment rating scale. *Journal of Psychosomatic Research, 11,* 213–218.

Horowitz, M. J. (1985). Disaster and psychological responses to stress. *Psychiatric Annals, 15,* 161–167.

Horowitz, M. J., Daniel, S. W., Kaltreider, N., Krupnick, J., Marmar, C., Wilner, N., & DeWitt, K. (1984). Reactions to the death of a parent. *Journal of Nervous and Mental Disease, 172*(4), 383–392.

Horowitz, M. J., Marmar, C., Weiss, D. S., DeWitt, K. N., & Rosenbaum, R. (1984). Brief psychotherapy of bereavement reactions. *Archives of General Psychiatry, 41,* 438–448.

Horowitz, M. J., Marmar, C. R., Weiss, D. S., Kaltreider, N. B., & Wilner, N. R. (1986). Comprehensive analysis of change after brief dynamic psychotherapy. *American Journal of Psychiatry, 143*(5), 582–589.

Horowitz, M. J., Weiss, D. S., Kaltreider, N., Krupnick, J., Marmar, C., Wilner, N., DeWitt, K. (1984). Reactions to the death of a parent. *Journal of Nervous and Mental Disease, 172,* 383–392.

Horowitz, M. J., Wilner, N., Marmar, C., & Krupnick, J. (1980). Pathological grief and the activation of latent self-images. *American Journal of Psychiatry, 137*(10), 1157–1162.

Hoyt, M. F. (1980–1981). Clinical notes regarding the experience of "presences" in mourning. *Omega, 11*(2), 105–111.

Irwin, M., & Pike, J. (1993). Bereavement, depressive symptoms, and immune function. In M. Stroebe, W. Stroebe, & R. Hansson (Eds.), *Handbook of bereavement.* Cambridge: Cambridge University Press.

Jacobs, J. A. (1967). A phenomenological study of suicide notes. *Social Problems, 15,* 60–72.

Jacobs, D. S., & Ostfeld, A. (1977). An epidemiological review of the mortality of bereavement. *Psychosomatic Medicine, 39,* 344–357.

Jacobs, S., & Ostefeld, A. (1980). The clinical management of grief. *Journal of the American Geriatrics Society, 28*(7), 331–335.

Jacobson, E. (1938). *Progressive relaxation* (2nd ed.). Chicago: Chicago Press.

Jacobson, E. (1970). *Modern treatment of tense patients.* Springfield, IL: Charles C Thomas.

Jourard, S. (1968). *Disclosing man to himself.* New York: Van Nostrand Reinhold.

Kalish, R. A. (1981). *Death, grief, and caring relationships.* Monterey, CA: Brooks/Cole.

Kaltreider, N. B., Becker, T., & Horowitz, J. J. (1984). Relationship testing after the loss of a parent. *American Journal of Psychiatry, 141*(2), 243–246.

Kaprio, J., Koskenvico, M., & Rita, H. (1987). Mortality after bereavement: A prospective study of 95,647 widowed persons. *American Journal of Public Health, 77*, 283–287.

Kastenbaum, R. J. (1969). Death and bereavement in later life. In A. H. Kutscher (Ed.), *Death and bereavement.* Springfield, IL: Charles C Thomas.

Kastenbaum, R. J. (1977). *Death, society and human experience.* St. Louis: C. V. Mosby.

Kaufman, I. C., & Rosenblum, L. A. (1967). The reaction to separation in infant monkeys: Anaclitic depression and conservation-withdrawal. *Psychosomatic Medicine, 29*(6), 648–675.

Kavanaugh, R. E. (1972). *Facing death.* Baltimore: Penguin Books.

Kennedy, E. (1977). *On becoming a counselor: A basic guide for non-professional counselors.* New York: Seabury Press.

Kiecolt-Glaser, J., & Glaser, R. (1992). Psychoneuroimmunology: Can psychological interventions modulate immunity? *Journal of Consulting and Clinical Psychology, 60*, 569–575.

Kim, K., & Jacobs, S. (1991). Pathological grief and its relationship to other psychiatric disorder. *Journal of Affective Disorder, 21*, 257–263.

Kim, K., & Jacobs, S. (1993). Neuroendocrine changes following bereavement. In M. Stroebe, W. Stroebe, & R. Hansson (Eds.) *Handbook of bereavement.* Cambridge: Cambridge University Press.

Klein, M. (1940). Mourning and its relationship to manic-depressive states. *International Journal of Psycho-Analysis, 21*, 125–153.

Klein, S. J., & Fletcher, W. (1986). Gay grief: An examination of its uniqueness brought to light by the AIDS crisis. *Journal of Psychosocial Oncology, 4*(3), 15–25.

Kollar, N. (1989). Rituals and the disenfranchised grief. In: K. Doka (Ed.), *Disenfranchised grief.* Lexington, MA: Lexington Books.

Koos, E. L. (1946). *Families in trouble.* New York: Columbia University Press.

Kraus, A. S., & Lilienfeld, A. M. (1959). Some epidemiological aspects of the high mortality rate in the young widowed group. *Journal of Chronic Disease, 10*, 207.

Krupick, J. L., & Horowitz, M. J. (1985, August). Brief psychotherapy with vulnerable patients: An outcome assessment. *Psychiatry, 48*, 223–233.

Krupp, G. R. (1965). Identification as a defense against anxiety in coping with loss. *International Journal of Psychoanalysis, 46*, 303–314.

Kübler-Ross, E. (1969). *On death and dying.* New York: Macmillan.

Kübler-Ross, E. (1983). *On children and death.* New York: Macmillan.

LaGrand, L. E. (1980) Reducing burnout in the Hopi and death education movement. *Death Education, 4*(1), 61–75.

Lammers, E. (1995). Children, death, and fairy tales. *Omega, 31*(2), 151–167.

Landis, G. H. (1977). *Your marriage and family living.* New York: McGraw-Hill.

Larson, D. (1993). *The helper's journey.* Champaign, IL: Research Press.

Lawrence, D. H. (1928). After the death of his mother. Introduction to *Completed Book of Poems.* New York: Penguin Books.

Lazare, A. (1979). *Outpatient psychiatry: Diagnosis and treatment.* Baltimore, MD: Williams & Wilkins.

Lazare, A. (1979). Unresolved grief. In A. Lazare (Ed.), *Outpatient psychiatry: Diagnosis and treatment.* Baltimore: Williams & Wilkins.

LeShan, L. (1963). A basic psychological orientation apparently associated with malignant disease. *The Psychiatric Quarterly, 26,* 314–330.

Levav, I. (1982). Mortality and psychopathology following the death of an adult child: An epidemiological review. *Israeli Journal of Psychiatry and Related Sciences, 19,* 23–33.

Levenson, H. (1973). Multidimensional locus of control in psychiatric patients. *Journal of Consulting and Clinical Psychology, 41,* 397–404.

Levitan, H. (1985). Onset of asthma during intense mourning. *Psychosomatics, 26*(12), 939–941.

Lewis, C. S. (1961). *A grief observed.* New York: Seabury Press.

Lieberman, M. (1978). Help seeking and self-help groups. In M. Lieberman & L. Borman (Eds.), *Self-help groups for coping with crisis.* San Francisco: Jossey-Bass.

Lifton, R. J. (1968). *Death in life: Survivors of Hiroshima.* New York: Random House.

Lifton, R. J. (1979). *The broken connection.* New York: Simon & Schuster.

Lindbergh, A. M. (1973). *Hour of gold, hour of lead.* New York: Signet Books.

Lindemann, E. (1944). Symptomatology and management of acute grief. *American Journal of Psychiatry, 101,* 141–148.

Littlefield, C. H., & Rushton, J. P. (1986). When a child dies: The sociobiology of bereavement. *Journal of Personality and Social Psychology, 51*(4), 797–802.

Lopata, H. (1969, April). Social psychological aspects of role involvement. *Sociology and Social Research, 58,* 285–298.

Lopata, H. Z. (1971). *Widowhood in an American city.* Cambridge, MA: Schenkman.

Lopata, H. Z. (1972). Role changes in widowhood: A world perspective. In D. Cowgill & L. Holmes (Eds.), *Aging and modernization* (pp. 275–304). New York: Appleton-Century-Crofts.

Lopata, H. (1973). Self-identity in marriage and widowhood. *The Sociological Quarterly, 14,* 407–418.

Lopata, H. Z. (1974). Loneliness: Forms & components. In R. S. Weiss (Ed.), *Loneliness: The experience of emotional and social isolation.* Cambridge, MA: The MIT Press.

Lopata, H. Z. (1979). *Women as widows: Support systems.* New York: Elsevier North Holland.

Lorenz, K. (1952). *King Solomon's ring.* London: Methuen.

Lund, D. A., Caserta, M. S., & Dimond, M. F. (1986). Gender differences through two years of bereavement among the elderly. *The Gerontologist, 26*(3), 314–320.

Lund, D. A., Caserta, M. S., & Dimond, M. F. (1993). The course of spousal bereavement in later life. In M. Stroebe, W. Stroebe, & R. Hansson (Eds.) *Handbook of bereavement*. Cambridge: Cambridge University Press.

Lundin, T. (1984). Morbidity following sudden and unexpected bereavement. *British Journal of Psychiatry, 144*, 84–88.

Lynch, J. J. (1977). *The broken heart*. New York: Basic Books.

MacDonald, W. S., & Oden, C. W. (1977). Aumakua: Behavioral direction visions in Hawaiians. *Journal of Abnormal Psychology, 86*, 189–194.

Maddison, D., & Viola, A. (1968). The health of widows in the year following bereavement. *Journal of Psychosomatic Research, 12*, 297–306.

Maddison, D., & Walker, W. (1967). Factors affecting the outcome of conjugal bereavement. *British Journal of Medical Psychology, 113*, 1057–1454.

Malinak, D. P., Hoyt, J. F., & Patterson, V. (1979). Adult's reaction to the death of a parent: A preliminary study. *American Journal of Psychiatry, 136*, 1152–1156.

Marris, P. (1968). *Widows and their families*. London: Routledge & Kegan Paul.

Martin, J. L. (1988). Psychological consequences of AIDS-related bereavement among gay men. *Journal of Consulting and Clinical Psychology, 56*, 856–862.

Martin, J. L. & Dean, L. (1993). Development of a community sample of gay men for an epidemiologic study of AIDS. *American Behavioral Scientist, 33*(5), 546–561.

Martin, T., & Doka, K. (1996). Masculine grief. In K. Doka (Ed.), *Living with grief after sudden loss*. Washington, DC: Hospice Foundation of America.

Martocchio, B. C. (1985). Grief and bereavement: Healing through hurt. *Nursing Clinics of North America, 202*, 327–341.

Maslach, C., & Jackson, S. (1979, May). Burned-out cops and their families. *Psychology Today, 59*.

Maslow, A. (1954). *Motivation and personality*. New York: Harper and Bros.

Mason, D. (1991). Genetic variations in the stress response. Susceptibility to experimental allergic encephalomyelitis and implication for human inflammatory disease. *Immunology Today, 12*, 57–58.

Mason, J. W. (1975). A historical view of the stress field. *Journal of Human Stress, I*, 6–12.

Matchett, W. F. (1972). Repeated hallucinatory experiences as part of the mourning process among Hopi Indian women. *Psychiatry, 33*, 184–194.

Mawson, D., Marks, J. M., Ramm, L., & Stern, R. S. (1981). Guided mourning for morbid grief: A controlled study. *British Journal of Psychiatry, 138*, 185–193.

May, R. (1953). *Man's search for himself*. New York: New American Library (Signet).

McCollum, A. T. (1974). Counseling the grieving parent. In L. Burton (Ed.), *Care of the child facing death*. Boston: Routledge & Kegan Paul.

Michalowski, R. (1976). The social meanings of violent death. *Omega, 7*, 83–93.

Miles, M. S. (1979). *The grief of parents: A model for assessment and intervention*. Unpublished manuscript.

Miles, M. S., & Crandell, E. K. R. (1983). The search for meaning and its potential for affecting growth in bereaved parents. *Health Values: Achieving High Level Wellness, 7*(1), 19–23.

Miles, M. S., & Demi, A. S. (1983–1984). Toward the development of a theory of bereavement guilt: Sources of guilt in bereaved parents. *Omega, 14*(3), 299–314.

Miles, M. S., & Demi, A. S. (1986). Guilt in bereaved parents. In T. A. Rando (Ed.), *Parental loss of a child.* Champaign, IL: Research Press.

Mor, V., McHorney, C., & Sherwood, S. (1986). Secondary morbidity among the recently bereaved. *American Journal of Psychiatry, 143*(2), 158–163.

Morgan, L. A. (1976). A re-examination of widowhood and morale. *Journal of Gerontology, 31*, 687–695.

Morillo, E., & Gardner, L. I. (1979). Bereavement as an antecedent factor in thyrotoxicosis of childhood: Four studies with survey of possible metabolic pathways. *Psychosomatic Medicine, 41*, 545–556.

Moss, M. S., & Moss, S. Z. (1983–1984). The impact of parental death on middle aged children. *Omega, 14*(1), 65–75.

Mother Teresa. (1996). *The joy in loving* (Compiled by J. Chalika & E. LeJoly). New York: Penguin Books.

Murphy, G. E., Armstrong, J. W., Jr., Hermele, S. L., Fischer, J., & Clendenin, W. W. (1979). Suicide and alcoholism. *Archives of General Psychiatry, 36*, 65–69.

Murphy, G. E., & Robins, E. (1967). Social factors in suicide. *JAMA, 199*(5), 81–86.

Neugebauer, R., Rabkin, J., Williams, J., Remein, R., Goetz, R., & Gorman, T. (1992). Bereavement reactions among homosexual men experiencing multiple losses in the AIDS epidemic. *American Journal of Psychiatry, 149*, 1374–1379.

Orbach, C. E. (1959). Multiple meanings of the loss of a child. *American Journal of Psychotherapy, 13*, 906–915.

Orbach, I., Weiner, M., Har-Even, D., & Eshel, Y. (1994/95). Children's perception of death and interpersonal closeness to the dead person. *Omega, 30*(1), 1–12.

Osterweis, M., Solomon, E., & Green, M. (Eds.). (1984). *Bereavement: Reactions, consequences and care* (Report by the Committee for the Study of Health Consequences of the Stress of Bereavement, Institute of Medicine, National Academy of Sciences). Washington, DC: National Academy Press.

Owen, G., Fulton, R., & Markusen, E. (1982–1983). Death at a distance: A study of family survivors. *Omega, 13*(3), 191–225.

Papadatou, D., & Papadatos, C. (1991). *Children and death.* New York: Hemisphere.

Pardeck, J., & Markward, M. (1995). Bibliotherapy: Using books to help children deal with problems. *Early Child Development and Care, 106*, 75–90.

Parker, A. T. (1988). A report on hospice in America. *Thanatose, 13*(1), 4–5.

Parkes, C. M. (1964). Recent bereavement as a cause of mental illness. *British Journal of Psychiatry, 110*, 198–204.

Parkes, C. M. (1965). Bereavement and mental illness: Part II. A classification of bereavement reactions. *British Journal of Medical Psychology, 38*, 1–26.

Parkes, C. M. (1971a). The first year of bereavement: A longitudinal study of the reaction of London widows to the death of their husbands. *Psychiatry, 33*, 444–467.

Parkes, C. M. (1971b). Psychosocial transitions: A field for study. *Social Science and Medicine, 5*, 101–115.

Parkes, C. M. (1972). *Bereavement: Studies in grief in adult life.* New York: International Universities Press.

Parkes, C. M. (1975). Determinants of outcome following bereavement. *Omega, 6*(4), 303–323.

Parkes, C. M. (1976). The broken heart. In E. S. Shneidman (Ed.), *Death: Current perspectives*. Palo Alto, CA: Mayfield.

Parkes, C. M. (1985). Bereavement. *British Journal of Psychiatry, 146,* 11–17.

Parkes, C. M. (1993). Bereavement as a psychosocial transition: Processes of adaptation to change. In M. Stroebe, W. Stroebe, & R. Hansson (Eds.), *Handbook of bereavement*. Cambridge: Cambridge University Press.

Parkes, C. M., & Brown, R. J. (1972). Health after bereavement. A controlled study of young Boston widows and widowers. *Psychomatic Medicine, 34*(5), 449–461.

Parkes, C. M., & Weiss, R. S. (1983). *Recovery from bereavement*. New York: Basic Books.

Paulley, J. W. (1984). Pathological mourning: A key factor in the psychopathogenesis of autoimmune disorders. *Psychosomatic Psychotherapy, 40,* 181–190.

Pelletier, K. R. (1977). *Mind as healer, mind as slayer*. New York: Delta.

Pennebaker, J. W., & O'Heeron, R. C. (1984). Confiding in others and illness rates among spouses of suicide and accidental death victims. *Journal of Abnormal Psychology, 93,* 473–476.

Peretz, D. (1970). Development, object-relationships, and loss. In B. Schoenberg, A. C. Carr, D. Peretz, & A. H. Kutscher (Eds.), *Loss and grief: Psychological management in medical practice*. New York: Columbia University Press.

Pincus, L. (1974). *Death in the family*. New York: Pantheon.

Pine, V. R. (1986). An agenda for adaptive anticipation of bereavement. In T. A. Rando (Ed.), *Loss and anticipatory grief*. Lexington, MA: Lexington Books.

Polak, P. R., Egan, D., Vanderbergh, R., & Williams, W. V. (1975). Prevention in mental health. *American Journal of Psychiatry, 132,* 146–149.

Pollock, G. N. (1961). Mourning and adaptation. *International Journal of Psychoanalysis, 43,* 341–361.

Rando, T. A. (1983). Investigation of grief and adaptation in parents whose children have died from cancer. *Journal of Pediatric Psychology, 8,* 3–20.

Rando, T. A. (1984). *Grief, dying and death: Clinical interventions for caregivers*. Champaign, IL: Research Press.

Rando, T. A. (1986a). A comprehensive analysis of anticipatory grief: Perspectives, processes, promises, and problems. In T. A. Rando (Ed.), *Loss and anticipatory grief*. Lexington, MA: Lexington Books.

Rando, T. A. (1986b). The unique issues and impact of the death of a child. In T. A. Rando (Ed.), *Parental loss of a child*. Champaign, IL: Research Press.

Rando, T. A. (1993). *Treatment of complicated mourning*. Champaign, IL: Research Press.

Range, L. M., & Calhoun, L. G. (1990). Responses following suicide and other types of death: The perspective of the bereaved. *Omega, 21*(4), 311–320.

Raphael, B. (1975). The management of pathological grief. *Australian and New Zealand Journal of Psychiatry, 9,* 173–180.

Raphael, B. (1977). Preventive intervention with the recently bereaved. *Archives of General Psychiatry, 34,* 1450–1454.

Raphael, B. (1978). Mourning and the prevention of melancholia. *British Journal of Medical Psychology, 51*, 303–310.

Raphael, B. (1980). A psychiatric model of bereavement counseling. In M. B. Schoenberg (Ed.), *Bereavement counseling: A multidisciplinary handbook*. Greenwood, CT: Greenwood Press.

Raphael, B. (1984). *The anatomy of bereavement*. London: Hutchinson.

Raphael, B., & Maddison, D. (1976). The care of bereaved adults. In O. W. Hill (Ed.), *Modern trends in psychosomatic medicine*. London: Butterworth.

Redmond, L. (1989). *Surviving when someone you know was murdered*. Clearwater, FL: Psychological Consultants Ed. Services.

Redmond, L. M. (1996). Sudden violent death. In K. Doka (Ed.), *Living with grief after sudden loss*. Washington, DC: Hospice Foundation of America.

Reed, M. D., & Greerwald, T. Y. (1991). Survivor victim status, attachment, and sudden death bereavement. *Suicide and life threatening behavior, 21*(4), 311–320.

Rees, W. D., & Lutkins, S. (1967). Mortality and bereavement. *British Medical Journal, 4*, 13–16.

Richmond, J. B., & Waisman, H. A. (1955). Psychological aspects of management of children with malignant diseases. *American Journal of Diseases of Children, 89*, 42–47.

Rochlin, G. (1965). *Griefs & discontents: The focus of change*. Boston: Little, Brown.

Rose, R. (1980). Endocrine responses to stressful psychological events. *Psychiatric Clinics of North America, 3*, 251–276.

Rosen, E. J. (1988). Family therapy in the case of interminable grief for the loss of a child. *Omega, 19*, 1987, 202–218.

Rosen, E. J. (1989). Hospice work with AIDS-related disenfranchised grief. In K. Doka (Ed.), *Disenfranchised grief*. Lexington, MA: Lexington Books.

Rosenblatt, P. C., Walsh, R. P., & Jackson, P. A. (1976). *Grief and mourning in cross-cultural perspective*. New Haven: HRAF (Human Relations Area Files, Inc.) Press.

Rynearsom, E. K. (1978). Humans and pets and attachments. *British Journal of Psychiatry, 133*, 150–155.

Sanders, C. M. (1979). The use of the MMPI in assessing bereavement outcome. In C. S. Newmark (Ed.), *MMPI: Clinical and research trends*. New York: Praeger.

Sanders, C. M. (1979–1980). A comparison of adult bereavement in the death of a spouse, child, and parent. *Omega, 10*(4), 303–322.

Sanders, C. M. (1980–1981). Comparison of younger and older widows in bereavement outcome. *Omega, 11*, 217–232.

Sanders, C. M. (1982–1983). Effects of sudden vs. chronic illness death on bereavement outcome. *Omega, 13*(3), 227–266.

Sanders, C. M. (1986). Accidental death of a child. In T. A. Rando (Ed.), *Parental loss of a child*. Champaign, IL: Research Press.

Sanders, C. M. (1989). *Grief: The mourning after*. New York: John Wiley & Sons.

Sanders, C. M. (1993). Risk factors in bereavement outcome. In M. S. Stroebe, W. Stroebe, & W. Hansson (Eds.), *Handbook of bereavement*. New York: Cambridge University Press.

Sanders, C. M., Mauger, P. A., & Strong, P. N. (1977). *A manual for the grief experience inventory*. Palo Alto, CA: Consulting Psychologist Press.

Saunders, C. (1975). *Terminal care.* London: Oxford Press.

Saxton, L. (1968). *The individual, marriage, and the family.* Belmont, CA: Wadsworth.

Schatz, W. H. (1986). Grief of fathers. In T. A. Rando (Ed.), *Parental loss of a child.* Champaign, IL: Research Press.

Schiff, H. S. (1977). *The bereaved parent.* New York: Crown.

Schleifer, S. J., Keller, S. E., Camerino, M., Thornton, J. C., & Stein, M. (1983). Suppression of lymphocyte stimulation following bereavement. *JAMA, 250*(3), 374–377.

Schlentz, M. (1978). A study of grief: The effect of death of parents on middle aged adults. *Archives of the Foundation of Thanatology, 7,* 157.

Schmale, A. H. (1958). Relationship of separation and depression to disease. *Psychosomatic Medicine, 20,* 259–277.

Schmale, A. H., & Iker, H. (1966). The psychological setting of uterine cervical cancer. *Annals New York Academic Science, 125,* 807–813.

Schmale, A. H., & Iker, H. (1971). Hopelessness as a predictor of cervical cancer. *Social Science and Medicine, 5,* 95–100.

Schneider, C. (1977). *Shame, exposure & privacy.* Boston: Beacon Press.

Schneidman, E. S. (1971, June). The enemy. *Psychology Today,* 74–80.

Schulz, R. (1978). *The psychology of death, dying, and bereavement.* Reading, MA: Addison-Wesley.

Schulz, R., & Aderman, D. (1974). Clinical research and the stages of dying. *Omega, 5*(2), 137–143.

Schwab, J. J., Chalmers, J. M., Conroy, S. J., Farris, P. B., & Markush, R. E. (1975). Studies on grief: A preliminary report. In B. Schoenberg, I. Berger, A. Kutscher, D. Peretz, & A. C. Carr (Eds.), *Bereavement: Its psychosocial aspects.* New York: Columbia University Press.

Schwartz, A. M. (1977). Comments in section on "The Parents." In N. Linzer (Ed.), *Understanding bereavement and grief.* New York: Yeshiva University Press.

Secundy, M. G. (1977). Bereavement: The role of the family physician. *Journal of the National Medical Association, 69*(9), 649–790.

Segal, S., Fletcher, M., & Meekison, W. G. (1986). Survey of bereaved parents. *Canadian Medical Association Journal, 134*(1), 38–42.

Seligman, M. E. (1975). *Helplessness: On depression, development and death.* San Francisco: W. H. Freeman.

Selye, H. (1956). *The stress of life.* New York: McGraw-Hill.

Selye, H. (1974). *Stress without distress.* New York: J. P. Lippincott.

Sheldon, A. R., Cochrane, J., Vachon, M. L. S., Lyall, W., Roger, J., & Freeman, S. (1981). A psychosocial analysis of risk of psychological impairment following bereavement. *The Journal of Nervous and Mental Disease, 169,* 253–255.

Shepherd, D. M., & Barraclough, B. M. (1974). The aftermath of parental suicide for children. *British Journal of Psychiatry, 129,* 267–276.

Sherr, I., Hedge, B., Steinhart, K., Davey, T., & Petrack, J. (1992). Unique patterns of bereavement in HIV: Implications for couselling. *Genitourinary Medicine, 68,* 378–381.

Sheskin, A., & Wallace, S. E. (1976). Differing bereavements: Suicide, natural, and accidental death. *Omega, 7,* 229–242.

Shneidman, E. S. (1976). A psychological theory of suicide. *Psychiatric Annals, 6*, 51–66.

Shuchter, S. R., & Zisook, S. (1990). Hovering over the bereaved. *Psychiatric Annals, 20*, 327–333.

Shuchter, S. R., & Zisook, S. (1993). The course of normal grief. In M. Stroebe, W. Stroebe, & R. Hansson (Eds.), *Handbook of bereavement*. Cambridge: Cambridge University Press.

Shuchter, S. R., Zisook, S., Kirkorowicy, B. S., & Riscj, C. (1986). The dexamethasone suppression test in acute grief. *American Journal of Psychiatry, 143*(7), 879–881.

Siggins, L. (1966). Mourning: A critical survey of the literature. *International Journal of Psychoanalysis, 52*, 259–266.

Silverman, P. (1974). Background to the development of the widow-to-widow program. In P. Silverman, D. MacKenzie, M. Pettipas, & E. Wilson (Eds.), *Helping each other in widowhood*. New York: Health Sciences.

Silverman, P. (1981). *Helping women cope with grief*. Beverly Hills, CA: Sage.

Silverman, P. (1987). In search of new selves: Accommodating to widowhood. In L. A. Bond & B. M. Wagner (Eds.), *Families in transition: Primary prevention programs that work*. Beverly Hills, CA: Sage.

Silverman, P. R., & Cooperband, A. (1974, May 18). *On widowhood: Mutual help and the elderly widow*. Paper presented at an Interdisciplinary Meeting of the Boston Society for Gerontologic Psychiatry.

Simonton, O. C., & Simonton, S. (1975). Belief systems and management of the emotional aspects of malignancy. *Transpersonal Psychology, 7*, 29–48.

Simpson, M. A. (1979). *The facts of death*. Englewood Cliffs, NJ: Prentice-Hall.

Singh, B. S., & Raphael, B. (1981). Post-disaster morbidity of the bereaved. *Journal of Nervous and Mental Disease, 169*(4), 208–212.

Solnik, A., & Green, M. (1959). Psychologic considerations in the management of deaths on pediatric hospital services: I. The doctor and the child's family. *Pediatrics, 24*, 106–112.

Solomon, G. F. (1969). Emotions, stress, the central nervous system, and immunity. *Annals of the New York Academy of Science, 164*, 333–343.

Spitz, R. A. (1945). Hospitalism: An inquiry into the psychiatric conditions in early childhood. *Psychoanalytic Study of the Child, 1*, 53.

Spitz, R. A. (1946). Anaclitic depression: An inquiry into the genesis of psychiatric conditions in early childhood. II. *Psychoanalytic Study of the Child, 2*, 313–342.

Stephenson, J. (1986). Grief of siblings. In T. A. Rando (Ed.), *Parental loss of a child*. Champaign, IL: Research Press.

Stern, K., Williams, G. M., & Prados, M. (1951). Grief reactions in later life. *American Journal of Psychiatry, 108*, 289–294.

Stillion, J. M. (1996). Survivors of suicide. In K. Doka (Ed.), *Living with grief after sudden loss*. Washington, DC: Hospice Foundation of America.

Stillion, J. M., & McDowell, E. E. (1996). *Suicide across the life span: Premature exits* (2nd ed.). Washington: Hemisphere Publishing.

Stillion, J., McDowell, E. E., & May, E. (1989). *Suicide across the life span: Premature exits*. Washington, DC: Hemisphere Press.

Stoddard, S. (1978). *The hospice movement.* New York: Vintage.

Stroebe, M. S., & Stroebe, W. (1983). Who suffers more? Sex differences in health risks of the widowed. *Psychological Bulletin, 93*(2), 279–301.

Stroebe, M. S., Stroebe, W., Gergen, K. J., & Gergen, M. (1981). The broken heart: Reality or myth. *Omega, 12,* 87–106.

Stroebe, W., & Stroebe, M. S. (1987). Bereavement and health. New York: Cambridge University Press.

Stroebe, W., Stroebe, M. S., & Dormittner, G. (1985). The impact of recent bereavement on the mental and physical health of young widows and widowers. In *Reports from the Psychological Institute* (No. 17). University of Tubingen, Germany.

Sullivan, H. (1956). The dynamics of emotion. In H. Sullivan (Ed.), *Clinical studies in psychiatry* (chap. 5). New York: W. W. Norton.

Taggartt, M. (1980). *Salvete et valete:* On saying goodbye to a deceased former parent. *Journal of Marital and Family Therapy, 6,* 117–120.

Taves, I. (1974). *Love must not be wasted.* New York: Thomas Y. Crowell.

Vachon, M. L. S. (1976). Grief and bereavement following the death of a spouse. *Canadian Psychiatric Association Journal, 21,* 35–44.

Vachon, M. L. S., Formo, A., Freeman, K., Lyall, W. A., Rogers, J., & Freeman, S. (1976). Stress reactions to bereavement. *Essence, 1,* 23–33.

Vachon, M. L. S., Rogers, J., Lyall, W. A., Lancee, W. J., Sheldon, A. R., & Freeman, S. J. (1982). Predictors and correlates of high distress in adaptation to conjugal bereavement. *American Journal of Psychiatry, 139,* 998–1002.

Vachon, M. L. S., Sheldon, A. R., Lancee, W. J., Lyall, W. A. L., Rogers, J., & Freeman, S. J. J. (1980). A controlled study of self-help intervention for widows. *American Journal of Psychiatry, 137,* 1380–1384.

Vachon, M. L. S., Sheldon, A. R., Lancee, W. J., Lyall, W. A. L., Rogers, J., & Freeman, S. J. J. (1982). Correlates of enduring distress patterns following bereavement: Social network, life situation and personality. *Psychological Medicine, 12,* 783–799.

van der Hart, O. (1983). *Rituals in psychotherapy: Transitions and continuity.* New York: Irvington.

Van Der Wal, J. (1989–1990). The aftermath of suicide: A review of empirical evidence. *Omega, 20*(2), 149–171.

van Gennep, A. (1960). *The rites of passage.* Chicago: University of Chicago Press.

Vernon, G. M. (1970). *Sociology of death: An analysis of death-related behavior.* New York: Ronald Press.

Videka-Sherman, L. (1982). Coping with the death of a child: A study over time. *American Journal of Orthopsychiatry, 52*(4), 699–703.

Videka-Sherman, L., & Lieberman, M. (1985). The effects of self-help and psychotherapy in intervention on child loss: The limits of recovery. *American Journal of Orthopsychiatry, 55*(1), 70–82.

Viney, L., Henry, R., Walker, B., and Crooks, I. (1992). The psychosocial impact of multiple deaths from AIDS. *Omega, 24,* 151–163.

Volkan, V. (1970). Typical findings in pathological grief. *Psychiatric Quarterly, 44,* 231–250.

Volkan, V. (1971). A study of a patient's "regrief work" through dreams, psychological tests and psychoanalysis. *Psychiatric Quarterly, 45,* 225–273.

Volkan, V., & Showalter, C. R. (1968). Known object loss, disturbances of reality testing and re-grief work as a method of brief psychotherapy. *Psychiatric Quarterly, 42,* 358–374.

Walker, R. N., McBride, A., & Vachon, M. L. S. (1977). Social support networks and the crisis of bereavement. *Social Science and Medicine, 11,* 35–41.

Weiner, A., Gerber, I., Battin, D., & Arkin, A. M. (1975). The process and phenomenology of bereavement. In B. Schoenberg, I. Gerber, A. Weiner, A. H. Kutschen, D. Peretz, & A. C. Carr (Eds.), *Bereavement: Its psychosocial aspects.* New York: Columbia University Press.

Weiner, H., Thaler, M., Reiser, M., and Mirsky, I. A. (1957). Etiology of duodenal ulcer. Relations of specific psychological characteristics to rate of gastric secretion. *Psychosomatic Medicine, 19,* 1–10.

Weisman, A. D. (1972). Psychosocial considerations in terminal care. In B. Schoenberg, A. C. Carr, D. Peretz, & A. H. Kutscher (Eds.), *Psychological aspects of terminal care.* New York: Columbia University Press.

Weiss, R. S. (1993). Loss and recovery. In M. Stroebe, W. Stroebe, & R. Hansson (Eds.), *Handbook of bereavement.* Cambridge: Cambridge University Press.

Weissman, M. M., & Klerman, G. L. (1977). Sex differences and the epidemiology of depression. *Archives of General Psychiatry, 34,* 98–111.

Wenckstern, S., & Leenaars, A. A. (1991). Suicide postvention: A case illustration in a secondary school. In A. A. Leenaars & S. Wenckstern (Eds.), *Suicide prevention in schools* (pp. 181–195). New York: Hemisphere.

Wetzel, R. D. (1976). Hopelessness, depression, and suicide intent. *Archives of General Psychiatry, 33,* 1069–1073.

White, E. B. (1952). *Charlotte's web.* New York: Harper & Brothers.

Wolff, C. T., Friedman, S. B., Hofer, M. A., & Mason, J. W. (1964). Relationship between psychological defenses and mean urinary 17-hydroxycorticosteroid excretion rates: I. A predictive study of parents of fatally ill children. *Psychosomatic Medicine, 26,* 576–591.

Worden, J. W. (1982). *Grief counseling and grief therapy: A handbook for the mental health practitioner.* New York: Springer.

Young, M., Benjamin, B., & Wallis, G. (1963). Mortality of widows. *Lancet, 2,* 454–456.

Zisook, S., & DeVaul, R. A. (1983). Grief, unresolved grief, and depression. *Psychosomatics, 45,* 370–399.

Zisook, S., & DeVaul, R. (1985). Unresolved grief. *American Journal of Psychoanalysis, 45*(4), 370–379.

Zisook, S., DeVaul, R. A., & Click, M. A. (1982). Measuring symptoms of grief and bereavement. *American Journal of Psychiatry, 139*(12), 1590–1593.

Index

Ablin, A. R., 205
Abused children, death of parent, 158
Accepting responsibility, 104–107
Accommodation, 34–35
Acting out emotional expectations, 63
Acute state of grieving, 26–27
Adaptive bereavement, 36
Adaptive nature of grief, 28
Adaptive resources of bereaved
    in children, 157–158
    in concurrent crises, 148
Aderman, D., 45
Adolescents, suicide and, 182
Age
    of adult child at parent's death, 231–232,
        233–235
    of bereaved, 134–137, 230
    bereavement of spouse and, 214
    of child at death, 198
    stress reactions and, 120
Agee, J., 9
AIDS-related death, 188–192
Alarcon, R. D., 118
Alarm, physiological, 53–55
Alarm stage, 83
Alcohol abuse, 147
Allen, B. G., 181
Altruistic egotism, 113
Ambivalence toward deceased, 22–23, 124–126
Anatomy of an Illness (Cousins), 282
ANCOVA (analysis of covariance), 140–141
Anderson, H., 232
Anger
    ambivalent, 66

appropriate, 67
in bereaved children, 158
in child's death, 201–203
confrontive, 66
displaced, 66
within family, 165–167
helpless, 67
after homicide, 186
internalized, 66–67
personality and, 121–122
Anniversary reactions, 111
    rituals and, 256
ANOVA (analysis of variance), Social
    Support by Marital Status by Gender,
    144
Antidepressants, 275
Anxiety
    death, 241–243
    fight-flight response and, 29
    loneliness, 228
    physical illness and, 29
    separation, 61–62
    therapy and, 131
Appetite loss, 56
Arkin, A. M., 150
Armstrong, J., 147
Atchley, R. C., 140
Attachment
    to deceased, 11, 27–29, 233
    parent-child, 156–157
    theory, 27–29
Attachment figure
    loss of, 156–157
    retrieving, 28